CW01635076

Enriching Awareness and Practice in the Pastoral and Reflective Supervision of Clergy

Enriching Awareness and Practice in the Pastoral and Reflective Supervision of Clergy

Edited by Peter Madsen Gubi

LEXINGTON BOOKS
Lanham • Boulder • New York • London

Published by Lexington Books
An imprint of The Rowman & Littlefield Publishing Group, Inc.
4501 Forbes Boulevard, Suite 200, Lanham, Maryland 20706
www.rowman.com

86-90 Paul Street, London EC2A 4NE

Copyright © 2023 by The Rowman & Littlefield Publishing Group, Inc.

All rights reserved. No part of this book may be reproduced in any form or by any electronic or mechanical means, including information storage and retrieval systems, without written permission from the publisher, except by a reviewer who may quote passages in a review.

British Library Cataloguing in Publication Information Available

Library of Congress Cataloging-in-Publication Data Available

ISBN 9781666909852 (cloth : alk. paper)
ISBN 9781666909869 (ebook)

∞™ The paper used in this publication meets the minimum requirements of American National Standard for Information Sciences—Permanence of Paper for Printed Library Materials, ANSI/NISO Z39.48-1992.

We would like to dedicate this book to all of our pastoral supervisees and trainees who, over many years, have taught us so much.

Contents

Acknowledgments

We would like to thank the Trustees of the Association for Pastoral Supervision and Education for their encouragement and support. We acknowledge the help and support of our editor and assistant production editor at Lexington Press, Megan White and Anna Keyser. Finally, we acknowledge the love and support of our various families who have had to endure our absence in the production of this book.

Introduction

Peter Madsen Gubi

The pastoral supervision of clergy (also called 'reflective supervision' in some Christian denominations) is increasingly recognised as essential for maintaining the well-being of clergy and in managing risk and safeguarding within the Church.[1] Arguably, pastoral supervision, in some form or other, has been informally carried out over hundreds of years, but it has been patchy, informal, lacking in training, and structure and accountability, if indeed it has existed at all. This book brings together the expertise of a number of experienced pastoral supervisors who each explore an area of focus that can occur within pastoral supervision, to enrich and deepen the awareness, knowledge, and skills of pastoral supervisors who work with clergy in a pastoral supervision context. Throughout the book, the terms 'pastoral supervision' and 'pastoral supervisor/supervisee' will be used. We recognise that the same discipline is recognised as 'reflective supervision' in many countries and denominations, and the content of this book is equally applicable to those who practice reflective supervision.

WHAT PASTORAL SUPERVISION IS

There is a growing recognition within several Christian denominations in the UK, and within the published research,[2] that pastoral ministry is increasingly complex, isolating, and 'messy' (e.g., lacking clear boundaries which can cause misunderstandings and create risk). Issues within society have become more complicated, there is less willingness to 'believe in' religion, and more apathy shown towards the Christian faith within Western societies. Consequently church attendance has fallen in many places leading to demoralisation among many clergy. There is also little training offered in theological colleges to prepare ministers for what they may face in pastoral work.[3] As a consequence, there are high rates of clergy stress and isolation and past-case reviews are highlighting occurrences of poor boundary-keeping, unwise decision-making, and spiritual and sexual abuse.[4]

As a way of responding to these issues, several denominations in the UK—the Methodist Church, the Church of England, the United Reformed Church, the Moravian Church, the Salvation Army and the Baptist Church—have considered (or are currently considering) pastoral supervision as a way of providing support—and being 'seen' to provide support—for their clergy. Pastoral supervision has been defined as

> a relationship between two or more disciples who meet to consider the ministry of one or more of them in an intentional and disciplined way. Such an arrangement allows each person being supervised to give an account of their work, to explore their responses, review their aims and develop their strategies and skills. Pastoral supervision is practised for the sake of the supervisee, providing a space in which their well-being, growth and development are taken seriously, and for the sake of those among whom the supervisee works, providing a realistic point of accountability within the body of Christ for their work as chaplains, local church ministers, spiritual directors, pastoral counsellors or youth workers.[5]

The Association of Pastoral Supervision and Education (APSE) also defines pastoral supervision as:[6]

- *a regular, planned, intentional and boundaried space* in which a practitioner skilled in supervision (the supervisor) meets with one or more other practitioners (the supervisees) to look together at the supervisees' practice;
- *a relationship* characterised by trust, respect, confidentiality, support and openness that gives the supervisee freedom and safety to explore the issues arising in their work;
- *spiritually/theologically informed*—works within a framework of spiritual/theological understanding in dialogue with the supervisee's world view and role;
- *psychologically informed*—draws on relevant psychological theory and insight to illuminate intra-personal and inter-personal dynamics;
- *contextually sensitive*—pays attention to the particularities of setting, culture and world-view;
- *praxis based*—focuses on a report of work and/or issues that arise in and from the supervisee's practice;

- *a way of growing* in vocational identity, role competence, self-awareness, spiritual/theological reflection, quality of presence, accountability, response to challenge, mutual learning;
- *attentive* to issues of fitness to practice, skill development, management of boundaries, professional identity and the impact of the work upon all concerned parties.

Pastoral supervision is an exploratory and reflective process in which one or more ministry practitioners meet together with a *trained, resourced, and approved supervisor/facilitator* to reflect on their vocation and practice. The intention of such regular and focused reflection on practice is to support a change of culture in the life of the Church from one which is often one of isolated and vulnerable practice to one of support and more safety for ministers, and for those among whom they work. *Pastoral supervision is not performance management nor ministerial oversight.*[7] The Methodist Church's policy of 'Responsible Grace: Supervising in the Methodist Church'[8] states that pastoral supervision has three main functions:

- to support the minister in their vocation and practice and its development;
- to safeguard the interests of those amongst whom ministry is practised, including those of children and vulnerable adults;
- to ensure that the ministry offered in the name of the denomination is collegially and accountably reflected upon in the light of God's mission and the purposes of the Church.

Research[9, 10] that has been conducted, thus far, into the value and limitations of pastoral supervision, has been very encouraging and highlights its necessity.

THE POSITIONING OF THE CONTRIBUTORS

This book is a result of a collaboration between the chapter contributors, most of whom are members of the Training, Research and Publication Sub-Group of APSE. Each contributor identifies as a Christian, and so the language of Christianity will permeate the book to offer the authentic voice of each writer. However, we hope that what is being discussed can be made applicable to pastoral supervision in other faith contexts and in contexts where there is no faith. Many of the contributors are also experienced psychotherapists, and so psychological insights will be interwoven in the chapters.

WHO THE BOOK IS WRITTEN FOR

This book is intended to increase and enrich the awareness, knowledge, and skills of pastoral supervisors who work with clergy in a pastoral/reflective supervision context. The content is also applicable to supervisors within a Clinical Ministerial Education context, and to all clergy who want to develop their awareness of interpersonal dynamics.

WHAT IS IN THE BOOK

In chapter 1, Bill Mullally addresses the important elements of presence and power in the pastoral supervisory relationship. He explores how an open, authentic and trusting environment can be created within reflective practice. This has regenerative and healing potential, whereby the practitioner will be better able to face the challenges of their work in order to competently and joyfully fulfil their vocation. He argues that there is a need for well-qualified, skilled, and spiritually sensitive supervisory support for every person in professional practice. Effective pastoral supervisors will understand the dynamics of power and presence to create a sacred space for practitioners to "come apart and reflect a while." Drawing upon fifteen years of experience in this field and recent research, Bill shares key insights and practices regarding power and presence in the supervisory relationship to create transformational possibilities for those who commit to the journey.

In chapter 2, Peter Madsen Gubi argues that pastoral supervision differs from other forms of reflective supervision in that it draws upon the spiritual insights and wisdom of faith traditions and narratives. His chapter advocates a model for reflecting theologically on issues that present in pastoral supervision.

In chapter 3, Gubi advocates a way of ethically and appropriately working with prayer in pastoral supervision. Prayer needs to be considered carefully like any other intervention, and incorporated with awareness, if indeed it is ever used.

In chapter 4, Mish Seabrook explores how to integrate a self-care focus into pastoral supervision. She explores the importance of self-care for the clergy, and how supervision can provide the reflective space to address the personal and professional issues regarding self-care. The potential challenges of addressing clergy self-care are explored. A practical approach to engaging with issues of self-care is outlined.

In chapter 5, Deanne Gardner explores the importance of diversity awareness in pastoral supervision, in order to develop greater awareness and enhance practitioners' work within the pastoral supervisory relationship. In the pastoral supervision arena, little is written specifically to address the importance of working with diversity within various faith settings. This chapter discusses diversity in the Body of Christ and how the pastoral supervisor may develop a curiosity that encourages inclusivity in their practice.

In chapter 6, Sally Bubbers draws on the ideas, language, and systems thinking of the Internal Family Systems (IFS) model by Richard Schwartz. She offers insights through the lens of IFS by introducing the language and concept of the role of 'parts' into pastoral supervision. These insights can bring awareness to places of stuckness, where the supervisee and/or supervisor may be struggling. At the same time, this can build up the confidence of the supervisee to find a way through.

In chapter 7, Bubbers outlines a basic understanding of the relationship between neurobiology and behaviour patterns that impact our daily lives. When a person becomes distressed or agitated, they have a reduced capacity to think clearly, analyse, or anticipate. This simple fact has enormous implications for communication within a pastoral supervisee's work context. This information can help the pastoral supervisor support the supervisee in decoding confusing situations, allowing for better communication through greater compassion and understanding. The chapter looks at the neurobiology of the triggering system, the window of tolerance, and the mapping of the autonomic nervous system (ANS) with reference to the Polyvagal Theory. Bubbers offers simple mindfulness practices which help bring the 'thinking brain' back online at times of stress. There will be a brief reference to attachment styles.

In chapter 8, Sally Nash offers a definition of shame and its differentiation to guilt, including contextual nature and idea that shame has an audience. Her chapter contains a brief introduction to biblical perspectives on shame and introduces four elements of her research-based typology and how they may manifest in pastoral supervision: personal, communal, structural and theological (illustrated with quotations from her research). Her chapter demonstrates how to recognise shame in supervisees' body language, words, shame/rage, and withdrawal dynamics, explores self-awareness and triggers for the supervisor, and looks at how best to respond to shame in the supervisee.

In chapter 9, Tuntufye Mwenisongole argues that it is crucial for someone to learn and understand the cultural backgrounds and religious forces, influences, and impacts which could hinder or promote the process of pastoral supervision. Drawing on his experience from Tanzania, his chapter further argues that pastoral ministry needs professional supervisors who will be sensitive to understanding the context of the workplace to make supervision applicable and effective. This chapter recommends that it is very important to understand the thinking, behaviour, and personal narratives (or stories) of a person in the environment of pastoral supervision.

Finally, in chapter 10, Deanne Gardner discusses clergy spouses' unique position in what might be considered to be a two-person career. Her chapter includes different role expectations and emotional demands made upon clergy spouses, and the value and importance of pastoral supervision for clergy spouses.

BIBLIOGRAPHY

Association of Pastoral Supervision and Education, "Definition and Ethos." https://www.pastoralsupervision.org.uk/home/about/definition-and-ethos. (accessed 1 August 2022).

Gubi, Peter Madsen. "Utilising Reflective Practice Groups as pedagogy in ordination training and theological development." *Practical Theology Journal* 12, no. 4 (2019): 366–78.

Gubi, Peter Madsen, and Tuntufye A. Mwenisongole. "A pilot evaluation study of pastoral supervision provision in the Moravian Church (British Province)." *Journal of Mental Health, Religion and Culture* 25, no. 2 (2022): 197–206. DOI: 10.1080/13674676.2022.2045924.

Hudson, Rachel. "Is there a need for specialist counselling for church ministers?" *Thresholds: Counselling with Spirit* (Autumn 2015): 10–13.

Leach, Jane, and Michael Paterson. *Pastoral Supervision: A Handbook.* London: SCM Press, 2015.

Methodist Church, *Responsible Grace: Supervising in the Methodist Church.* London: The Methodist Church, 2017.

Methodist Church of Great Britain, "Reflective Supervision Report," Methodist.org.uk, 2021, 640. https://www.methodist.org.uk/media/21766/conf-2021-40-reflective-supervision-report.pdf (accessed 1 August 2022).

Mullally, Bill. "The effect of presence and power in the pastoral supervisory relationship." *HOLINESS: The Journal of Wesley House Cambridge* 3 no. 1 (2019): 5–34.

NOTES

1. Peter Madsen Gubi and Tuntufye A. Mwenisongole, "A pilot evaluation study of pastoral supervision provision in the Moravian Church (British Province)." *Journal of Mental Health, Religion and Culture* 25, no. 2 (2022): 197–206. DOI: 10.1080/13674676.2022.2045924.

2. Rachel Hudson, "Is there a need for specialist counselling for church ministers?" *Thresholds: Counselling with Spirit* (Autumn 2015): 10–13.

3. Peter Madsen Gubi, "Utilising Reflective Practice Groups as pedagogy in ordination training and theological development," *Practical Theology Journal* 12, no. 4 (2019): 366–78.

4. Bill Mullally, "The effect of presence and power in the pastoral supervisory relationship," *HOLINESS: The Journal of Wesley House Cambridge* 3 no. 1 (2019): 5–34

5. Jane Leach and Michael Paterson, *Pastoral Supervision: A Handbook* (London: SCM Press, 2015), 1.

6. Association of Pastoral Supervision and Education, "*Definition and Ethos*." https://www.pastoralsupervision.org.uk/home/about/definition-and-ethos. (accessed 1 August 2022).

7. Leach and Paterson, "Pastoral Supervision," 1–4.

8. Methodist Church, *Responsible Grace: Supervising in the Methodist Church* (London: The Methodist Church, 2017).

9. Gubi and Mwenisongole, "A pilot evaluation study of pastoral supervision," 197–206.

10. The Methodist Church of Great Britain, "Reflective Supervision Report," Methodist.org.uk, 2021, 640. https://www.methodist.org.uk/media/21766/conf-2021-40-reflective-supervision-report.pdf (accessed 1 August 2022).

Chapter One

The Effect of Presence and Power in the Pastoral Supervisory Relationship

Bill Mullally

Paul Vitello reported in the *New York Times*:

> Members of the clergy now suffer from obesity, hypertension and depression at rates higher than most Americans. In the last decade, their use of antidepressants has risen, while their life expectancy has fallen. Many would change jobs if they could.[1]

More than a decade later, this pattern of unhappiness and health issues within the context of ministry appears to remain prevalent, not only in America, but also in the United Kingdom and Europe, with grave concern for the potential consequences.

> Without good pastoral support, the demands of ministerial practice are likely to lead to burnout, inattention to boundaries, and a lack of focus on the patterns of ministry and church life that supports the deeper purposes of God. Without reflective attention to boundaries, those in ministry and those among whom they minister are put at risk. Without reflective attention to the detail of church life and ministerial practice in relation to the deep purposes of God, the church's mission is at risk. Both at the individual and the institutional level, survival strategies take over.[2]

In this new millennium, those in Christian ministry are seeking what it means to be church, and how to offer relevant leadership and support within their community, in a society that is changing more rapidly than in any previous era. As Johnston states,

> The challenge is for the church to be seen to respond to the social milieu in which it seeks to articulate and enact its faith in such a way that all aspects of its life, including the structural application and use of power, make sense of the realities encountered.[3]

My own personal journey as a minister in the church, having held responsibilities at local, national, and international levels, has convinced me that pastoral supervision can be a key instrument in developing greater resilience for those in ministry to effectively deal with the tasks and challenges they face.

Pastoral supervision creates an opportunity for those in ministry to reflect and process issues that arise within their work. This practice needs be an essential and regular part of the practitioner's life and work—encouraging freedom and safety to explore issues, through the confidentiality, trust, and support within this reflective space. As Boyatzis and McKee state, 'We need to attend to ourselves, and to others, in mind, body, heart and spirit. Mindfulness, hope, and compassion enable us to be resilient and function effectively even in the face of challenges.'[4] Ideally, these qualities are at the heart of the pastoral supervision experience. In this chapter, I explore two key issues, presence and power, which influence and affect the creation of a space that is both sacred and safe for those who participate in pastoral supervision. As I have reviewed, engaged in, and reflected on the discourses within literature concerning the purpose and process of pastoral supervision, I have discovered that there is little said about presence, or the dynamics of power, in the supervisory relationship. In my experience, these crucial elements of presence and power within the supervisory relationship matter, although they are often not reflected on, acknowledged, or openly addressed. Yet, they exist and influence the individuals involved, in a conscious and subconscious way. The existence of these dynamics can affect the processes of communication, vulnerability, and transparency, which in turn can influence the depth of the trusting relationship, and consequently affect the supervisory experience and its potential benefit.

In this chapter, I explore how a deeper knowledge of these two factors within pastoral supervision could enhance, and develop, the supervisory experience as a transformational encounter for those involved, that will better support the supervisees concerned and equip them to face the challenges in their ministry today. This chapter is an adaptation and extension of an article that I have previously published.[5]

Having been supervised and having offered supervision myself for a period of almost thirty-five years within different contexts of ministry, I am convinced that a central and crucial element of effective supervision is the supervisory relationship itself. Rogers states that a deep human encounter lies at the centre of all helping relationships when he says, "If I can provide a certain type of relationship, the other person will discover within himself the capacity to use that relationship for growth, and change and personal development will occur."[6] The Reflective Practice Journal, which provides a framework to promote critical reflection on formation and supervision in ministry in various contexts and from diverse Christian traditions, says,

> Good practice relies on ongoing reflection. The capacity for critical self-reflection is an essential dimension of any habitus for ministry and religious leadership. Pastoral supervision is itself a practice that occurs in relationships that encourages such critical reflection in ministry.[7]

I perceive that inherent in the call to ministry and religious leadership is an obligation before God to understand oneself and how one's use of presence and power can influence the effectiveness of this call and the quality of one's leadership. Thus, I will explore how this can be enhanced through the process of pastoral supervision. I will outline the meaning and context of pastoral supervision in ministry and consider the aspects of presence and power as they relate to the Divine, the supervisory relationship, and the individual's work context.

PASTORAL SUPERVISION IN MINISTRY

Owing to the wide number of contexts in which the term 'supervision' is used, its meaning is often fraught with confusion and misunderstanding. If one reflects upon it, supervision is received by us, in one form or another, throughout our whole lives: parental supervision, educational supervision, work supervision, professional supervision, and so on. Feinberg says that "the term supervision falls victim to . . . death by a thousand qualifications."[8] For many, the term 'supervision' conjures up the notion of oversight, seniority, greater experience, and more responsibility. There is often the connection between supervision and power over a person who is less experienced than us and in need of monitoring, evaluation, and control, and there are times when this is necessary and even essential. Pohly comments, "Supervision is a term that is loaded with baggage. . . . It suggests a hierarchy of superiority/inferiority and dredges up threatening associations with the past."[9] Yet, supervision, as used to describe professional reflective practice, can have profound effects on those who participate and can lead to life-changing outcomes, both personally and in the workplace.

Paterson shares the invitation of Noel Davis: "We who supervise will know we are living in an age of wisdom when we venture beyond the familiar in our practice, range wider than routine in our interactions, delve beneath the old certainties, break from the programmed, and regularly find ourselves and those we supervise taking a different way home."[10] This type of deep listening and wisdom-evoking presence is not a new discipline, although the term 'supervision,' used in this sense, is a comparatively recent development. Carroll says, "supervision has been around for over a century and in that time it has developed substantially."[11] While this may be true within the professional caring industry, in my experience, this has not been the case in formal pastoral supervision within the church, until in recent years. Since qualifying as a cross-professional supervisor in 2009, I have often observed a failure for provision of a professional reflective space, where needs can be identified and strengths harnessed to process and resolve issues, both at a personal and an organisational level.

Pastoral supervision is defined by the Association of Pastoral Supervision and Education as being a:

> regular, planned, intentional and boundaried space . . . a relationship characterised by trust, respect, confidentiality, support and openness that gives the supervisees freedom and safety to explore the issues arising in their work. It is spiritually and theologically informed and works within a framework of spiritual/theological understanding in dialogue with the supervisee's world view and work. It is psychologically informed . . . contextually sensitive . . . and praxis based. It is a way of growing in vocational identity, role competence, self-awareness, spiritual/theological reflection, quality of presence, accountability, response to challenge, and mutual learning; and attentive to issues of fitness to practice, skill development, management of boundaries, professional identity and the impact of the work upon all concerned parties.[12]

In this chapter, the supervisory context is pastoral in nature and approached from a Christian viewpoint. Just as Christ, called the Good Shepherd (John 10:11),[13] sets the pastoral example, pastoral supervision implies an encounter that practices a caring attitude and a peaceful presence and necessitates a careful use of power to create a safe space and a spiritual openness. Pohly affirms this as he speaks of "Christ's own oversight and shepherding"[14] and hence pastoral supervision moves beyond the secular understanding of supervision and seeks to create what can be termed 'sacred space.'

While there is much that can be said about pastoral supervision in its practice and purpose, I propose that an understanding of the elements of presence and power, and their effect on the supervisory relationship, is crucial to both engaging in the process and benefiting from the experience.

PRESENCE IN THE PASTORAL SUPERVISORY RELATIONSHIP

Effective supervision happens when the people involved intentionally meet for the particular purpose of reflection upon their work, and are willing to participate and to share of themselves, and their experience, within the context of their work. This requires an understanding that presence can mean different things to different people; all have boundaries which need to be recognised and respected.

> The more we can understand the ways in which the world looks different through different cultural lenses, the more able we are to work well across cultures.[15]

This awareness can hugely influence one's outlook, understanding, and response to the challenges one faces in ministry, and what one perceives God is saying through circumstances, through others, and through Scripture.

Even within a comparatively homogenous group can lie a diversity which must be taken into account—including gender, marital state, sexual orientation, age, place of origin, individual backgrounds, culture, and context. This makes for a rich dynamic that in itself takes on its own identity and pace according to the needs and inclinations of those involved.

Supervisees serving within the church and community have indicated that meaningful presence in pastoral supervision gives encouragement and accountability, and can simplify and clarify issues. This quality of presence allows for different perspectives to be considered, as well as providing the opportunity for the supervisee to listen to themselves in the presence of another.

Bobby Moore in his book *Reflexive Supervision* helpfully reminds us of the importance of trust in the supervisory relationship. He says,

> supervisees will allow supervisors to influence them to the degree to which they sense the supervisor as trustworthy. . . . Trust, however, is not a given at the onset of any relationship. We often begin with caution, testing out the ground and gradually opening up more and more as we go along. It takes time and effort to build trust, and perhaps even more so when survival is at stake.[16]

Ideally, the supervisee experiences the supervisor as someone who is 'there for them,' and the supervisor's presence communicates support, compassion, and a sensitivity that enables an easy environment in which to speak and to process thoughts and emotions. This quality of presence within pastoral supervision creates a thinking environment that can be very different to that which is common in our culture, even within many forms of church interaction. As expressed by a supervisee, "presence . . . takes effort, particularly to listen, as we're used to waiting for the gap in conversation and giving our opinions."

Our Western culture is one that tends to emphasise: "Think the way others are thinking. Think to impress. Think to avoid ridicule. Think to get a promotion. Think to out-manoeuvre."[17] Even if the thinking is not as obviously a 'survival of the fittest' mentality as described by Kline, the inclination of those in ministry can often be to 'rescue' the other.

In contrast, the pastoral supervisory experience is ideally a different and more helpful encounter; rather than rushing into 'rescue' by offering a solution, the supervisor uses their presence to enable the supervisee to find the answer within themselves, through adept listening, reflecting, and using pertinent questions that educe other perspectives and possibilities.

This focus on the use of skilful questions is amplified by Davys and Beddoe: "supervision is about asking questions which in turn leads to more questions. This develops learning, which is not necessarily about answers."[18] Pastoral supervision is an opportunity for the supervisee to develop the practice of becoming more consciously present to themselves, to their thoughts, their emotions and their physical responses, and to their own inner experience. Silsbee defines presence as a "state of awareness, in the moment, characterized by the felt experience of timelessness, connectedness and a larger truth."[19] Being 'fully present' involves the giving of time, genuine attention, compassion, deep thoughtfulness and prayer, which can all be encapsulated in a word—love. The ongoing experience of this level of presence within supervision can develop within the supervisee the skill of being intentional, which has been described by supervisees as a 'giving of oneself wholly'—a 'laying aside of all other distractions and applying concentration,' and of 'being aware of the importance of this particular moment in time.' Thus, through the supervisor's attentive presence, over time the supervisee becomes more aware of the spiritual discipline of being more present to themselves and to the whisper of God. This potentially impacts not only the quality of supervision but, over time, can also benefit the quality of other interactions as the supervisee develops a heightened alertness to each particular context and learns the art of being more fully present to themselves, to the other, and to God's presence, in those situations. The conscious choice to be fully present can deepen empathy and create meaningful conversations, which can lead to a sense of assurance, well-being, and deep-down sense of peace. This empowering experience, which is both exemplified and facilitated by the competent supervisor, is expressed in the reflection made by one supervisee, "We should, perhaps, think of ourselves as midwives—we assist others to give birth to solutions!"

Another metaphor that may be helpful to comprehend the experience of pastoral supervision is the parallel to the journey to the promised land, which

Brueggemann termed an "ongoing pilgrimage."[20] The reflective and validating presence within the supervisory relationship can reassure the supervisee that whatever they are going through is not necessarily as uncommon as they might otherwise have perceived it to be. In other words, pastoral supervision is an opportunity to explore territory that one may not have explored before, to have someone intimately travel alongside you, sharing not only the conversation and the nurture, but also the beauty, the silences, the challenges and the discomforts, while all the time having a sense of a distant destination that it is not yet in sight.

While we are likely to find ourselves in supervisory relationships with people of our own faith, it is worth considering that there may be valuable experience in being present to people from other faith backgrounds. As Ballard states, "it is all too easy to 'close Scripture down' by our own blindnesses, obstinacy and even 'orthodoxies'"[21] as we presume our understanding of the Divine as the only possibility. If one looks closely at the Scriptures, there is evidence that God Himself does not ignore the gifts that the 'pagan' brings; even to the record of wise men bearing gifts for the Christ-child, who came from the East—in other words, they came from lands beyond Judaism. Rohr challenges,

> When another's experience of God isn't exactly the way I would describe it, doesn't mean that they haven't had an experience of God or that their experience is completely wrong. . . . Could it not be that this Hindu, this Sufi, this charismatic, this Jewish woman has, in fact, touched upon the same Eternal mystery that I am seeking?[22]

The experience of Christian leaders seeking deep encounter, who have chosen to move beyond the boundaries and barriers of their own religious persuasion, has been recorded as remarkably life enriching. To quote Merton:

> Therefore, the question of contacts and actual communication between contemplatives of the various traditions no longer presents very great obstacles. A little experience of such dialogue shows at once that this is precisely the most fruitful and the most rewarding level of ecumenical exchange. . . . Indeed, it is illuminating to the point of astonishment to talk to a Zen Buddhist from Japan and to find that you have more in common with him than with those of your own compatriots who are little concerned with religion or interested only in its external practice.[23]

Ultimately, the purpose of pastoral supervision is surely to explore and more deeply understand, within the context of one's work, how to "enable the community of faith critically to understand the faith and to express answers to the questions: Who is God? Where is God to be found today and what does this God require of us here and now?"[24]

Pastoral supervision creates the space to ponder such questions as these within one's own context—and, as recorded throughout Judeo-Christian history, each story of the Bible is also "an account of human response."[25] What is essential for using this reflective space to 'make meaning' within ministry is that participants are clear about the purpose of their meeting, which Paterson describes as "the intentional dialogue between Soul, Role and Context,"[26] and which may be exemplified by Palmer's phrase "the journey towards an undivided life."[27] Pastoral supervision uses a rich toolbox of creative tools that can evoke a greater awareness of God's presence and guidance in the work context, as expressed by a supervisee: 'Sometimes the power of God's Spirit confirms . . . (the) decision you should take, and this realisation can be unsettling and uncomfortable.'

It is usual for the pastoral supervisor to enquire of the supervisee what will be helpful to invite the presence of God within the session, and the response to this is different for different people—for example, spending some moments in mindful, quiet, praying together or lighting a candle. Together, supervisor and supervisee trust that God will illuminate and guide the journey—that the Divine is present not only in the conversation but also in the pauses and silent reflection, which are integral to meaningful pastoral supervision. As commented upon by one supervisee, 'The presence of God is vital to the dynamic of supervision.' Divine presence within the pastoral supervisory relationship is underpinned by the truth and promise of the "one God and Father of all, who is over all, and through all, and in all" (Ephesians 4:6). God's presence is not only found in the mystical and invisible but also in the very way that the supervisor and supervisee are present to each other and give witness to what is unfolding. A parallel to this may be drawn from when Jesus encourages his disciples, "Let us go off by ourselves to some place where we will be alone and you can rest a while" (Mark 6:31). He models the need not only for acts of kindness within community, but also an opportunity to draw apart and to reflect—to be still to hear God.

Pastoral supervision provides a sacred space for the supervisee to share their own 'history': as articulated by Ballard, "That God is present 'by, with and under' the historical reality of the creature. History itself can thus be sacramental, the place of meeting with the divine."[28] Schillerbeeckx reminds us that, "human encounter with Jesus is, therefore, the sacrament of encounter with God."[29]

As already discussed, the pastoral supervisory process creates a sense of 'pilgrimage' and, at the personal level, there may be a parallel with Christ's journey to the cross, to resurrection and ascension.

> All bring our own expertise and experiences, our prejudices and ignorance to the process . . . and need to work through them, perhaps unlearn them, so that they do not get in the way and suppress the voice of the Spirit. We also have to be open to learn new things about ourselves, about God, about the world, that can either be exciting or fascinating or, perhaps, fearsome and difficult. It is necessary to work through them and come out the other side.[30]

In other words, there needs to be a 'dying' to old habits and mindsets to enable a new and different way of being, and this is an ongoing journey that will take a lifetime to accomplish. The pastoral supervisor can provide helpful support and accompaniment during the joys and challenges of ministry.

Moore proposes that the level to which supervisees will trust supervisors is directly related to the level to which they experience the supervisor's credibility, reliability, and intimacy.[31] Trust is enhanced when supervisees know that their supervisor has *credibility*, that they have 'credentials'—they are qualified, competent, and bring a breadth of knowledge and skill regarding effective supervision. When supervisors have 'credence' by demonstrating their belief in the value and truth of the supervision encounter, they establish a collaborative encounter where "shared wisdom that can emerge from the learning relationship."[32] Moore adds, "supervisees will be more inclined to trust supervisors if they have confidence that those supervisors will follow through on their promises," that they demonstrate reliability by being consistent, dependable, and "show that they are prepared to go the extra mile."[33] He continues, "effective supervisors are skilled in emotional intelligence that adds intimacy to the equation. When intimacy is high, then supervisees get an emotional sense that it matters to supervisors that they achieve their learning goals."[34]

It is important to emphasise that relationships are built through the quality of presence, which relies upon covenanted boundaries to ensure that the psychological safety of the supervision experience is not compromised, especially as self-disclosure can be challenging for some people, and there may be occasions when some invisible, but significant, line may be unhelpfully crossed. Meaningful presence is determined by effective boundaries which are reliant on wise use of power. Thus, the issue of power within pastoral supervision needs to be reflected upon to ensure that the presence of the Divine, and the presence of the supervisor and of the supervisee to themselves and to their interpersonal dynamics, is not clouded or contaminated.

POWER IN THE PASTORAL SUPERVISORY RELATIONSHIP

An understanding of power in the pastoral supervisory relationship is "better explored than ignored," state Hawkins and Shohet,[35] because, as bluntly put by Morgan, "Power influences who gets what, when and how."[36] I propose that the quality of presence may be helpfully established or contaminated by the use, or misuse, of power, which I seek to clarify here. Power can be defined simply as, "the medium through which conflicts of interest are ultimately resolved."[37] This ever-present, yet mostly invisible element, termed 'power,' needs to be understood and acknowledged for successful pastoral supervision to take place. The role of the supervisor, and their understanding and use of power, is essential to offer the most helpful interventions. What is modelled within pastoral supervision may well impact the way that those in ministry use power within the context of their vocation and work. "Powerlessness . . . tends to breed bossiness rather than true leadership. In large organizations . . . it is powerlessness that often creates ineffective desultory management and petty, dictatorial, rules-minded managerial styles."[38] Benefiel and Holton advocate that "the goal [in supervision] is always critical reflection and professional growth, not power or control. The problem with power and control in the supervisory relationship, as elsewhere, is that it does not circulate; it tends to accumulate, to become increasingly asymmetric."[39]

So, how is power exercised and, especially as it applies to pastoral supervision, how is it exercised for ministerial growth and accountability? Power in the church is an interesting and sometimes confusing concept. We seek and trust in the power of sovereign God. We are living in the age of the Spirit whose power draws out and leads to the completion of what Jesus began (Acts 1:8; John 14:25–26). In relation to power, the New Testament writings identify a set of functions for the oversight of the first Christian congregations as the new covenant community:

> Bishops were to 'take care of God's church' (1 Timothy 3:5); deacons were those who served (1 Timothy 3:13); and elders whom Paul had earlier called 'overseers,' whose duty it was 'to shepherd the church of God' (Acts 20:28) were to exercise 'rule' over others (1 Timothy 5:17), though precautions were urged that they should 'tend the flock of God . . . exercising the oversight . . . with humility.' (1 Peter 5:2–5)[40]

Yet, "power can often be considered a dirty word in church circles," state Leach and Paterson: "A proper emphasis on servanthood in ministry can be easily confused with a refusal to name and exercise properly the power which the authorisation of the church confers and with which charismatic gifts are invited."[41] So, Christian leaders have power, both divine and human, which is used in, and through, the church and the community of faith. A discerning spirit, and great wisdom, are needed to know when to exercise power over, and when to empower; when to exercise God-given authority and when to make room for the power of God to move and inspire the individual, groups, and the community. These are issues that can be better understood in their unique context when deliberated upon within the safe space of pastoral supervision.

Inherent in power, and the use thereof, is authority. The perception of authority is that it belongs to a person who has been given such power to make and enforce decisions. It can also refer to someone who is an expert (authority) in a field (e.g., supervision). A clear understanding of the authority/power that is invested is crucial to recognise, because it affects the way pastoral supervision is offered and the ways in which those involved will relate to each other. To have a greater understanding of the dynamics of power within the pastoral supervisory relationship/s, it can be helpful to consider the five types of power identified by French and Raven: *reward*, *coercive*, *legitimate*, *expert* and *referent* power.[42] Johnston gives a succinct definition of these types of power, the first four of which he discusses herewith:

> Briefly, *reward power* is evident when the person with power has the capacity to offer a reward or benefit to the one they seek to influence. *Coercive power* exists when, rather than reward, punishment can be inflicted for failure to comply. *Legitimate power* involves situations in which a person believes that the one with power has a recognised right to exercise authority by virtue of a number of things including but not limited to cultural conditioning and social or organizational structures. . . . *Expert power* is grounded in knowledge, experience or ability that a particular person may have or have access to which is needed by others.[43]

It is evident that some forms of power will not be helpful within the context of pastoral supervision, and that power needs to be wisely used. Pastoral supervision holds the potential for redistribution of all types of power and, in particular, for a significant increase in referent power: "*Referent power* is not coercive or rewarding in nature, rather it is by virtue of the strength of association that power is transferred from one to another."[44] This provides the opportunity for the *expert power* of the supervisor to develop *referent power* within the supervisee. Furthermore, Johnston proposes this "*referent power* . . . could well lead to the exercise of a more healthy power within the wider church context, which in turn can impact community at large."[45]

Pastoral supervision, within a ministerial context, has at its centre the belief that God is present, that He ultimately holds the power, directs the activities, inspires the mind and heart, and brings the change. "For where two or three gather in my name, there am I with them" (Matthew 18:20). One supervisee observed, "There can be a kind of 'energy transfer' between people who are keenly in tune with God and one another." This power enables us to share, listen, and respond appropriately to situations, both within supervision and within ministry, often confirming what we already know and what we should do, where God is 'the source, the driver, the power of change and progress.' Brueggemann states the Bible provides us with "an alternative identity, an alternative way of understanding ourselves, an alternative way of relating to the world. It offers a radical and uncompromising challenge to our ordinary ways of self-understanding."[46] He continues to state that, "theological reflection is the training of the imagination so that we are freed to discern the Spirit and to let the Scripture, in all its maddening obscurity as well as glory, lead us where it will."[47]

Even with Christian leaders who seek to follow God, power dynamics introduce challenges and opportunities with regard to perceived, and actual, power. Power operates in the in-between spaces in contexts and relationships. Just as a leader cannot lead without followers, individuals and groups cannot exercise power independent of context and relationships. It is important to recognise that there is an asymmetrical power dynamic in any supervisory relationship. As Johnston notes, "the interactions within the group, influence the resultant contribution of each member,"[48] and this plays out even in a 'group of two.' The task at hand, and the desired outcome, should direct and influence the presence and practice of power.

The issue of power naturally raises the issue of vulnerabilty. As the supervisee chooses to open themselves to the supervisor, there is naturally a sense of vulnerability. And, as human beings, we are sometimes slow to allow this—as, in a sense, we are giving 'power over us' to another. It is of note that,

> to be trusted with the story of another is to be given power. The more honest and vulnerable a person is encouraged to be, the more powerful will be the interventions we make and the more important it becomes that we are in touch with what the Holy Spirit is doing and with the dimensions of our own personalities and experiences that are likely to get in the way.[49]

An issue to be aware of, and named, within the supervisory relationship, is dual roles. Unexplored roles have the potential to negatively influence the supervisory relationship, as a supervisor might hold other roles that could influence issues and impact other areas of the work. This raises the question as to whether a person who holds a position of authority over the supervisee can effectively fulfill the task of pastoral supervisor, or whether there is a danger that the person's role can potentially obstruct, or distort, the effectiveness of the supervision. This is especially true of hiearchical provision of supervision which can effect power and crosses boundaries.

Leach and Paterson advocate that the team leader needs to be alert to the complexity of the dynamics of their own power.[50] The supervisor has the power to use, or not to use, their power as best suits the needs of the supervisee at that particular time, and in that particular context. Even when dual roles do not present themselves, the pastoral supervisor needs to still hold awareness that they may be perceived by the supervisee as holding expert power. Spoelstra and Pienaar state, "only the strong can afford to be weak, . . . in fact, the strong, by being weak, become even stronger."[51] I propose that an effective pastoral supervisor needs to embrace this 'weak power,' which, at times, Jesus modelled, to create safety and space for supervisees to experience self-examination and pastoral encounter. 'The pastoral supervisor is therefore always a powerful person and needs to be aware of that power and use it for good.'[52]

The pastoral supervisor also needs to be aware that power is not only about authority that is attached to the position of an individual but can also be inherent in the nature and behaviour of a participant. It is recognised that certain people hold more power because of their personality. Indeed, one person can have power over another, even though their roles may be equal.

To summarise, wherever there are issues of boundaries, as in pastoral supervison, there are also related issues of power, and issues of power will be particularly apparent if a person in that context holds a role of authority.

BOUNDARIES—THE INTRINSIC LINK OF PRESENCE AND POWER

Whenever one is in the presence of another, power dynamics exist, and establishing and upholding mutually respectful boundaries is central to creating meaningful presence. A safe, secure, compassionate experience of the presence of the other, inviting the presence of God, is needed within pastoral supervision for the supervisee to allow presence to oneself—an opening of the 'inner gate' to one's thoughts, and also to one's bodily reactions, emotions, anxieties, vulnerabilities, intuitions, and dreams. For such a level of safety to exist in the pastoral supervisory relationship, there need to be clear boundaries. Issues of damaged boundaries are invariably linked to issues of power that is wielded inappropriately.

A helpful analogy in this regard is one's own skin—a flexible membrane that both protects one from infection and damage and contains that which is within. Without the boundary of our skin, there would not be adequate containment for us or for others. It is interesting to note that when we cross the boundaries of appropriate social conduct, our metaphors of speech relate closely to that of breaking the boundary of skin; we refer to a person 'being abrasive,' of 'feeling wounded' or 'scarred.' Appropriate boundaries are essential for the healthy functioning of the supervisory relationship, and when issues of power arise, these boundaries are at risk of being breached. The pastoral supervisor encourages respectful boundaries, which create containment, for the benefit of the supervisory process and of the supervisee, as well as for the professional role of the supervisor. When both supervisor and supervisee hold such boundaries in awareness, the personal power of each individual can be effectively released. When one ignores boundary needs, both the safety of the relationship and the supervisee's personal power to create the change needed for self are at risk. Personal power can be seen as the power to navigate one's emotional faculties into the position of responding helpfully, rather than reacting, in all forms of communication. This personal power is the by-product of practising healthy boundaries, of knowing what is 'me' and 'my stuff,' and what is not—what is 'you' and 'your stuff,' while remaining committed to the supervisory task at hand. When we empower others, we ourselves become empowered to be part of meaningful change.

Such effectively boundaried space that allows personal reflection and growth, is captured in the 1 Corinthians 13 passage on love, which denounces egotistical practices such as boasting and focusing on wrongdoing, and rather advocates the practice of qualities such as patience, kindness, trust, hope, and perseverance. As stated in Proverbs 25:28, "Like a city whose walls are broken through is a person who lacks self-control." Thus, the pastoral supervision covenant is an agreement to uphold boundaries that ensure each person's emotional containment, which is essential for psychological well-being. An effectively boundaried supervisory space enables the supervisor and supervisee to 'stay in their own psychological skin' and not invade, or damage, the space and integrity of the other. Palmer proposes that a "circle of trust consists of relationships that are neither invaded or evaded."[53] By keeping within one's own boundaries, one is able to see the other's perspective, recognise one's own perspective (how life is within my skin), and to leave the supervisee free, yet supported, to make the choices they need to make for themselves. In this lies the power of pastoral supervision. Therefore, the effective *referent power* of the supervisee depends primarily on the *expert power* of the supervisor. Kadushin emphasises that "the supervisor must accept, without defensiveness or apology, the authority and related power inherent in his [or her] position. Use of authority may sometimes be unavoidable. The supervisor can increase effectiveness if he [or she] feels, and can communicate, a conviction in his [or her] behaviour."[54]

The supervisor's awareness of their authority in this role is of particular importance, because a key part of this work is to be alert to risk and safeguarding issues, as there may arise situations where the supervisee could be at risk of being abused or be at risk of perpetrating unethical or abusive behaviour. In such times, the supervisor evokes a collaborative conversation about the possibility of risk and identifying steps to ameliorate these. This approach stems from a shared trust and accountability for ethical awareness and professional practice that draws on the expert and legitimate power of the supervisor, and which calls on the referent power of the supervisee. However, there may be times when it is the supervisor's responsibility to ensure that action is taken. At such times, every effort should be made to liaise with, and involve, the supervisee in this decision. As for example, the Methodist Church in Britain stipulates, "In the case of serious and immediate risks of harm the supervisor may, if consent is withheld by the supervisee, notify a safeguarding team and/or the minister in oversight of the situation and record that they have done this on an Agreed Record."[55]

My experience over the years, as well as relevant literature, convinces me that pastoral supervision, where the supervisor's *expert power* is used to develop the supervisee's *referent power*, is a helpful practice. It provides suitable and effective means of supporting leaders in ministry and establishes a way of interacting that encourages deeper listening skills, which leads to deeper respect, deeper understanding and self-discovery. This process invites the presence of God and evokes that presence to self and to others.

IMPLICATIONS

The Methodist Church in Britain commissioned a research project in 2019–2020, three years after the implementation of pastoral supervision. While the research revealed some negativity and resistance to supervision, the majority of participants interviewed held a positive attitude towards supervision, for example:

- *76 percent: improved connection with God's presence and own sense of vocation.*
- *73 percent: improved well-being and reduced anxiety and stress.*
- *70 percent: improved ability to use time more intentionally.*
- *68 percent: improved ability to identify and manage risk.*
- *74 percent: improved ability to clarify role and boundaries.*
- *65 percent: improved relationship with colleagues.*
- *71 percent: improved sense of accountability.*[56]

While the feedback from this survey is encouraging, my experience has been that, despite the possibilities that supervision offers, or perhaps because of them, there has been a resistance to the idea that I could significantly benefit from participating in pastoral supervision. Many think that it is intended only for those who are new to the ministry, or that attending pastoral supervision is a sign of weakness, or that self-exposure will minimise their status and reveal their vulnerabilities. Others are concerned that because of the confidential nature of their work, they cannot reveal, or share, about others or about themselves. Unless the pastoral supervisory space is proven to be safe and beneficial, there will be those who are suspicious and guarded about a supervisory process that is unfamiliar to them, and who consequently will not venture in.

The implications of power and presence need to be recognised and addressed, so as to create a safe, transformational, sacred space within the pastoral supervisory relationship. As some ministers share their experience of the blessing of effective pastoral supervision, it is becoming more likely that those who are reticent may reconsider their viewpoint. To successfully embrace pastoral supervision requires a positive personal conviction of the need to participate in pastoral supervision, the quality of and commitment to the covenant relationship entered into, and a skilled pastoral supervisor.

The Importance of Personal Conviction of Those in Ministry to Participate in Pastoral Supervision

When one considers attending pastoral supervision, the issue of whether it is by personal conviction or by mandatory requirement of an institution has interesting implications. Personal arrangement gives one the opportunity to be voluntarily involved, to choose one's own pastoral supervisor, to influence the agenda and to hold one's own sense of personal power. In contrast, institutional requirement of supervision is frequently identified with mentoring or line management. It often has the institution's needs for productivity, control, and outcomes at its centre; and such supervision is guided towards these ends. While these goals are necessary for the successful running of an institution, they often fail to meet the deeper personal needs of those who are being supervised.

If those in ministry do not have the support they need, they may be prone to burnout or disillusionment, leading to ineffective work, potentially more conflict issues and greater risk of health challenges that would impact productivity or could even lead to resignation. Yet, something more than 'survival' is called for:

> If our roles were more deeply informed by the truth that is in our souls, the general level of sanity and safety would rise dramatically.[57]

As Maya Angelou expresses, "the question is not how to survive, but how to thrive with passion, compassion, humour and style."[58] The needs of the institution are better served when its members have the professional support that can contribute towards their self-motivation and commitment, to empower them towards achieving their desired goals, including their personal well-being. I propose that the church needs to be actively promoting and supporting those in ministry to receive quality pastoral supervision. As Paterson states, "many practitioners are struggling to keep the inner motivational pilot lights lit (never mind stoking the fire in the bellies) and that too many are sick and tired of being hosed down by policies and performance indicators that extinguish the joy they once knew at work."[59]

Covenant Relationship

To achieve the balance of power that is required for the delicate and yet potent work of pastoral supervision, I propose that the creation of a supervisory covenant is essential, one that is similar to, but not identical to, a contract. According to Pyle and Seal, covenants and contracts have common elements, but also significant differences.

> Contracts are based on responsibility; covenants are based on relationships. Contracts define boundaries and bind, covenants provide for growth and becoming. Contracts are legalistic and enforceable; covenants focus on accountability and redemption. . . . Covenant is intentional. It grows out of our relationship with God. God's covenant with us colours and shapes our understanding of our covenanting with each other. It provides structure for relationships, with God and others.[60]

In biblical terms and in Christian practice, the term 'covenant' is used to describe the mutual agreement of structure and accountability. Pastoral supervision, according to Pohly, affirms the relational nature of covenant between God and people, which has as its objective, "the well-being and mission of an entire nation."[61] It is this covenant relationship that exists between God and self that enables those in Christian service to exercise that same covenantal relationship with each other. Hawkins and Shohet state,

> Supervision is a joint endeavour in which a practitioner, with the help of a supervisor, attends to themselves as part of their relationships and the wider systemic context, and by so doing improves the quality of their work, transforms their relationships, continuously develops themselves, their practice and the wider profession.[62]

So, the supervisory covenant creates the context and purpose for pastoral supervision, exploring the goals of this 'pilgrimage' and consensually determining how it is managed.

Vital Role of the Pastoral Supervisor

The professionalism, training and insightful skills of the pastoral supervisor are paramount to the effectiveness of the supervisory process. Leach and Paterson remind us "that to sit with someone as their supervisor is to be in a position of power. . . . Awareness of the power you have, and how to use it for the good of those you work with, is an essential dimension of all Christian practices."[63] Unless the supervisor gives attention to creating *referent power,* and thus facilitates the supervisee's presence to self and to God's Spirit, the much-needed benefits of pastoral supervision are unlikely to be accomplished. Hawthorne asserts that there may be times when the supervisor abdicates or manipulates power. She states, "with the role of supervisor comes the responsibility to be aware of your own power and learn ways of utilising this power in ways that are: appropriate, well intentioned, anti-oppressive and sensitive to the particular background of the supervisee."[64] This also necessitates working with the supervisee to "explore dimensions of risk in their work including those relating to safeguarding self and others; the use of power by self and others and the negotiation of boundaries."[65]

The effective pastoral supervisor has an awareness of how crossing boundaries and mishandling power will affect the sense of presence in the supervisory relationship, obstructing, or contaminating, the potential work of the supervisee. As Benefiel and Holton state, "supervision is always alert to the issues of equality, to the call to respect deep democracy and its many voices, to be open to change in perspectives."[66] The supervisor, in order to effect greater presence to self, to others, and to the issue at hand, recognises and calls to attention those thought patterns that are blocking progress. "Supervisors are challenged to enhance the quality and depth of the supervisory conversation by making the questioning of assumptions a contextual necessity."[67]

While there is discussion regarding the inherent, asymmetrical power balance in the pastoral supervisory space, it could be helpful to further explore whether this issue with power has less to do with the tasks of supervision and more to do with the attitude and skill of the supervisor. As observed by Weld,

> Key to enabling the transformative function in supervision is the supervisory relationship, which should be built on a foundation of openness and honesty, providing a working partnership that models respect, care, empathy, careful use of humour, challenge and holistic recognition of the worker as a professional being.[68]

It is important to note that the work of the effective pastoral supervisor is, in itself, challenging, and that it should be required of the supervisor to also be receiving supervision.[69] The supervisor him/herself needs a reflective space to ensure these elements of presence and power are understood and effectively managed, to create a pastoral supervisory process that generates a reflective, healthy, and transformational space.

CONCLUSION

Where does a person in ministry go when they are discouraged, burned out, or facing challenges in their work? Those in ministry need the assurance of confidentiality and of an empathetic, nonjudgmental ear, from one who has the professional skills to be able to support the practitioner to tease out the tangle of work overload, complicated relationships, and competing priorities. Professional pastoral supervision is an essential and beneficial practice for those in ministry, and for the wider church, and this is an area that needs to be developed and 'normalised' in the lives of those who respond to this vocation.

After seven years since the commencement of the pastoral supervision programme within the Methodist Church in Britain, the findings indicated that

> participants were aware of the beneficial impact of supervision on both their individual health and wellbeing and also that of the organisation as a whole. The opportunity to share problems and difficulties and to celebrate and learn from what has been successful was acknowledged to decrease feelings of isolation, reduce the risk of mental health issues and increase a sense of empowerment and resilience, all of which contribute to reducing defensive attitudes, to better planning and decision making and improved relationships. The ability to stay with uncertainty and inaction with increased equanimity was also specifically mentioned.[70]

Benefiel uses the word 'harmony' as she identifies the need in organisation to provide an environment where there is congruence between work and our moral/ethical values and family responsibilities and where everyone is treated justly:

> [where] people can find meaning, significance and success through work, and where personal and workplace values align to greater outward harmony and inner spiritual life . . . to grow holistically and build relationships themselves while they are serving.[71]

She also notes that when these factors are in place, it 'improves [parishioner] care.'[72] Weld affirms,

> Good supervision can create shifts in thinking and behavior that contribute to positive, long-lasting change . . . in directions which support . . . powerful professional and personal development, always aimed at increasing the level of service we provide to others.[73]

To achieve this quality of care, the various aspects that determine effective pastoral supervision, including presence and power, need to be reflected upon, as these are imperative to creating a safe, open, authentic and trusting environment within the pastoral supervisory relationship. This has the potential to positively impact the personal well-being of those in ministry and their greater sphere of influence, benefiting not only the worker but also the organisation and the community.

In ending this chapter, let us reflect on Jane Leach's statement as she recalls the journey of supervision within the Methodist Church in Britain,

> as we have risked what matters most deeply to us within structured supervisory relationships, we have started to hear God's voice. This is a voice calling to us not only from a simplified past, but in the midst of the cacophonous present, calling us, not only as individuals, but as the body of Christ, into a new future that we have not yet imagined.[74]

BIBLIOGRAPHY

Association of Pastoral Supervision and Education, "Definition and Ethos." https://www.pastoralsupervision.org.uk/home/about/definition-and-ethos (accessed 1 August 2022).

Ballard, Paul. "The Bible in Theological Reflection: Indications from the History of Scripture," *Practical Theology* 4, no. 1 (2011): 35–47.

Benefiel, Margaret, and Geraldine Holton. *The Soul of Supervision: Integrating Practice and Theory.* New York: Moorehouse Publishing, 2010.

Benefiel, Margaret. *Soul at Work: Spiritual Leadership in Organisations*. Dublin: Veritas Publications, 2005.

Bochen, Christine. *Thomas Merton: Essential Writings*. Ossining, NY: Orbis Books, 2000.

Boyatzis, Richard, and Annie McKee. *Resonant Leadership: Renewing Yourself and Connecting with Others Through Mindfulness, Hope and Compassion.* Boston: Harvard Business School Press, 2005.

Brueggemann, Walter. *The Bible Makes Sense.* Louisville: Westminster/John Knox Press, 2001.

Carroll, Michael. "One More Time: What Is Supervision?" *Psychotherapy in Australia* 13, no. 3 (2007): 34–40.

Davys, Allyson, and Liz Beddoe. *Best Practice in Professional Supervision: A Guide for the Helping Professions.* London: Jessica Kingsley, 2010.

de Gruchy, John. *Theology and Ministry in Context and Crisis: A South African Perspective.* New York: Harper & Row Publishers, 1966.

Feinberg, Joel. *Reason and Responsibility: Readings in Some Basic Problems of Philosophy*. Belmont, CA: Dickenson Publishers, 1968.

French, John, and Bertram Raven. "The Bases of Social Power," *Classics of Organization Theory*, eds. Jay Shafritz and Steven Ott. Orlando: Harcourt College Publishers, 2001.

Hawkins, Peter, and Aisling McMahon. *Supervision in the Helping Professions.* London: Open University Press, 2020.

Hawkins, Peter, and Robin Shohet. *Supervision in the Helping Professions.* Maidenhead: Open University Press, 2012.

Hawthorne, Lillian. "Games Supervisors Play," *Social Work Journal* 20, no. 3 (1975): 179–83.

The Holy Bible. *The NIV Study Bible—New International Version*. Grand Rapids, MI: Zondervan Bible Publishers, 1985.

Johnston, Richard. "The Relevance of Non-Directive Consultancy for Contemporary Church Ministry." Unpublished MA dissertation, University of Sheffield at Cliff College, 2004.

Kadushin, Alfred. *Supervision in Social Work*. New York: Columbia University Press, 1992.

Kanter, Rosabeth. "Power Failure in Management Circuits," in *Classics of Organization Theory,* eds. Jay Shafritz and Steven Ott. Orlando: Harcourt College Publishers, 2001.

Kline, Nancy. *Time to Think: Listening to Ignite the Human Mind*. London: Ward Lock. Cassell Illustrated, 1999.

Leach, Jane. *A Charge to Keep: Reflective Supervision and the Renewal of Christian Leadership.* Nashville: Wesley's Foundery Books, 2020.

Leach, Jane, and Michael Paterson. *Pastoral Supervision: A Handbook.* London: SCM Press, 2015).

The Methodist Church of Great Britain, "*Reflective Supervision Report*," Methodist.org.uk, 2021. https://www.methodist.org.uk/media/21766/conf-2021-40-reflective-supervision-report.pdf (accessed 1 August 2022).

Moore, Bobby. *Reflexive Supervision: A Workbook for Learning Within and Across Professions*. CreateSpace Independent Publishing Platform, 2017.

Morgan, Gareth. *Images of Organization*. Thousand Oaks, CA: Sage Publications, 1997.

Mullally, Bill. "The effect of presence and power in the pastoral supervisory relationship." *HOLINESS: The Journal of Wesley House Cambridge*, 3 no. 1 (2019): 5–34

Palmer, Parker. *A Hidden Wholeness: The Journey Toward an Undivided Life.* San Francisco: Jossey-Bass, 2004.

Paterson, Michael. *Between a Rock and a Hard Place: Pastoral Supervision Revisited and Revisioned*. Independently Published, 2020.

Pohly, Kenneth. *Transforming the Rough Places: The Ministry of Supervision*. Ohio: Whaleprints, 1993.

Pyle, Mary, and William Seal. *Experiencing Ministry Supervision: A Field-Based Approach*. Nashville: Broadman & Holman Publishers, 1995.

Reflective Practice Journal: Formation and Supervision in Ministry. "Editorial Policy," 31 May 2022, https://www.reflective-practice-journal.org/author-guidelines (accessed 4 September 2022).

Rogers, Carl. *On Becoming a Person: A Therapist's View of Psychotherapy*. London: Constable, 1961.

Rohr, Richard. *Yes, and . . . , Daily Meditations*. Cincinnati: Franciscan Media, 2013.

Schillerbeeckx, Edward. *Christ the Sacrament of the Encounter with God.* New York: Sheed and Ward, 1963.

Silsbee, Doug. *Presence-Based Coaching: Cultivating Self-Generative Leaders through Mind, Body and Heart*. San Francisco: Jossey-Bass, 2008.

Spoelstra, Herman, and Wynand Pienaar. *Negotiation: Theories, Strategies and Skills*. South Africa: Juta and Company, 1999.

Vitello, Paul. "Taking a Break from the Lord's Work," *New York Times*, 1 August 2010, https://www.nytimes.com/2010/08/02/nyregion/02burnout.html. (accessed 1 August 2022).

Weld, Nicki. *A Practical Guide to Transformative Supervision for the Helping Professions: Amplifying Insight*. London: Jessica Kingsley Publishers, 2012.

NOTES

1. Paul Vitello, "Taking a Break from the Lord's Work," *New York Times*, 1 August 2010, https://www.nytimes.com/2010/08/02/nyregion/02burnout.html. (accessed 1 August 2022).

2. Jane Leach, *A Charge to Keep: Reflective Supervision and the Renewal of Christian Leadership* (Nashville: Wesley's Foundery Books, 2020), 12.

3. Richard Johnston, "The Relevance of Non-Directive Consultancy for Contemporary Church Ministry." Unpublished MA dissertation (University of Sheffield at Cliff College, 2004), 16.

4. Richard Boyatzis and Annie McKee, *Resonant Leadership*: *Renewing Yourself and Connecting with Others Through Mindfulness, Hope and Compassion* (Cambridge, MA: Harvard Business School Press, 2005), 63.

5. Bill Mullally, "The effect of presence and power in the pastoral supervisory relationship," *HOLINESS: The Journal of Wesley House Cambridge*, 3 no. 1 (2019): 5–34.

6. Carl Rogers, *On Becoming a Person: A Therapist's View of Psychotherapy*. (London: Constable, 1961), 33.

7. *Reflective Practice Journal: Formation and Supervision in Ministry*. "Editorial Policy," 31 May 2022, https://www.reflective-practice-journal.org/author-guidelines (accessed 4 September 2022).

8. Joel Feinberg, *Reason and Responsibility: Readings in Some Basic Problems of Philosophy* (Belmont, CA: Dickenson Publishers, 1968), 48.

9. Kenneth Pohly, *Transforming the Rough Places: The Ministry of Supervision*. (Ohio: Whaleprints, 1993), 2.

10. Michael Paterson, *Between a Rock and a Hard Place: Pastoral Supervision Revisited and Revisioned* (Independently Published, 2020), unpaginated.

11. Michael Carroll, "One More Time: What Is Supervision?" *Psychotherapy in Australia* 13, no. 3 (2007): 34–40.

12. Association of Pastoral Supervision and Education, "Definition and Ethos." https://www.pastoralsupervision.org.uk/home/about/definition-and-ethos. (accessed 1 August 2022).

13. The Holy Bible. *The NIV Study Bible—New International Version* (Michigan: Zondervan Bible Publishers, 1985).

14. Pohly, *Transforming the Rough Places*, 10.

15. Peter Hawkins and Aisling McMahon, *Supervision in the Helping Professions,* 5th ed. (London: Open University Press, 2020), 119.

16. Bobby Moore, *Reflexive Supervision: A Workbook for Learning Within and Across Professions* (CreateSpace Independent Publishing Platform, 2017), 58–59.

17. Nancy Kline, *Time to Think: Listening to Ignite the Human Mind* (London: Ward Lock. Cassell Illustrated, 1999), 31.

18. Allyson Davys and Liz Beddoe, *Best Practice in Professional Supervision: A Guide for the Helping Professions* (London: Jessica Kingsley, 2010), 239.

19. Doug Silsbee, *Presence-Based Coaching: Cultivating Self-Generative Leaders through Mind, Body and Heart* (San Francisco: Jossey-Bass, 2008), 21.

20. Walter Brueggemann, *The Bible Makes Sense* (Louisville: Westminster/John Knox Press, 2001), 10.

21. Paul Ballard, "The Bible in Theological Reflection: Indications from the History of Scripture," *Practical Theology* 4, no. 1 (2011): 35–47.

22. Richard Rohr, *Yes, and . . . , Daily Meditations* (Cincinnati: Franciscan Media, 2013).

23. Christine Bochen, *Thomas Merton: Essential Writings* (Ossining, NY: Orbis Books, 2000), 171.

24. John de Gruchy, *Theology and Ministry in Context and Crisis: A South African Perspective* (New York: Harper & Row Publishers, 1966), 55.

25. Ballard, "The Bible in Theological Reflection," 35–47.

26. Paterson, "Between a Rock and a Hard Place," unpaginated.

27. Parker Palmer, *A Hidden Wholeness: The Journey Toward an Undivided Life* (San Francisco: Jossey-Bass, 2004), vii.

28. Ballard, "The Bible in Theological Reflection," 35–47.

29. Edward Schillerbeeckx, *Christ the Sacrament of the Encounter With God* (New York: Sheed and Ward, 1963), 15.

30. Ballard, "The Bible in Theological Reflection," 35–47.

31. Moore, *Reflexive Supervision*, 59.

32. Ibid.

33. Moore, *Reflexive Supervision*, 61.

34. Ibid.

35. Peter Hawkins and Robin Shohet, *Supervision in the Helping Professions,* 4th ed. (Maidenhead: Open University Press, 2012), 122.

36. Gareth Morgan, *Images of Organization* (Thousand Oaks, CA: Sage Publications, 1997), 170.

37. Ibid.

38. Rosabeth Kanter, "Power Failure in Management Circuits," in *Classics of Organization Theory,* eds. Jay Shafritz and Steven Ott (Orlando: Harcourt College Publishers, 2001), 343.
39. Margaret Benefiel and Geraldine Holton, *The Soul of Supervision: Integrating Practice and Theory* (New York: Moorehouse Publishing, 2010), 138.
40. Pohly, *Transforming the Rough Places*, 10.
41. Jane Leach and Michael Paterson, *Pastoral Supervision: a Handbook* (London: SCM Press, 2015), 199.
42. John French and Bertram Raven, "The Bases of Social Power," *Classics of Organization Theory,* eds. Jay Shafritz and Steven Ott (Orlando: Harcourt College Publishers, 2001), 321.
43. Johnston, "The Relevance of Non-Directive Consultancy," 11.
44. Ibid.
45. Johnston, "The Relevance of Non-Directive Consultancy," 16.
46. Brueggemann, *The Bible Makes Sense*, 10.
47. Brueggemann, *The Bible Makes Sense*, 37.
48. Johnston, "The Relevance of Non-Directive Consultancy," 87.
49. Leach and Paterson, *Pastoral Supervision*, 200.
50. Leach and Paterson, *Pastoral Supervision*, 226.
51. Herman Spoelstra and Wynand Pienaar, *Negotiation: Theories, Strategies and Skills* (South Africa: Juta and Company, 1999), 131.
52. Leach and Paterson, *Pastoral Supervision*, 201.
53. Palmer, *A Hidden Wholeness*, 64.
54. Alfred Kadushin, *Supervision in Social Work* (New York: Columbia University Press, 1992), 112.
55. The Methodist Church of Great Britain, "*Reflective Supervision Report*," Methodist.org.uk, 2021, 640. https://www.methodist.org.uk/media/21766/conf-2021-40-reflective-supervision-report.pdf (accessed 1 August 2022).
56. The Methodist Church of Great Britain, "Reflective Supervision Report," 592.
57. Palmer, *A Hidden Wholeness*, 17.
58. Paterson, "Between a Rock and a Hard Place," (unpaginated).
59. Ibid.
60. Mary Pyle and William Seal, *Experiencing Ministry Supervision: a Field-Based Approach* (Nashville: Broadman & Holman Publishers, 1995), 50.
61. Pohly, *Transforming the Rough Places*, 10.
62. Hawkins and Shohet, *Supervision in the Helping Professions*, 5.
63. Leach and Paterson, *Pastoral Supervision*, 4.
64. Lillian Hawthorne, "Games Supervisors Play," *Social Work Journal* 20, no. 3 (1975): 179–83.
65. The Methodist Church of Great Britain, "Reflective Supervision Report," 653.
66. Benefiel and Holton, *The Soul of Supervision*, 138.
67. Ibid.
68. Nicki Weld, *A Practical Guide to Transformative Supervision for the Helping Professions: Amplifying Insight* (London: Jessica Kingsley Publishers, 2012), 130.
69. Leach and Paterson, *Pastoral Supervision*, 226.

70. The Methodist Church of Great Britain, “Reflective Supervision Report,” 594.

71. Margaret Benefiel, *Soul at Work: Spiritual Leadership in Organisations* (Dublin: Veritas Publications, 2005), 150.

72. Benefiel, *Soul at Work*, 151.

73. Weld, *A Practical Guide to Transformative Supervision*, 130.

74. Jane Leach, *A Charge to Keep*, 16.

Chapter Two

Reflecting Theologically in Pastoral Supervision

Peter Madsen Gubi

Pastoral supervision is different from other forms of reflective and supportive supervision, in that it draws from the wisdom and insight of spiritual and faith traditions in order to discern how that wisdom might inform practice. Yet, it is probably true to say that much of what happens in month-to-month pastoral supervision is more psychologically informed than theologically informed. The two disciplines need not conflict each other, but insights from psychology can be invaluable to arriving at theological responses and application for the practitioner. This chapter explores a way of bringing the theological and spiritual more into focus in pastoral supervision, so that they can appropriately be facilitated and integrated. In this chapter, I will write from a Christian perspective as that is the language in which I can most authentically express my theological and spiritual insight and understanding. However, that is not to denigrate the wisdom and insight that can come from other faith traditions and scripture. Indeed, it is hoped that pastoral supervisors of any faith and spirituality may find much in this chapter that resonates with them, albeit that they might express the process, insights, and wisdom differently, using the language which they find most authentic.

JUSTIFYING PASTORAL SUPERVISION THEOLOGICALLY

From a Christian perspective, the theological justification of pastoral supervision is already covered in the literature.[1, 2, 3, 4, 5] In addition, the Uniting Church in Australia Ministerial Education Commission[6] states that it is through relationships that God is revealed. God is active throughout history and is known and revealed. Through the life of Jesus, God is revealed, not as a theoretical or abstract principle, but in the actuality of a human person in the midst of human living, among the joys and sorrows, the needs and aspirations of ordinary human beings. The gospel is that the kingdom of God is among us, that the rule and purposes of God are realised in human engagement. "*For where two or three gather in my name, there am I with them*" (Matthew 18:20). God is revealed, again and again, in the events of our lives and in our meeting with each other. Pastoral supervision, therefore, is a meeting together in the fellowship of the Holy Spirit, which will lead us into truth.

One aim of pastoral supervision, from a theological and spiritual perspective, is to seek to know where God is in the events and engagements of our ministry or work context, and thus to know where we need to be and what we need to do in response to the activity of God in our lives. The disciples' learning was done 'at the coal-face' with Jesus. They saw and experienced the activity of God in His ministry. Jesus used parables, stories of an everyday kind, as the metaphors to frame the disciples' understandings of what they were experiencing, and as a way to penetrate to the deeper meaning of what they witnessed. This was the pastoral supervision that they experienced out of the covenantal relationship with their Lord.

Pastoral supervision is concerned with the congruity (i.e., appropriate and wise integration) between belief and practice. The primary focus is on what happens at the intersection of what one believes and how one lives out that belief. It is at this intersection that the possibility of integration occurs. Pastoral supervision is 'confessional' in the sense that in advocating wholeness, and it requires that people not only acknowledge and face their strengths and weaknesses but also accept and integrate them. It is only as people confess their weaknesses and strengths that the whole person can be addressed in the supervisory relationship. Pastoral supervision is reflective. Pastoral supervision occurs within a conversation in which people reflect critically on their personhood, ministry, work, and faith. Pastoral supervision is reflective in that the pastoral supervisor assists people in seeing themselves and their ministry (or work) more accurately, clearly, and creatively. Having seen themselves, people can decide to make the changes that they need to make. In reflecting on their ministry or work with a pastoral supervisor, the supervisee can have what they reflect on, reflected have back to them from another angle of vision. It is when people take ownership and responsibility for decisions and their future, that the possibility of integration occurs. Pastoral supervision is revelatory. One of the goals of pastoral supervision is to promote honesty. Pastoral supervision is tolerant of a person's weaknesses and shortcomings. It understands, but does not tolerate, dishonesty and self-deception. Pastoral supervision calls for authenticity and integrity. Its function is to encourage openness to the tradition, culture, and experience: places where God reveals God's 'self.' God continues to work in our lives, bringing new and creative ways into being within us. Pastoral supervision provides a process that can enable people to reflect on the movement of the spirit of God in their lives. The process of pastoral supervision helps us to consider what difference God's presence makes in our life and assists in the 'movement toward insight' about God's ongoing revelation in the world. Pastoral supervision is about gaining 'wisdom' and grace. Central to all critical reflection is wisdom. In all evaluation, we experience assessment, wisdom and grace. From a theological viewpoint, evaluation reveals and activates both God's wisdom and grace. It is in these terms, that we experience pastoral supervision. Pastoral supervision has a belief in the future. The 'becoming human' process which is provided for and actively encouraged in pastoral supervision, specifically implies belief in a future. God is always the 'God in front of us' and 'alongside us.' The present moment is not locked-in, not finished. It is open to the future and, for this reason, we are able to trust the 'process'; to grow means to allow for future change, optimistically and hopefully. In spite of the current struggle, there is hope of becoming a more integrated person and a more effective pastor/professional. There is present in pastoral supervision a vision of and toward the future. Pastoral supervision is contextual. It operates at many different levels of ministry and work, within and outside the church. The key to pastoral supervision is the facilitation of theological reflection in different vocational contexts.

REFLECTING THEOLOGICALLY AS AN ADDITIONAL MODE

One of the commonly utilised models for reflective supervision in various helping professional contexts, is Hawkins and Shohet's[7] seven- eyed process model. This model also underpins much of the understanding of the pastoral supervision process (i.e., what happens in the pastoral supervisory process), except for the theological/spiritual. These modes (or lenses, or aspects of focus in the supervision process) can be summarised as:

Mode 1: The focus is on the supervisee and what has been observed about them. Attention is concentrated on the content of the interaction between supervisee and supervisor—what supervisees say and how they say it, how they present themselves, and what they choose to talk about.

Mode 2: The focus is on what the supervisee did and how she or he responded to the situation. Attention is paid to the strategies and interventions/responses used by the supervisee and his or her reason for using them. The goal is to develop the supervisee's choices and skills in intervention/response.

Mode 3: The focus is on the relationship between supervisee and any others in the situation that she or he is reflecting on. Attention is paid to what was happening, consciously and unconsciously, in the relationship between the supervisee and others involved in the situation that is being reflected on, what images and metaphors might emerge, and what changes in voice and posture occurred in both parties. The goal is to develop the supervisee's insight and understanding of the relationship.

Mode 4: The focus is on the supervisee's process. Attention is paid to how the supervisee is consciously and unconsciously affected by the work/encounter with the others, and includes reflection on the supervisee's development and self-support, as well as issues of countertransference.

Mode 5: The focus is on the supervisory relationship. Attention is paid to how the supervisory relationship might unconsciously be playing out, or paralleling, the hidden dynamics of the work/encounter with the other. The goal is to enable the supervisee to surface unaware dynamics including issues of transference.

Mode 6: The focus is on the supervisor's process. Attention is paid to the supervisor's own here-and-now experience in the supervision; what feelings, thoughts, and images are emerging, and issues of countertransference.

Mode 7: The focus is on the wider context in which the supervisee's work is taking place. Attention is paid to social, cultural, political, and economic contexts as well as organisational factors affecting the supervisee, and possibly those in the situation/encounter that is being reflected on.

Good supervision usually involves movement between modes, and these modes are not chronological but rather they are aspects of the supervisory dynamic and process that come into 'view' and which *may* need to be attended to and facilitated in any session. However, in pastoral supervision, there is an eighth mode (or lens) to the supervisory process—that of theological/spiritual reflection; and it is the integration of this eighth mode/lens that this chapter seeks to develop. In pursuing how this might occur, there is an inevitable overlap with many of the modes expressed above. The theological doesn't stand 'apart' as separate, as to identify a situation that requires critical reflection is, in itself, an act of theology.[8]

MODE 8: THE THEOLOGICAL/SPIRITUAL MODE

Very little is written about how the theological and spiritual can be integrated into pastoral supervision. In exploring how pastoral supervisors might encourage this, I draw on Swinton and Mowat's[9] model of 'Practical Theological Reflection' and Gubi's[10, 11] 'Foci of Reflexivity' to formulate what I am now calling 'Mode 8: the theological/spiritual mode.'

Swinton and Mowat's[12] model of Practical Theological Reflection encompasses a four-stage approach, which can be summarised as:

Stage 1: *Current Praxis*: This is the stage of identifying a situation that requires critical reflection. This is likely to be what the pastoral supervisee wants to explore in pastoral supervision;
Stage 2: *Cultural/Contextual*: This is the stage of thinking about the situation, bringing insights from personal awareness, current theory and practice to the situation;
Stage 3: *Theological*: This is the stage where an implicit and explicit theological lens, or narrative, from established tradition and practice is brought to bear on the situation, in order to tease out areas of resonance and dissonance with established ways of thinking;
Stage 4: *Reformulating Revised Practice*: This is the stage at which new forms of practice, or new ways of thinking about current practice, emerge and are promoted in a way that is authentic and faithful.

In addition, Gubi's[13, 14] 'Foci for Reflexivity' consists of five stages and can be summarised as:

Stage 1: *Developing a growing awareness of how I am feeling about a situation that I have encountered or I am encountering.* This is likely to be what the pastoral supervisee wants to explore in pastoral supervision;
Stage 2: *Becoming aware of what this is tapping into for me in terms of my psychological processes.* This might be where a pastoral supervisee begins to make links with previous experiences and injuries at a feeling level in seeking to understand the part that they are now playing in the current situation that is being reflected on;
Stage 3: *Making sense of how I am feeling and responding.* This might be where a pastoral supervisee gains moments of connection and enlightenment of transferential/counter-transferential responses and behaviours;
Stage 4: *Sensing the presence and action of God and discerning God's purpose.* This is where links and insights can be discerned and made to

higher forms of wisdom—i.e., to where God might be at action through the struggle that is being reflected on;

Stage 5: *Deciding to cooperate with God by trying out a different way of thinking and being.* In this stage, the pastoral supervisee begins to discern how he or she doesn't have to reenact old behaviours and responses but can use the insights gained from the reflection to develop a different way of being as they pursue the path of phronesis (practical and higher wisdom and grace).

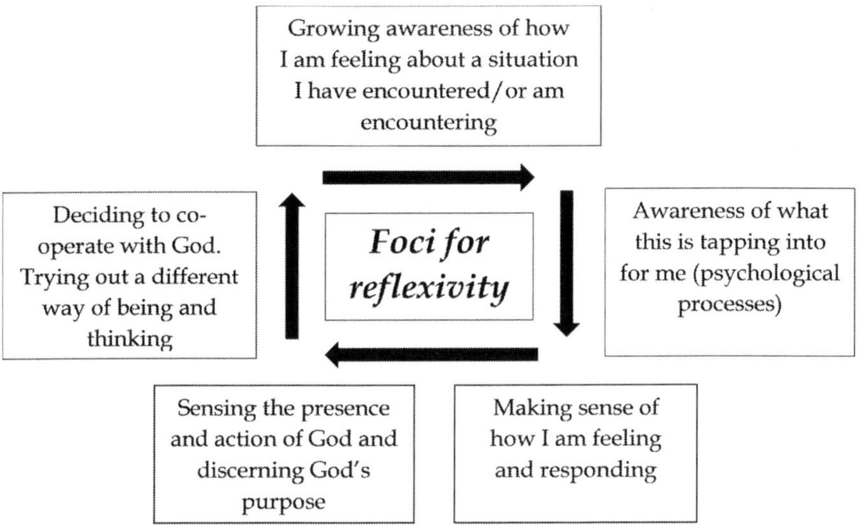

Figure 2.1

For the purposes of pastoral supervision, these two models can be combined to inform the approach to theological reflection that I now elaborate on in this chapter:

As stated before, these stages do not follow chronologically in pastoral supervision, but rather the focus of what is being reflected on may oscillate between the stages and modes of pastoral supervision. It is to the operationality of this combined approach, in the context of pastoral supervision, that I now turn. In doing so, we will be considering how these stages of the theological/spiritual mode may be evident using two case studies.

Table 2.1: Mode 8: Theological/Spiritual Reflection Mode in Pastoral Supervision

Stages of the theological/ spiritual mode	*Swinton and Mowat*	*Gubi*
Stage 1 *Bringing the experience into the now*	*Current praxis*	Developing a growing awareness of how I am feeling about a situation that I have encountered or am encountering.
Stage 2 *Reflecting and psychologically informing*	*Cultural/Contextual*	Becoming aware of what this is tapping into for me in terms of my psychological processes. Making sense of how I am feeling and responding.
Stage 3 *Reflecting and theologically/spiritually discerning*	*Theological*	Sensing the presence and action of God and discerning God's purpose.
Stage 4 *Moving forward with insight*	*Reformulating Revised Practice*	Deciding to co-operate with God by trying out a different way of thinking and being.

MODE 8 IN PRACTICE

Case Study 1: Ewan and Bob

To help us think about this approach to reflecting theologically/spiritually in pastoral supervision, I use a case study that Ewan Kelly[15] writes in his book *Personhood and Presence*, because it represents the kind of situation that may present in pastoral supervision.

> Shortly after being appointed to my first chaplaincy post, I was asked by the nursing staff in the neurosurgical unit to see a 39-year-old shipbuilder who had recently been diagnosed with an aggressive, inoperable brain tumour. Bob's considerable, yet understandable, distress was rendering his family and the ward staff helpless and upset. Could I offer him some support? On approaching Bob and introducing myself, I was met at first by stony silence, and then by a very angry man who told me in no uncertain terms to get out of his sight. I retreated somewhat sheepishly. However, the next day I decided to try again, this time whilst his family were present. Bob roared at me before I could utter a greeting—I could take my God elsewhere because God was no use to him (or words to that effect!). Active treatment was not an option for Bob, and he went home soon after to the care of his own doctor and palliative care services. I never saw Bob again. However, I did see his wife. Ironically, she came over to

the chaplaincy centre later that day to apologize for Bob's behaviour. However, it gave me the opportunity to apologize to her because I realized I had far from offered person-centred care—I had not respected Bob's wishes and had invaded his privacy. In short, I felt guilty because I felt I had added to his distress and had not acted in Bob's best interests. However, Jean graciously brushed aside my apology and began to talk. She needed to express her despair, sense of hopeless, struggle with lack of control and all her anxiety about the uncertainty of what the future may hold for Bob, herself, and the rest of the family. Jean also spontaneously told me something of Bob's story. It transpired Bob was originally from the Western Isles of Scotland and had been brought up in a familial and church culture where he absorbed the understanding that good things happened to those who were hard working and faithful to God and the wicked got what they deserved. On leaving school, Lewis and its restrictive Calvinistic church culture, Bob came to Glasgow to do his apprenticeship. In his early twenties, he met Jean, they fell in love and got married. Unfortunately, their first child had died in infancy. This hit Bob hard. The local minister had been very supportive of Jean at the time, but Bob would have nothing to do with him. After Jean had finished recounting their shared life together with all its ups and downs and her struggle at times to deal with Bob's occasional angry outbursts, I suggested Jean might like some support front her local minister in the days ahead. Not to invade Bob's space but to enable her to have someone outside the family to talk to about her concerns. Jean welcomed this. She had heard of the minister, Alice, by repute, and it was agreed that I phone Alice to alert her to Jean's situation. I was then able to set up an introductory meeting with Jean and Alice in the chaplaincy prior to Bob's discharge. A few months later Alice rang me to tell me that Bob had died in the local hospice, still angry and full of existential questions, but less so than in the immediacy of his diagnosis. She was still seeing Jean regularly, in the manse, not in her home. Bob had known that Jean was getting support from Alice, but he did not want her in his house. Bob had requested a Humanist funeral, but Jean was now planning a short memorial service for Bob with Alice's help to be held in the church.

Stage 1: Bringing the Experience into the Now

Stage 1, Bringing the Experience into the Now, would involve the pastoral supervisee sharing the narrative of the situation with the pastoral supervisor. In terms of facilitation, the pastoral supervisor would be listening carefully, and might focus on what they are 'noticing,' both in the supervisee and in their own self, as the supervisee shares his or her experience.

Stage 2: Reflecting and Psychologically Informing

Stage 2, Reflecting and Psychologically Informing, involves the exploration of how the supervisee is feeling, and of what may be going on for the 'other' in the situation. In Ewan's case study, he offers the following insight on the 'other' in the situation:

> I can only surmise about the real source of Bob's anger directed at me. The first time we met, his anger was not about me as a human being but was about me being a chaplain (the second time, he would undoubtedly have been angry at me ignoring his initial request and yet his rage was disproportionate to this). Bob probably transferred his deep-seated feelings about his oppressive religious upbringing onto me as a perceived representative of the Church. In addition to representing ecclesial (and perhaps familial) authority figures from the past, I assume I also embodied for him an unjust, cruel and judgemental God who he perhaps deemed responsible for the hugely significant loss of his first child, now his own identity and, very soon, his life. All of this, of course, is only speculation.

While the supervisee's insight may hold 'truth,' the pastoral supervisor might also notice that Ewan is inexperienced as a chaplain. He may, therefore, have something to prove to others and to himself—maybe he is on probation or under assessment. This could be teased out. The other staff don't know how to help Bob. This may possibly leave Ewan buying into meeting a need, and possible expectation of others, to lessen the anger, and maybe even buying into his own needs for him to be the rescuer, fixer, saviour or hero. Bob's anger is almost certainly transference/projection. Ewan is able to recognise this after some reflection, but he doesn't recognise it before his second attempt at visiting. Why that was may be the focus of some reflection. Ewan's second visit may be indicative of a need to be rescuer, fixer, or 'saver of souls.' Might there be possible cultural implications of what it means to be 'a man,' which is inherent in Bob's Scottishness? A man may be expected to produce offspring as a sign of his virility, and so Bob may see himself as having 'failed' as a man. Bob's 'over-reaction' may be a repressed reaction to his own repression as a boy. If Ewan couldn't help Bob, might he have transferred his need to help onto Jean?

Throughout stage 2, there is a gentle facilitation of the supervisee's process and an exploration of possibilities in the 'other's' process to seek some psychological insight—in this case, Bob's process. Always, the supervisor is checking out with the supervisee how what is being shared may, or may not, be speaking into the situation.

Stage 3: Reflecting and Theologically/ Spiritually Discerning

Stage 3 is where the theological and spiritual are drawn on in the process of reflection. Again, some sharing of theological 'surmising' is appropriate:

- Bob may have been taught that God is a just God who will protect him. Therefore, feels very let down by God—but is God a just and protective God? What evidence for this way of thinking is found in Scripture?
- Bob was brought up in a strict Church tradition that taught 'good things happened to those who are faithful.' Yet, life events ran counter to the teachings of his Church's tradition. Does that make Bob a bad person? Might Bob think that it made him a bad person?
- Ewan may hold the theological view that 'I am my brother's keeper'—but, how much am I my brother's keeper? What does it mean in practice to be my brother's keeper? Is 'keeping' a form of empowerment or disempowerment? What part do self-agency, autonomy, and personal responsibility play? How do we work out our own salvation with fear and trembling?;
- Ewan may hold the theological view that it is the Christian's task to 'seek and save that which is lost' (i.e., the lost sheep)—but, is it always the Christian's task to 'seek and save that which is lost'? What might the impact be of acting from that theological base on the other?
- Ewan may have a problem with anger because anger is not one of the fruits of the Spirit—and yet, the psalms of lament give permission for folks to be angry with God;
- Ewan may have felt a responsibility to facilitate a conversation about death and making peace with God.

It is important that, at this stage, the supervision session doesn't become an intellectual discussion about theology. The purpose here is to 'mine' theological narrative for possible understanding and to discern how the supervisee's process, and the 'other's' process, may be helped or hindered by theological assumptions and beliefs. Other facilitative 'wonderings' at this stage might be:

- I'm wondering where you perceive God to be in this situation?
- I'm wondering, if you were to act from a place of higher wisdom (i.e., God), what might that course of action look like, or be?
- How does higher wisdom speak into this situation?
- Are there any passages or stories from scripture that speak into this situation for you?

Stage 4: Moving Forward with Insight

The final stage, then, is to discern a way through the situation through 'cooperating with God,' or to reflect on what insights have been gained by the supervisee from having reflected on the situation in pastoral supervision. Responses in this case might be:

- I'm wondering what ways you (the supervisee) could have handled the situation differently?
- I'm wondering if you (the supervisee) hadn't returned, Bob may have felt abandoned, yet again, by God's representative; yet, by returning for a second visit, you arguably hadn't respected Bob's wishes. It's sometimes difficult to know what the best thing to do is.
- Could you (the supervisee) have sought advice from a more experienced hospital chaplain, if there was another chaplain in the hospital?
- With Bob, returning for a second visit wasn't the right thing to do in retrospect—but with another person, might it be exactly the right thing to do?
- In light of what Ewan learned about Bob from Bob's wife after Ewan's failed second visit, could the information have been helpful beforehand?
- There may have been some issues of power that were not considered by Ewan. Bob may have become more aware of his powerlessness in light of Ewan's position. There were possibly socioeconomic and sociodemographic differences to bear in mind
- How do you want to move forwards from here with the wisdom and insight you have gained?
- What learning are you left with for the next time?
- Where might God be in this?

Personal discernment, based on phronesis (or practical and higher wisdom and grace) is called for in this stage, based on an awareness of one's own psychological and theological processes, and with an awareness of what is feeding into whatever action is ultimately decided on.

Case Study 2: Michael and Jane

Michael is an experienced vicar who found himself in a situation that he brought to pastoral supervision. A lady, called Jane, started attending his church. After a few Sundays, he noticed her sitting in the pew after service, in tears. So, he went over to see if he could be of any support to her. As he listened, Jane shared that she had been told by God to leave her husband (which she did out of obedience to God), and God told her that he would send her someone called Michael, who would become her new husband. As she sat in Michael's services, she had become more and more convinced that vicar Michael was the man that God had told her about. As Michael listened, he began to feel uncomfortable at what he was hearing. He had no feelings for Jane but empathised with her distress and courage in telling him. He could see the genuineness of Jane, and that this was a wrestle, for Jane, with her faith. Michael listened empathically and sensitively, trying not to show any of his discomfort, but eventually he told Jane that whilst he appreciated the strength of Jane's calling, he had no sense that God had called him to her, and that he had to let her down. However, rather than just reject Jane, Michael recommended someone he knew to whom Jane could turn confidentially in order to work out what was going on for her and to explore what his rejection might mean to her at a spiritual level. Jane was clearly disappointed but thanked Michael and left.

In the following months, Michael started bumping into Jane regularly at the local supermarket. She would even approach him at the petrol pump and slip him a note saying, 'call me.' It felt to Michael as if she was deliberately waiting for him at the places that she knew he frequented. This increased Michael's discomfort to the point that he wasn't sure how to handle the situation. He felt that he was being stalked, but still felt compassion for Jane. Jane even started rumours in the parish that Michael was gay because he wasn't responding to her overtures. Michael began to find it increasingly difficult to be her priest and to serve her communion—yet, worship was public worship, and he couldn't just ask her to leave his church. What could he do?

Stage 1: Bringing the Experience into the Now

Again, stage 1, Bringing the Experience into the Now, would involve the pastoral supervisee sharing the narrative of the situation with the pastoral supervisor. In terms of facilitation, the pastoral supervisor would be listening carefully, and might focus on what she or he is 'noticing,' both in the supervisee and in his or her own self, as the supervisee shares his or her experience.

Stage 2: Reflecting and Psychologically Informing

Stage 2, Reflecting and Psychologically Informing, involves the exploration of how the supervisee is feeling, and of what may be going on for the 'other' in the situation. In this case, Michael's discomfort with the situation might be facilitated:

- What is Michael's sense of threat about for him?
- Are there previous experiences or injuries that this is tapping into for him?
- How realistic is that threat?
- How comfortable is Michael with sexual matters or with his own sexuality?

His sense of 'threat' and of 'not knowing how to handle the situation' might be worked with to enable him to find strategies for coping and safeguarding his own welfare:

- Are there things that Michael can put in place to ensure his own safety (e.g., putting strategies in place to make sure that he is never alone with Jane; finding a different supermarket to shop in, etc.)?
- Are there members of Michael's team that he could alert to the situation while being confident in their discretion?
- Might this be serious enough a matter for involving the police (stalking)?
- How is Michael with being thought of as gay in his church community?

Consideration could also be given as to what might be going on for Jane psychologically. This might involve acknowledging the possibility of erotic transference[16] and of the possible existence of mental health issues, which may invoke a greater sense of compassion and empathy for Jane, while attending to Michael's own needs and safety.

Stage 3: Reflecting and Theologically/ Spiritually Discerning

Stage 3 is where the theological and spiritual are drawn on in the process of reflection. Again, some sharing of theological 'surmising' is appropriate:

- What does Michael understand about what it means to be 'called'?
- How might Michael know if Jane's call is genuine, or if it is the result of dysfunction?
- Some recalling of, or resonances with, various callings in the Bible may be helpful (or not);
- What might it mean to Jane to be rejected by Michael, and from the church, at a spiritual level?

Michael could be reminded of how sensitively he heard Jane, and of how he recognised that this was a spiritual matter for Jane. Some references to how Jesus responded to others might be appropriately woven into the session. Michael could be assured that his decision to refer Jane to someone else was wise, rather than to try and offer her the support himself.

Stage 4: Moving Forward with Insight

The final stage, then, is to discern a way through the situation through 'cooperating with God,' or to reflect on what insights have been gained by the supervisee from having reflected on the situation in pastoral supervision. Responses in this case might be:

- I'm wondering what ways you (Michael) could have handled the situation differently?
- How do you want to move forwards from here with the wisdom and insight you have gained from your reflections?
- Are there any risk or safeguarding factors that we need to report, or that you need extra support for?
- What learning are you left with for if this happens another time?
- Where might God be in this?

Again, personal discernment is called for in this stage, based on an awareness of one's own psychological and theological processes, and with an awareness of what is influencing whatever action is ultimately decided on.

CONCLUSION

Pastoral situations are often messy, in that there often isn't a right thing to do, or a right course of action to take. Yet, there may be many wrong courses of action. Pastoral supervision offers the supervisee the opportunity to reflect on process (i.e., the supervisee's, the 'other's,' the organisational context's) which is informed by psychological and theological insights. In pastoral supervision, it is the highest wisdom and grace that the pastoral supervisor and supervisee seek to discern together, either to inform future interaction, affirm the work, or seek to learn from the experience—and to find God in the mess.

BIBLIOGRAPHY

Cameron, Helen. *Living in the Gaze of God: Supervision and Ministerial Flourishing.* London: SCM Press, 2018.

Gubi, Peter Madsen. "Theological Thoughts About Reflective Practice Groups." Pp. 74–96 in *Reflective Practice Groups for Clergy: Offering Pastoral Supervision, Well-being Support and Spiritual Formation in Community*. Peter Madsen Gubi, Jan Korris, and William West. Chester, UK: Chester University Press, 2020.

______. "Utilising Reflective Practice Groups as Pedagogy in Ordination Training and Theological Development." *Practical Theology* 12, no. 4 (2019): 366–78. DOI: 10.1080/1756073X.2019.1609254.

Hawkins, Peter, and Robin Shohet. *Supervision in the Helping Professions.* Maidenhead, UK: Open University Press, 2012.

Kelly, Ewan. *Personhood and Presence: Self as a Resource for Spiritual and Pastoral Care*. London: Bloomsbury, 2012.

______. "Risking the Embodied Self: A Theology of Presence in Pastoral Supervision." Pp. 40–52 in *Enriching Ministry: Pastoral Supervision in Practice*, eds. Michael Paterson and Jessica Rose. London: SCM Press, 2014.

Leach, Jane. *A Charge to Keep: Reflective Supervision and the Renewal of Christian Leadership.* Nashville: Wesley's Foundery Books, 2020.

Leach, Jane, and Michael Paterson. *Pastoral Supervision: A Handbook.* London: SCM Press, 2015.

Swinton, John, and Harriet Mowat. *Practical Theology and Qualitative Research.* London: SCM Press, 2006.

The Uniting Church in Australia Ministerial Education Commission. Pastoral Supervision: Introducing a Process of Reflection on Ministry Experience. Unpublished document, 2001.

Ward, Pete. *Perspectives on Ecclesiology and Ethnography.* Grand Rapids, MI: William B. Eerdmans Publishing Company, 2012.

NOTES

1. Ewan Kelly, "Risking the Embodied Self: A Theology of Presence in Pastoral Supervision," in *Enriching Ministry: Pastoral Supervision in Practice*, eds. Michael Paterson and Jessica Rose (London: SCM Press, 2014), 40–52.

2. Jane Leach and Michael Paterson, *Pastoral Supervision: A Handbook* (London: SCM Press, 2015).

3. Helen Cameron, *Living in the Gaze of God: Supervision and Ministerial Flourishing* (London: SCM Press, 2018).

4. Peter Madsen Gubi, "Theological Thoughts About Reflective Practice Groups," in *Reflective Practice Groups for Clergy: Offering Pastoral Supervision, Well-being Support and Spiritual Formation in Community*. Peter Madsen Gubi, Jan Korris, and William West (Chester, UK: Chester University Press, 2020), 74–96.

5. Jane Leach, *A Charge to Keep: Reflective Supervision and the Renewal of Christian Leadership* (Nashville: Wesley's Foundery Books, 2020).

6. The Uniting Church in Australia Ministerial Education Commission. Pastoral Supervision: Introducing a Process of Reflection on Ministry Experience (Unpublished document, 2001).

7. Peter Hawkins and Robin Shohet, *Supervision in the Helping Professions* (Maidenhead, UK: Open University Press, 2012).

8. Pete Ward, *Perspectives on Ecclesiology and Ethnography* (Grand Rapids, MI: William B. Eerdmans Publishing Company, 2012).

9. John Swinton and Harriet Mowat, *Practical Theology and Qualitative Research* (London: SCM Press, 2006).

10. Peter Madsen Gubi, "Utilising Reflective Practice Groups as Pedagogy in Ordination Training and Theological Development," *Practical Theology* 12, no. 4 (2019): 366–78. DOI: 10.1080/1756073X.2019.1609254.

11. Gubi, "Theological Thoughts About Reflective Practice Groups."

12. Swinton and Mowat, *Practical Theology and Qualitative Research*, 95–97

13. Gubi, "Utilising Reflective Practice Groups."

14. Gubi, "Theological Thoughts About Reflective Practice Groups."

15. Ewan Kelly, *Personhood and Presence: Self as a Resource for Spiritual and Pastoral Care* (London: Bloomsbury, 2012): 88–90.

16. Erotic transference is a term used to describe the feelings of love and the fantasies of a sexual or sensual nature that a client experiences about their therapist (or a parishioner about their priest).

Chapter Three

Prayer in Pastoral Supervision

Peter Madsen Gubi

Many would probably argue that the use of prayer has a natural home in pastoral supervision, particularly when both the pastoral supervisor and supervisee are of the same faith. After all, pastoral supervisors and supervisees meet, in encounter, to explore and discern spiritual and theological issues—and prayer is at the centre of all spirituality[1]. However, I will argue in this chapter that the ethical considerations of the integration of prayer are just as applicable in pastoral supervision as they are in other helping professional contexts. Its use in a natural setting does not preclude ethics! In considering the issues, I will draw on research and writing that I have conducted and published on prayer—albeit it that these were written about and researched in the context of counselling and psychotherapy.[2, 3]

As a pastoral supervisor, I have rarely prayed *with* a pastoral supervisee, even when working with people of faith—but I certainly have prayed *for* them, and I have always asked their permission to do so. I have never just presumed it was OK. I have sometimes (although not always) prayed with others in my role as priest—again, always asking their permission, but also trying to discern if they could say 'no' if they wanted to (which is mostly met with a quizzical look of 'of course it is OK! What a strange question to ask . . .'). I have had others pray with me, and I have sometimes found it to be a cathartic and healing experience. However, I have also had others pray with me without asking, on the presumption that it would be acceptable to me as a Christian priest. The thought of asking if it would be OK had probably never crossed their mind, because praying is firmly embedded in much of Christian culture, in that Christians often always begin and end meetings with a prayer, or hold difficult situations in prayer, or pray on behalf of self and others. While I have gone along with it and haven't challenged it at the time, sometimes it has felt uncomfortable and inappropriate—especially when the prayer becomes about what the pray-er wants to happen, rather than praying for God's will to be done in a situation. So, even in pastoral supervision, we cannot assume that it is OK to pray. This chapter will look at the implications for practice in the use of prayer in pastoral supervision, drawing heavily on recommendations that I have made for other professions as a result of my research.[4]

PRAYER IN PRACTICE

There is certainly no evidence in the published literature, that prayer influences pastoral supervision—although anecdotally, I know that it does. However, it is important that there is an informed debate about the value of prayer as an intervention in pastoral supervision, and that the limitation and value of such practice is critically evaluated to determine what it means in practice. So, what might 'considerations for good practice' look like in the integration of prayer in pastoral supervision?

At *a philosophical level*, all pastoral supervision can be regarded as prayer in that prayer pervades the atmosphere and environment in which the pastoral supervisor and supervisee are in 'communion' (encounter) at a spiritual level. Prayer is an attitude that is inherent in the pastoral supervisor's way of being, providing a context for silence, defining the quality of attention, and qualifying the sense of being a part of something bigger to which the work can be entrusted. Prayer provides an existential perspective, or frame of reference, that makes the work more meaningful at a spiritual and theological level. This can be motivational for the pastoral supervisor and provides a way of understanding and contextualising the process of their work.

At a *covert level*, prayer is a valuable, integral, and necessary part of the pastoral supervisor's supportive practice. It is a personal and private practice in which the pastoral supervisor uses prayer: to ground and attune herself in preparation for the work, enabling a deeper level of presence, stillness, balance, and concentration; to place the work in the care of a higher being, enabling connection with the 'here and now' and containment; to add an extra healing dimension to the work through the use of intercessory prayer on behalf of the supervisee, which also enables the spiritual aspect of the work to be kept in focus; to still the mind, aiding peace, calm, meaning, purpose, and direction at times of stuckness, panic, and anxiety. This helps the pastoral supervisor to stay with the sometimes 'not knowing' and the 'aloneness,' enabling the connection with the supervisee to be maintained and enhanced; to stay with the intense feelings of helplessness; as part of a spiritual discipline that enables the pastoral supervisor to acknowledge her own spirituality, prevent burnout, and maintain balance in her life through fostering a forum in which self-reflection, self-respect, and self-care are intrinsic.

The pastoral supervisor may also be upheld by the supervisee's prayer at this level, providing that such practice is not explicitly encouraged, but who instead accepts it in the 'spirit' in which it is offered, even though at an unconscious level it may indicate issues of attachment and insecurity. The ethical use of prayer at the covert level is determined by the intent of the pastoral supervisor, in that praying for the supervisee utilises a spiritual resource on behalf of their supervisee. This can strengthen the relationship between pastoral supervisor and supervisee because it taps into the forces that become powerfully operative in the transcendent encounter. If the supervisee knows that the pastoral supervisor does this on her behalf, it can add to their sense of being cared for and can reduce the sense of abandonment and separation that they may feel between sessions. However, it is important to avoid an unhealthy preoccupation with a supervisee in prayer life. It is preferable to gain their consent, but it may be unethical to withhold such a practice if the pastoral supervisor believes in the effectiveness of praying for their supervisees away from their presence. This has to be balanced against the perceived reaction of the supervisee if s/he knew that intercessory prayer was being enacted on his/her behalf without his/her permission. When the pastoral supervisor prays on the supervisee's behalf, it is ethically less problematic to use the 'Thy will be done' approach. This approach to prayer gives the work a more meaningful perspective by reminding the pastoral supervisor that the process is part of something bigger than what takes place in the room, and is largely undetermined, full of 'unknowing,' and out of their control. The practice also serves to remind the pastoral supervisor that her accountability is also to something greater, as well as to the supervisee. This can prevent complacency.

At the *overt level* (i.e., praying with a supervisee), prayer can be used tentatively with a supervisee who is open to the process of prayer. However, the use of prayer needs to be carefully considered and contracted for (i.e., explicitly agreed between pastoral supervisor and supervisee). Praying overtly is most likely to occur at the beginning of a session; at the end of a session; at the termination of the supervisory relationship; at times of difficulty; through the use of silence; through the use of ritual; through transpersonal imaging (i.e., imagining what God or Higher Wisdom might say, or do, in this situation); and as a way of communicating appropriate values to the supervisee that are compatible with intrinsic pastoral supervision values (e.g., "We pray for Sam who we know is of great worth to you, and who is loved intensely by you, even though he can't yet see, or know, it for himself").

CONSIDERATIONS FOR GOOD PRACTICE

Each of these three levels (i.e., philosophical, covert, and overt) has to be *equally underpinned* by an ethical awareness based on the values of Fidelity, Autonomy, Beneficence, Non-maleficence, Justice, and Self-Respect, which form the ethical framework for good practice in many ethical frameworks or codes.[5] Considerations for good practice advocated here are underpinned by: 1) an awareness of potential ethical issues; 2) an awareness of how prayer can be integrated ethically; 3) an awareness of the quality and characteristics of the prayer being used; and 4) a considered awareness of issues of tension and difficulty for the pastoral supervisor.

Developing an Awareness of Potential Ethical Issues

The first consideration for good practice is the development of an awareness of potential ethical issues. These are summarised in Table 3.1[6] but are not definitive.

An awareness of, and insight into, these difficulties is important in preventing the pastoral supervisor from colluding with defences and resistance. However, the ethical difficulties, although cautionary, are not prohibitive if prayer is integrated appropriately into practice. A good pastoral supervisor knows of potential risks when entering into a pastoral supervisory relationship, but an awareness of the potential risks enables her to facilitate more appropriately without withholding the cathartic opportunity. While the ethical difficulties may seem insurmountable, in my experience, practitioners whose work includes prayer have often carefully reflected on the issues and have reached a place of understanding of the issues where they have found the use of prayer to be less implicated with ethical dilemmas than Table 3.1 suggests.

How Prayer Can Be Integrated Ethically

The second consideration for good practice is an awareness of how prayer can be pragmatically, but ethically, integrated. It may be useful for the pastoral supervisor to conduct a formal assessment of the supervisee's spiritual history. This enables the pastoral supervisor to communicate an acceptance of the supervisee's spirituality, and to gain a better sense of the supervisee's worldview and spiritual practice. Perhaps, the use of pre-contact information or a symbolic environment (often discreet religious symbols in the room or on jewellery) to communicate acceptance of spirituality may indicate greater openness to prayer. Supervisees who are in touch with their own spirituality can often become aware of the pastoral supervisor's openness to spirituality

Table 3.1. Summary of Ethical Difficulties of Using Prayer in Pastoral Supervision

Pastoral supervisor's process	Supervisee's process
• Fear of appropriateness of personal disclosure	• Fear of authentic self before God may inhibit pastoral supervision
• How authentic can the pastoral supervisor really be?	• Prayer can be used to deny or distort truth
• Potential blurred boundary issues	• Prayer can be used to avoid difficult issues
• How will prayer impact on the supervisee?	• Prayer can be used to manipulate the pastoral supervisor and God
• Potential power and mutuality differential	• Prayer can be used to avoid listening to self
• Will prayer benefit or burden the supervisee?	• Prayer can be used to avoid challenging self
• Fear of collusion with inauthentic prayer	• Prayer can be used to avoid taking responsibility
• Prayer can inhibit the challenging of the supervisee	• Compliance with pastoral supervisor's expectation
• Diversion of attention away from supervisee to God	• Transference issues may be present
• Countertransference issues	• Conflictual issues with God may inhibit pastoral supervision if prayer is used
• Issues of competency—inadequate training	• Prayer can be used as a defence against insight and self-understanding
• Is adequate supervision available?	• Prayer can foster inappropriate intimacy
• Possible issues of compliance with supervisee's requests and words	• Prayer may inhibit disclosure
• Reliance on God versus reliance on self-determination	• The supervisee may fear judgement if prayer is used by the pastoral supervisor, and be inhibited
• Prayer may be unrecognised by insurance companies	• Prayer can be used as a way of avoiding possible change
• Insufficient research to justify use	• Prayer can be used as wish-fulfilment rather than as transcendental acceptance
• Prayer not just a technique	• Prayer can compromise supervisee's beliefs
• Danger of regarding prayer as panacea for all ills	• Prayer can be used to create a spiritual one-upmanship on the pastoral supervisor
• Praying for particular outcomes inappropriate	• Prayer can be used as indirect communication with pastoral supervisor
• Danger of imposing pastoral supervisor's values, beliefs, and prayer practice on supervisee	• Prayer can foster spiritual inadequacy in the supervisee
• Possible violation of work-setting boundaries	• Prayer can be used to foster states of magical superstition, victimhood, and helplessness
• Need to work within supervisee's religious framework which the pastoral supervisor may not subscribe to	
• Integrity of the pastoral supervisor may be at risk	

- Difficulty of knowing how to introduce prayer into the session
- Prayer can detract from immediacy of the supervisee's experiencing
- Prayer can be indirect communication with the supervisee
- Prayer can reveal hopes and expectations for supervisee
- Prayer can be a place to dump issues without exploration
- Difficult to psychologically explore an act of reverence and mystery—different language
- Prayer can be presented as a 'quick fix,' leaving the supervisee unable to explore ongoing pain
- Prayer can dilute the pastoral supervision process
- Prayer can be used to bypass the complexities of the pastoral supervision process
- Prayer can be frightening or repellent if the supervisee is associated with strict religious or abusive upbringing
- A supervisee who prays regularly may be reluctant for the pastoral supervisor to use prayer if she feels that her prayer should have been enough, or if she has been told that she is resisting God's grace by others

through their presence, way of being, and unconscious communication. Instead of a formalised procedure, the integration of prayer may rely more on a sensitive awareness of the supervisee's needs and an intuitive sensing of the appropriateness of the situation and the supervisee. It is likely that the pastoral supervisor has informally gained a sense of her supervisee's coping strategies and spirituality as the relationship has unfolded, so the integration of prayer is more often informed by the quality of attunement and connection between the pastoral supervisor and supervisee. It is therefore more likely to be a relational and intuitive process, based on an awareness of the appropriateness of prayer for the supervisee. Prayer must *not* be mechanistic and routine (except perhaps in the provision of silence at the beginning of the session) and must *not* be attributed to external sources (e.g., the Holy Spirit—"I feel led by the Holy Spirit to pray . . ."), except where such attribution actually stems from discernment that comes from the pastoral supervisor's conscious awareness.

The Quality and Characteristics of the Prayer

The third consideration for good practice is an awareness of the quality and characteristics of prayer. Prayer must have a quality of naturalness about it, with the notion of prayer being introduced with the tentative quality of 'feeling your way' that emerges out of a sense of respect for the supervisee (e.g., "Some people have found this helpful, and I wonder if you feel it would be appropriate . . ."). The prayer has to feel relevant to the context and the 'moment' of what is being shared and must not interrupt the agenda or take the supervisee away from experiencing the 'felt sense' of the moment. Prayer has to respect the supervisee's autonomy, and attention needs to be paid to potential issues of deference and compliance. In checking out issues of deference and compliance, it is important to gain the supervisee's consent, although to gain formal written consent 'in the moment' might detract from the intimacy of the moment, and lead to an intellectualisation of the phenomenon in which the simplicity and power of the experience is lost. It is important that the supervisee is able to refuse prayer, and it seems important that the pastoral supervisor is reflexive about her supervisees 'never refusing prayer,' to honestly ascertain if her method of introducing prayer can enable a supervisee to refuse it. If prayer occurs with the pastoral supervisor's eyes closed, the practitioner may more fully engage with the prayer experience itself, but she may miss having a sense of the supervisee's way of being as he prays. The use of silence at the beginning of a session may be the most appropriate form of prayer at this stage of the session, as it enables the supervisee to gain stillness and a focus for the work. It provides a spiritual space which facilitates the supervisee in focusing on their awareness, or on the essence of their deepest self (authenticity) which allows the unconscious to speak. The prayerful space also acknowledges the spiritual and theological context of the work in a subtle way. Praying with words may inhibit the expression of certain emotions. Lengthy prayer and routine, mechanistic prayer are not appropriate. Any verbal prayer needs to be focussed on the supervisee's needs and be a simple acknowledgement of what they want to bring. Praying at times of difficulty may take the supervisee away from experiencing the aloneness and the fear of the experience. However, after that has firstly been experienced and explored, prayer at these times may be beneficial at a time when their autonomy feels diminished. Meditative prayer (or mindfulness) may also be appropriate at times when the supervisee is experiencing panic, as such prayer can carry anxiety-reducing traits. The use of ritual to aid completion, resolution, a letting go, and a committal, can also be an appropriate place for prayer to be integrated in pastoral supervision. However, it is important that the supervisee does not expect instant healing or revelation from any ritual, but is able to continue to work on the issues as, and when, they recur. It is also important that the pastoral supervisor checks out that the supervisee does not feel that the pastoral supervisor would be disappointed if revelation or closure did not occur. This can enhance the supervisee's authenticity. Christian practices such as the 'laying on of hands' and 'speaking in tongues' are existentially powerful to those who encounter them. It is important that these types of ritual are not routine or mechanistic, and that the pastoral supervisor reflects carefully on her need to introduce such practices. Again, such practices need to have a quality of naturalness about them for both pastoral supervisor and supervisee. They also need to emerge from a discernment of the 'felt sense' of the moment.

Silence that fosters a connectedness to the sacred is a less controversial, but nevertheless overt, use of prayer. While prayer has the potential to disempower the supervisee, prayer also has the potential to empower him/her. This can be seen in the supervisee taking responsibility for the praying, in the way that the content of prayer changes over time, and in the ability of the supervisee to ask for prayer. All of these can be regarded as signs of developing autonomy. Some of the common uses of prayer in pastoral supervision are at the end of a session, or at the termination of working relationship. Using prayer at these times is less intrusive to the process of the session. Prayer for intervention, which introduces connotations of magic (e.g., instant healing and miracles), victimhood, and helplessness, is not appropriate. Using prayer to end the working relationship can act as a way of consolidating the gain, enabling closure and termination of the work at both a practical and a spiritual level.

Issues of Tension and Difficulty for the Pastoral Supervisor

The fourth consideration for good practice is an awareness of the possible areas of tension and difficulty for the pastoral supervisor. Prayer should not be used to impose or communicate the pastoral supervisor's values to the supervisee, because the supervisee may be unable to challenge what is being prayed, and the use of prayer in this way is open to manipulation and abuse. However, values that are compatible with the pastoral supervision values (e.g., the supervisee is a person of worth and of value) may be appropriately imparted and sanctified through prayer.

Prayer may also be a useful medium through which the supervisee is more able to hear the pastoral supervisor's insight and awareness of the supervisee and of her process. Rather than being an indirect communication with the supervisee which may be regarded as the antithesis of pastoral supervision, prayer can be regarded as a direct communication with the supervisee, if God is considered to be at the centre of the supervisee. Some pastoral supervisors may be reluctant to enable their supervisee to explore their motivation for, and act of, praying. However, if prayer is to be integrated into pastoral supervision, it must not be treated any differently from any other intervention. Exploration of whatever happens is an implicit part of pastoral supervision, and prayer is no different. A pastoral supervisor could explore the supervisee's need to pray before the prayer. Others might wait and let the exploration happen in a natural and unobtrusive way. Others might explore the supervisee's process after the prayer. Out of respect for the supervisee, it is important to travel alongside the supervisee through the prayer (even if the content does not feel comfortable for the pastoral supervisor), and then to facilitatively 'unpick' the process, or appropriately challenge the supervisee by sensitively, congruently, but tentatively sharing the supervisor's insights and awareness of the supervisee to further facilitation and exploration. If prayer is to be used, it must not assume a 'sacredness' that excludes it from the way that other interventions are worked with.

Self-disclosure of the pastoral supervisor's spirituality might also be an area of potential tension. Disclosure of the pastoral supervisor's spirituality can enable a more profound connection for supervisees who want to explore spiritual issues, because exploring spiritual material may be problematic for some supervisees. However, the sharing of spiritual beliefs may lead to an unhelpful transference phenomenon, or inappropriately influence the supervision agenda.

SUPERVISION ISSUES

For some pastoral supervisors, bringing issues of prayer to their own pastoral supervision may be highly problematic. Some pastoral supervisors may not feel free to explore their practice of prayer because of a fear of not being understood; a fear of being judged; a fear of losing respect and credibility; a fear of being thought of as transgressing; a fear of exposure by the supervisor; a lack of trust in how the supervisor will treat the disclosure; and a fear of condemnation and dismissal of something that is important and precious to the supervisee. However, it is equally important for pastoral supervisors that prayer can be discussed in their own supervision, even when some supervisors might regard it as 'normal practice.'

CONCLUSION

However, prayer is no more problematic than other intervention, nor should it be treated any differently from any other intervention within the context of pastoral supervision. Prayer in pastoral supervision needs to be approached with a knowledge and awareness of the possible ethical difficulties and be integrated in a manner that is respecting of, and enhancing of, the supervisee's autonomy, and in a way that fosters the supervisee's well-being. Arguably, all interventions are to some extent problematic, and need the same degree of careful ethical consideration. No intervention must be regarded as a panacea for all ills. To regard prayer in this way can be disrespecting of the supervisee. If prayer can be empowering, then arguably it is unethical to withhold it if the supervisee has a healthy spirituality, and prayer is an important part of their spirituality. If the pastoral supervisor also shares that spirituality and is cautious in her approach, and in her awareness of her supervisee, then the process should be open to any intervention (or 'mode of relating') that can enhance the supervisee's growth and practice (depending on how 'growth' is psychologically and spiritually defined), and that can enable the alliance to deepen relationally. The purpose of this chapter has not been to advocate the use of prayer in pastoral supervision, nor has it been to take the use of prayer for granted and to treat it as a 'norm' because that is what happens in other areas of Christian practice. The integration of prayer is intrinsically pragmatic and has to be characterised by an openness and acceptance of what is meaningful to the other.

BIBLIOGRAPHY

Gubi, Peter Madsen. "An exploration of the use of prayer in mainstream counselling." *British Journal of Guidance & Counselling* 29, no. 4 (2001): 425–34.

———. "Practice behind closed doors—challenging the taboo of prayer in mainstream counselling culture." *Journal of Critical Psychology, Counselling and Psychotherapy* 2, no. 2 (2002): 97–104.

———. *Prayer in Counselling and Psychotherapy: Exploring a Hidden Meaningful Dimension.* Jessica Kingsley Publications, 2008.

———. "A qualitative exploration into how the use of prayer in counselling and psychotherapy might be ethically problematic." *Counselling and Psychotherapy Research* 9, no. 2 (2009): 115–21.

———. *What Counsellors and Spiritual Directors Can Learn from Each Other.* Jessica Kingsley Publications, 2017.

Magaletta, Philip R. and Peter A. Brawer. "Prayer in Psychotherapy: A Model for its use, Ethical Considerations, and Guidelines for Practice." *Journal of Psychology and Theology* 26 (1998): 322–30.

McMinn, Mark R. *Psychology, Theology, and Spirituality in Christian Counseling.* Tyndale House Publishers, Inc., 2012.

Richards, P. Scott, and Allen E. Bergin. *A Spiritual Strategy for Counseling and Psychotherapy*. American Psychological Association, 1997.

Rose, Jessica. *Sharing Spaces?: Prayer and the Counselling Relationship*. Darton, Longman & Todd, 2002.

Sperry, Len. *Spirituality in clinical practice: Incorporating the spiritual dimension in psychotherapy and counseling*. Psychology Press, 2001.

Tan, Siang-Yang. "Religion in clinical practice: Implicit and explicit integration." Pp. 365–87 in *Religion and the Clinical Practice of Psychology*, ed. Edward P. Shafranske. American Psychological Association, 1996.

NOTES

1. Len Sperry, *Spirituality in Clinical Practice: Incorporating the Spiritual Dimension in Psychotherapy and Counselling* (Psychology Press, 2001).

2. Peter Madsen Gubi, *Prayer in Counselling and Psychotherapy: Exploring a Hidden Meaningful Dimension* (London: Jessica Kingsley Publications, 2008).

3. Peter Madsen Gubi, *What Counsellors and Spiritual Directors Can Learn from Each Other* (London: Jessica Kingsley Publications, 2017).

4. Gubi, "Prayer in Counselling and Psychotherapy."

5. See the Association for Pastoral Supervision and Education's Code of Conduct, https://www.pastoralsupervision.org.uk/ (accessed 03/10/2022).

6. See Peter Madsen Gubi, "An exploration of the use of prayer in mainstream counselling." *British Journal of Guidance & Counselling* 29, no. 4 (2001): 425–34; Peter Madsen Gubi, "Practice behind closed doors—challenging the taboo of prayer in mainstream counselling culture." *Journal of Critical Psychology, Counselling and Psychotherapy* 2, no. 2 (2002): 97–104; Jessica Rose, *Sharing Spaces?: Prayer and the Counselling Relationship* (Darton, Longman && Todd, 2002); Philip R. Magaletta and Peter A. Brawer, "Prayer in Psychotherapy: A Model for Its Use, Ethical Considerations, and Guidelines for Practice." *Journal of Psychology and Theology* 26 (1998): 322–30; P. Scott Richards and Allen E. Bergin, *A Spiritual Strategy for Counseling and Psychotherapy* (American Psychological Association, 1997); Mark R. McMinn, *Psychology, Theology, and Spirituality in Christian Counselling* (Tyndale House Publishers, Inc., 2012); Siang-Yang Tan, "Religion in clinical practice: Implicit and explicit integration." Pp. 365–387 in *Religion and the Clinical Practice of Psychology*, ed. Edward P. Shafranske (American Psychological Association, 1996).

Chapter Four

Supervisee Self-Care in Pastoral Supervision

Michelle Seabrook

"How are you?" "I'm fine thanks." In this chapter, I will invite you to delve into the issues around supervisee self-care in pastoral supervision. For context, supervision is pivotal in managing my own self-care, and I have been interested in the self-care of those who help others for many years. Having had several 'helping' roles across a wide range of professions, I was unprepared for the toll this work would take, alongside the more expected joys of the work. Thankfully, I was given the opportunity to have supervision to explore the impact of helping others. My supervisor was challenging and containing, full of wit and warmth, and I developed a solid supervisory relationship that helped me situate my 'self' and my well-being within my work. It became very clear to me that unless I looked after myself, I would not be able to help others. It was also clear that saying this and doing this were very different, and were sometimes challenging concepts! I am still learning and developing my own self-care needs, and supervision continues to be a cornerstone of my self-care. I have evolved into a supervisor who places the restorative aspects of self-care at the heart of supervision.

The aim of this chapter is to explore the issues around self-care in pastoral supervision and to invite you to reflect on how present self-care is in the supervision that you offer. Placing self-care within supervision is not a new concept. Within the realms of the wider helping professions, the recognition that practitioner self-care is an important aspect of supervision is well-known. I will define self-care, and issues for consideration for self-care in pastoral supervision will be highlighted. Reflective prompts for both the supervisor and the supervisee will be used throughout. These may be useful to encourage supervisors to reflect on their own thinking around self-care and can also be used in practice to facilitate a reflective discussion with supervisees about their self-care.

WHAT IS SELF-CARE?

Self-care is a globally understood concept.[1] It can be described as taking proactive, deliberate steps to improve and maintain individual resilience and well-being.[2] Self-care is more than a buzzword, and, for those that work to help others, self-care is essential and obligatory. Self-care can mitigate the negative effects of working within the helping professions, through engaging with activities that nourish, and balance, and maintain resilience and well-being, so that the professional can continue to do their role. So, adopting self-care practice should not be as a reaction to crisis or distress; for those who help others, it should be a constant commitment. Perhaps what is also relevant, in the context of pastoral supervision, is the understanding of self-care, not only as an individual process, but one that is integrated into the culture of the role, and one that is organisationally driven.

From my perspective, to fully engage with the issues around self-care in pastoral supervision, we need to widen the frame of reference. Pastoral work can come under the umbrella of a helping/human services profession and, if it is understood as such, many issues of self-care that are relevant for the wider helping professions will be applicable to pastoral supervision. In order to help others in a professional role, the professional needs to take care of themselves. This appears to be a simple, straightforward idea, but the execution may be less than straightforward.

Addressing self-care takes many forms. Norcross and Vandenbos provide useful and comprehensive checklists of the various areas of self-care, such as recognition of hazards, focussing on rewards, physicality, relationships, boundaries, and spirituality, among others.[3] While their book is primarily aimed at psychotherapists, it is highly relevant across the range of helping professions, as the nature of therapeutic work which is likened to being a 'calling' will have a particular connection with pastoral work. The authors recognise the link between faith and social support, and a sense of purpose and hope.[4] While self-care can be secular, faith-based spirituality will be of particular importance when understanding the well-being of the pastoral supervisee. During times of stress, faith can be a source of both comfort and meaning. Butler et al. note that "Spiritual self-care practice creates space to reflect on our own inner needs and our role or place within the world and universe."[5] Research has linked faith and coping behaviours which may particularly resonate with pastoral supervision but may also have relevance outside of pastoral specific supervision.[6]

Butler et al. suggest that self-care can be addressed in six stages.[7] These are physical, professional/workplace, relationship, emotional and psychological, and spiritual, in turn. The domains are intrinsically linked, but it could be argued that within the pastoral roles, there is potentially a dominance of the spiritual stage. Similarly, Burns, Chapman and Guthrie also advocate for self-care to be the "ongoing development of the whole person."[8] Addressing the whole person in supervision requires acknowledgements and discussion of the proactive self-care activities that can reduce the impact of the work. There is no one way to 'do' self-care. In supervision, it can be useful for supervisors to explore the activities that nourish the supervisee. This can be a useful insight into the maintenance of their well-being, particularly if the supervisee speaks of not having time, or not feeling able to undertake the self-care activities. These clues to potentially impaired well-being can act as a springboard for discussion into how well the supervisee *really* is. Given that the range of activities that nourish the supervisee's well-being can be vast, it's important that supervisors encourage supervisees to adopt a proactive, well-being-maintaining self-care approach, rather than as a reaction to a self-care crisis.

The importance of including supervision as part of a plan of self-care cannot be underestimated. Supervisees may not be able to recognise early signs that they are becoming impaired. Their view of their well-being may be skewed by their commitment to their calling, their obligations to the community, or personal issues of stress, for example.[9] The value of reflecting with another is a crucial part of being a reflective practitioner and addressing the crossovers between personal and professional self-care issues. It is often an objective view that illuminates subjective reflections. Yet, supervisees proactively attending to their self-care is not something that can be assumed. Some may do a very convincing job of 'talking the talk.' This can be a challenge for supervisors to be able to fully assess and understand the well-being needs of the supervisee. A supervisor who explicitly focusses on self-care provides a reflective space for the supervisee to think about their well-being, and an arena to have self-care scrutinised, challenged, and celebrated. But, in my opinion, in order to do this, the supervisor needs to adopt and maintain a curious approach to the supervisee's self-care and situate this at the heart of the supervision dynamic.[10]

HOW DOES SELF-CARE FIT INTO PASTORAL CLINICAL SUPERVISION?

According to the Association for Pastoral Supervision and Education, pastoral supervision is having "a regular, planned, intentional and boundaried place."[11]

They specify that supervision should be attentive to issues that impact fitness to practice and the impact of the work. In Kelly's study on theological reflective practice, 83 percent of the respondents believed that supervision provided a reflective space which, in turn, enhanced their resilience.[12] Having a restorative element of supervision is well established across the helping professions, but in order for supervisors to truly address supervisee self-care, to know 'how their supervisee is,' it is worth investing time during the supervision session for understanding your supervisees' baseline for their well-being. While there are numerous models that may offer insight into this, perhaps the Seven-Eyed model of supervision could be of use here. The model provides a process of exploring the systemic and relational aspects of the supervisee, the individuals or groups who are receiving support from the supervisee, the supervisor and supervisee dynamic, the context of the work, and the wider contexts.[13] Particularly relevant here is mode four—'focusing on the supervisee.' This element highlights the importance of the supervisor attending to how the supervisee is impacted by the work, their emotional reactions to the work, and their general well-being.[14] Milne and Reiner offer an alternative model called 'The Tandem Model.' Here, they use the metaphor of supervisor and supervisee as riding a tandem bike, where the supervisor is operating the controls, but the overall aim is to work together, and both supervisor and supervisee contribute to the transactional process.[15] They use the following definition:

> Supportive clinical supervision addresses supervisees' emotional experience of their workplace, and their personal functioning in that context. It is a formal, case-focused, and intensive relational process. . . . The main intended outcomes for supervisees are reductions in personal distress and enhanced wellbeing.[16]

Both models may offer supervisors a framework for situating supervisee self-care in supervision; with the Tandem Model being highly specific about the intention of situating supervisee wellbeing as the focus of the supervisory interaction. So, be warned, if attending to self-care in supervision feels like going through the motions, an add-on, or a checkbox item, rather than embedded into the process, this can create barriers in fully addressing supervisee self-care.

The supervision appointment may start off with the throwaway question of 'How are you?,' that is answered with an equally throwaway 'social norm' comment of "I'm fine thanks,' without considering that that seemingly simple question is an opportunity to delve deeper and to examine the layers of meaning and understanding. To counteract this, it is suggested that the 'how are you?' question is approached as an opportunity for deeper critical reflection, a concept that will be covered in greater depth later in the chapter. Unless this seemingly simple question is responded to with honesty, and the answer scrutinised by the supervisor, there may be an opportunity missed to fully engage with self-care at depth. Fundamentally, without attending to self-care in pastoral supervision at depth, we fail to attend to the needs of the individual on a micro level.

REFLECTIVE EXERCISE:

Think about a supervisee you are working with and the exchanges you have around their well-being.

- How has this been initially contracted for within supervision?
- What models/theories have you used to explain your rationale for this?
- What discussions do you have with your supervisee around attending to their self-care needs?
- What do you know about the self-care activities they undertake to maintain their well-being? How regularly do you ask them about this?

How might you introduce this or revisit supervisee self-care?

WHAT ARE THE SELF-CARE ISSUES FOR PASTORAL SUPERVISION?

Awareness of the issues that may impair well-being, and therefore need addressing through self-care, is important to be understood by the supervisor. There is often an overlap between the professional role and personal issues of self-care. The vocation is more than a 'job'—it's a reflection of the person. Despite many in the helping professions attempting to separate the personal and professional, this overlap may be particularly challenging for those in ministry, especially those who are experiencing spiritual exhaustion. Spiritual exhaustion can be understood as having diminished hope, increased awareness of own's own limitations, and spiritual suffering.[17]

It is recognised that many clergy may not be trained therapists, yet the work required will involve skills that are similar to working within the mental health professions or therapeutic support.[18] Research that measured burnout and vicarious traumatisation in clergy, indicated comparable results to other mental health professionals.[19] Hendron, Irving, and Taylor highlight that pastoral professions are potentially hazardous. The ongoing exposure and bearing witness to others' pain can contribute to symptoms of vicarious trauma.[20] Burns et al. highlight that there may be unrealistic expectations of the role due to the identities of the professional and the personal being intrinsically interlinked, which then creates an unhelpful internalised view of these expectations. They also highlight issues of social isolation that may be specific to the pastoral roles. This factor will be highly relevant for pastoral supervision.[21] In practical terms for supervisors, this means creating an environment that encourages recognition and disclosure of these matters. Furthermore, Bledsoe's research also highlights the importance of support systems alongside intentional self-care practices, with the aim to achieve balance and boundaries in the role.[22] The need for support systems speaks to the importance of having pastoral supervision.[23, 24]

Those who help others as their professional role are not immune to the everyday stressors that can occur. Yet, there may be assumptions around someone's professional role as offering immunity to everyday stress. It is important, therefore, for supervisors to normalise the everyday issues that have an impact on the supervisee. Additionally, helping roles are often emotionally demanding, and there is an unpredictability as to what issue will be presented, sometimes spiritual support being the first port of call following a highly traumatic event and, as a result of this, the supervisee may experience a challenge in their sense of safety in the world, which can have a long-term deleterious impact on the well-being of the professional. So, while we can acknowledge the importance of attending to supervisee self-care in supervision, there may be a conflict between the ideal and the reality.

CHALLENGES IN ADDRESSING SUPERVISEE SELF-CARE

Life Events, Past and Present

Everyday stressors will have an impact on supervisee well-being. It is important, therefore, to situate supervisee self-care within the wider framework of their life and history. There may be personal factors that have influenced their calling that are relevant to their self-care. Alongside this, there may be current issues that cause stress, such as illness, relationship issues, family and community dynamics and demands, financial problems, social and global issues, feelings of isolation and loneliness, lack of wider support, and other everyday issues which are important to recognise and explore in supervision.[25, 26]

The notion of being a 'wounded healer' is also relevant here. The concept captures the experiences of distress, trauma, and the historical psychological 'wounds' that shape an individual earlier on in their life, and often lead them to being drawn to a profession where they help others with their 'wounds.'[27] The 'wounded healer' concept can be traced back to Greek mythology, linked to religious texts, and perhaps most well-known from Jung.[28] Research has suggested that some in the ministry have previous trauma linked to their childhood and upbringing, and the impact that this has on their ministerial role has been profound.[29] Nolte and Dreyer discuss the importance of recognising a pastor's woundedness and the potential inner conflicts that this may present while they are reflecting on their views about their own experiences, their own humanness, and their ministry.[30] They encourage pastors to explore this as a gift of insight, and to be honest and transparent about their own struggles. In supervision, this would mean developing an environment that allows for an honest dialogue between supervisor and supervisee that encourages this honest and transparent exploration, rather than slipping into providing spiritual 'bypass,' where exploration of the trauma, and how this may impact on the work, is glossed over with a spiritual cliché.[31]

REFLECTIVE EXERCISE:

You are meeting a new supervisee for the first time. They are keen to start addressing the challenges in their role, but you recognise the importance of balancing addressing the current issues with understanding who your supervisee is. You begin to ask them about their history and what has led them to the work they do. The supervisee is curious as to why you need to know this. What is your rationale?

While it is useful to be honest and transparent about personal woundedness, it's important to acknowledge that self-care goes beyond the individual. To truly address self-care, we need to engage with issues around the culture of the professional and the intersections of the person's identity. All factors that impact the individual should be considered. Simpson's research argues for an intersectional trauma-informed approach in ministry, so that there is dialogue that enhances a readiness for the impact of the work.[32] It's also important for the organisational/church expectations to be examined in supervision, in order to interrogate how the profession encourages exploring the impact of the work, alongside the balance in acknowledging personal wounds that will be relevant for the professional well-being, and how best to support this. Therefore, in supervision, it is useful to engage in dialogue that captures the intersections of personal and professional issues that can impair the well-being of the supervisee.

Reflective prompts to use as discussion points with the supervisee:

- What has drawn you to the vocation you are in?
- Do you have previous experiences of trauma or distress that have influenced you?
- How does 'who you are,' across generations, inform your ability to attend to your self-care needs?
- How does the culture of the profession help or hinder you in addressing your self-care?

What have you understood as the expectations of your role and your calling, and how does the church/organisation enable you to look after yourself in the pursuit of helping others?

Vicarious Trauma

The impact of bearing witness to another's distress can be understood as 'vicarious trauma.[33, 34] The term captures the self-view and worldview changes that occur in a person as a result of engaging with another's trauma. It is the act of the indirect exposure that impacts on the supervisee. The effects of vicarious trauma are understood to develop over time, after ongoing interactions with other's trauma. It is recognised that many members of the community may seek faith-based counsel following a traumatic life event.[35] So, the potential for vicarious trauma is relevant for those supervising pastoral supervisees. Symptoms of vicarious trauma can be similar to those who have experienced the trauma firsthand; these will include intrusive imagery, nightmares, hyperawareness of safety, reduced motivation at work, and physical manifestations of stress and trauma.[36] If we understand that reactions to trauma are a normal reaction to an abnormal event, then vicarious trauma reactions can also be understood in this way and will require supervision that reflects this understanding. Nikischer's paper highlights the impact that simply researching and working indirectly with trauma will have on an individual and the importance of organisational recognition and support protocols that are needed to minimise the effects of working with trauma.[37] Once again, we are reminded of the need to address supervisee well-being beyond the individual, and have embedded organisational support.

Burnout

The concept of 'burnout' arose from Maslach's research, and has since been globally adopted as a common term for those feeling depersonalisation, emotional exhaustion and impaired feelings of accomplishment that are linked to work.[38] It results in a disconnect and conflict between what a person feels about their role and what they need to do in their role. Iosim's research on Romanian social workers and clerics suggests that supervision for those working in a helping role reduces symptoms of burnout.[39] Chandler's research into the impact of burnout on spiritual practice of spiritual leaders noted that they can experience isolation, stress, frustration, loneliness, and a depletion of spiritual nourishment. Interestingly, in Chandler's study, those that recognised symptoms of burnout, and felt able to address it, reported burnout as the catalyst for changing their circumstances.[40] So, there is hope, even in times of burnout.

Compassion Fatigue

'Compassion fatigue' is a term coined by Figley and is an occupational hazard of working with trauma.[41] Being exposed to the painful experiences of others can result in experiencing pain ourselves, and potentially overidentifying with the suffering. While the symptoms can be similar to burnout and vicarious trauma, it is recognised that those with compassion fatigue may be compelled to continue, rather than take time to repair. For those who hold a key role in the community, and commitment to their church, this is potentially problematic conflict as there may be a disconnect between the internal experience of the pastoral leader and that which is shown to the public. So, supervision that allows this to be explored is crucial.[42]

To some extent, these issues that impact on supervisee well-being are an inevitable outcome. Yet, they are an unwelcomed and unpredicted result of helping others. Shrode's research highlights the extra complexities that will be present for the clergy and, while the research is not supervision specific, it highlights a number of issues that are particularly relevant for pastoral supervision. The research raises the importance of acknowledging the importance of unaddressed trauma, or a supervisee being aware of trauma yet being noncommittal on addressing it. There may be a potential collusion or dismissing of supervisee trauma by using scripture as a 'pat answer' rather than exploration and support, and the importance of a trauma-sensitive culture and an emotionally healthy leadership.[43]

There is the potential that the unwelcomed aspects of the professional role may be seldom discussed at the start of pursuing a professional helping role or calling. It could be suggested that the understanding of the need to attend to self-care develops, alongside gaining experience in the role, as the symptoms of the impact of the role begin to emerge. To spend some time reflecting on these issues is essential for attending to the self-care needs of the supervisee, by the supervisor attuning and encouraging an open discussion about the impact of work. This can highlight to the supervisee when they need to increase their self-care activities.

Reflective prompts to use in discussion with the supervisee or for supervisor reflections:

- How much were you prepared for the potential negative impact of your work?
- How has this been explained in supervision? What would help enhance your understanding?
- How often do issues around the potential negative impact of the work get discussed? Who instigates these discussions, and why?
- How can we integrate explicit and ongoing discussions of the concepts of burnout, compassion fatigue, and vicarious trauma in supervision?

Given the context of the pastoral role, it is likely that supervisees will be engaging in work that is linked to trauma. The potential effects of engaging with this work are described above. In order to work with supervisee self-care when they are working with trauma, supervision also needs to be trauma-informed. Trauma-informed supervision understands the potential negative effects of the work and works with the supervisee to ensure a supervisory environment that has safety, trust, choice, collaboration, and empowerment.[44]

FACILITATING THROUGH THE BARRIERS

To encourage an honest dialogue about the potential negative impact of the work, supervisors need to clarify their understanding of the self-care needs of the supervisee. Supervisors also need to give 'permission' for the supervisee to be honest about their needs. This can be done at the start of a supervisory agreement but should also be included in reviews of the supervision arrangement and, if needed, the supervisee can be reminded of this throughout the supervisory process. The supervisor needs to adopt an active role in addressing supervisee self-care, rather than assuming or expecting that the supervisee will disclose.

There are a number of obstacles for both the supervisor and the supervisee to overcome when it comes to attending to self-care in an honest, transparent and open manner. I would suggest that both supervisor and supervisee adopt a curious approach to well-being in order to encourage an open dialogue within supervision. Davys and Beddoe offer a number of barriers that stifle looking at supervisee feelings within supervision.[45] They highlight the supervisee fear of being overwhelmed by the feelings, fear of judgment, and fear of distortion. Being overwhelmed by feelings acknowledges that the supervisee's emotional response may be painful and upsetting; thus, the supervisee may wish to avoid expressing these feelings as there is risk of feeling shame or feeling vulnerable. In terms of judgments, there may be supervisee fear that the supervisor will perceive them as being less competent, or overly involved. The fear of distortion is related to supervisory encounter, that the supervisee may wish to be perceived as robust, that an emotional response is not appropriate in supervision, or that the supervisor may not be able to contain the emotional response of the supervisee. They encourage supervisors to take the lid off and help their supervisees examine their self-care and emotional response to the work. I too, like the authors, see exploring emotion in supervision is a jointly held responsibility of both the supervisor and supervisee, but disclosure can be problematic.

My own research highlighted a potentially unhelpful dynamic within supervision around the difficulties in disclosing issues of self-care.[46] Both the supervisees and supervisors acknowledged that disclosure can be problematic for a supervisee as they want to maintain a professional facade and are worried about what the supervisor would think, and supervisees were uncertain whether they were 'allowed' to bring their difficulties to supervision.[47] Supervisees may believe that it is inappropriate, irrelevant, or too personal.[48] For pastoral contexts, there are similar issues around disclosure due to concerns of the views of those they serve or their superiors.[49] The supervisees may experience feelings of shame around disclosure of self-care issues, so it is vital that supervisors provide a supervisory environment that encourages disclosure and exploration of the issues that may be a barrier to this.

Supervisors may also wish to pay close attention to how issues around self-care are disclosed. Language exploration and listening to the linguistic clues are key skills in supervision. Metaphor can be a helpful tool for supervisees to introduce a potentially difficult topic, by using something to represent or symbolise something of significance.[50] So, it is important for supervisors to explore a metaphor when it is presented, in order to uncover the underlying issue that is being introduced into the supervisory space in a more palatable manner by the supervisee. The other linguistic clues that supervisors may wish to tune into is language that is hesitant, or which minimises the significance of a self-care issue, such as laughter or humour that is used to avoid the seriousness of the matter, or lengthy pauses which may mean that the dialogue is potentially problematic.[51, 52]

Reflective prompts to use as discussion points with the supervisee:

- What does distress look and feel like for you? How will I know that you need help with this?
- What may be the barriers in being fully honest about your feelings?
- What might be helpful in overcoming these barriers?
- What might be unhelpful?

IMPORTANCE OF THE SUPERVISORY RELATIONSHIP ON SUPERVISEE SELF-CARE

The influence of the supervisory relationship is crucial in addressing supervisee self-care.[53] Yet, it is recognised that there is a power dynamic in supervision that may impact on how self-care is addressed. The supervisor will be evaluating the supervisee, including their well-being and engagement with self-care. It may be a challenge for supervisors to get the balance between the educative, evaluative, and restorative aspects of supervision, while still maintaining a good supervisory relationship.

A qualitative meta-analysis on supervisees' experiences, by Chircop Coleiro, Creaner and Timulak, found that in order to encourage disclosure of self-care, the supervisor needs to foster an environment that feels safe and allows for supervisee vulnerability and cultural sensitivity.[54] Also, that feedback is sought, and the power dynamics are acknowledged. Essentially, the quality of the supervisory relationship will influence the extent of supervisee disclosure. Supervisee disclosure can be problematic if they believe that exploring their issues around self-care are not welcome in supervision, or the supervisee wants to maintain a version of themselves that is without flaw or vulnerability for fear of their professionalism being questioned.[55] Perhaps this is where the issue of supervisors challenging their supervisees about their self-care can be difficult to navigate. Receiving feedback from a supervisor can be a difficult part of the supervision process, and if this is layered upon a supervisee's wariness of their well-being being scrutinised, or it evokes feelings of shame, it is important for supervisors to help their supervisees learn the skill of receiving feedback and remain open to learning. Yet, for confronting self-care issues, there may be an added difficulty, given the personal nature of self-care. So, as a supervisor, you may need to facilitate a preemptive discussion with your supervisee regarding how to approach challenging them on their self-care issues.[56]

The importance of invitation is relevant here. If we take into account the inherent power dynamic in supervision, it is understandable that supervisees may feel a need for the supervisor to set the tone of how self-care is brought into the supervision space. It is simply not enough to assume that the supervisee feels able to disclose without 'permission' or guidance from the supervisor. To this end it may be useful to also explore how previous experiences of supervision have impacted on the supervisee's understanding of what is expected.

REFLECTIVE EXERCISE:

You've been working with a supervisee for a number of years, and you feel that you know your supervisee very well. You are aware that they have a tendency to place others' needs ahead of their own. You notice that they are showing signs of stress and you become increasingly concerned that they may be feeling burnt out. You raise your concerns with your supervisee, who dismisses and minimises the symptoms by saying, "It's just a busy time." How do you encourage a more open, yet challenging, dialogue about this issue without the conversation being dismissed or shut down?

IMPLICATIONS FOR PRACTICE: THE GOLDEN QUESTION

The idea of the 'Golden Question' arose from my research into supervisee self-care in clinical supervision.[57] It captures the importance of the supervisors inviting their supervisees to proactively engage with issues around their self-care through the use of a simple question, 'How are you'?, and treats this everyday question as a springboard into the layers of supervisee wellbeing. The idea can be used to encourage an exploration as to the supervisee's understanding of exploring self-care in supervision, their previous experiences of this, and the issues that help or limit their disclosure of self-care issues. Use the question as a prompt into exploring your supervisee's personal history and how this may emerge in their work and how they relate to others. Supervisors are encouraged to explore the supervisee response to being questioned, or challenged, about their self-care, and their potential feelings of guilt or shame. There also may be scope for wider contextual issues about role expectation and the support had from leadership. Also, as supervisors, we are skilled listeners, going beyond the words used, alert to the linguistic clues that indicate something that is being presented by the supervisee that requires particular attention. Listen for the verbal clues around the supervisee's response to exploring their self-care, such as hesitation, language that attempts to minimise their emotional response, using laughter as a diversion technique, or using metaphor as a way to introduce a self-care issue.

To implement this into practice, I would suggest that supervisors should invite their supervisees to engage in a reflective conversation, using some of the prompts from this chapter, that attends to the process of addressing self-care, so that obstructions can be brought out into the open and an honest discussion can take place. I encourage supervisors to commit to engage in a deliberate, proactive approach to engaging with their supervisees' issues around self-care that may be of concern but, also importantly, to highlight the well-being maintenance that is being engaged with and how this helps. It could therefore mean that an existing supervisory dyad may wish to make a new contract around how self-care issues will be invited, explored, and reviewed. Supervisors who will be working with new supervisees may want to have an explicit discussion at the start of work together that explores these issues, and thus give clarity on the expectations around exploring issues of self-care.

Think about the supervision you offer:

- Reflect on your current approach to addressing self-care in the supervision you offer. How much do you attend to it and why?
- Who instigates conversations around supervisee self-care? Why is this?
- How much do you know about your supervisee's self-care process and activities?
- What will you do differently to engage with your supervisees about their self-care?

How does addressing self-care in supervision get reviewed? What is helpful about this? What needs improving?

SUMMARY

The aim of this chapter was not only to invite and provoke reflections on supervisory practice in relationship to self-care, but was also to provide some prompts that could be used in practice within supervision. These prompts aim to encourage both supervisor and supervisee to examine the process of exploring self-care, so that self-care issues can be investigated in depth. Supervisors hold the tension between being supportive, educational, and challenging, and it is important to recognise there will be a number of aspects to consider that are at play when exploring supervisee well-being. So, an environment that allows for exploration of these layers is crucial. Supervision that supports self-care can help maintain the balance between supervisee distress and growth. So, use the 'how are you?' question to prompt a deeper, more transparent exploration of self-care, and place supervisee well-being at the heart of the supervisory process.

BIBLIOGRAPHY

Association of Pastoral Supervision and Education. "Definition and Ethos." Accessed 22nd March 2022. https://www.pastoralsupervision.org.uk/home/about/definition-and-ethos/.

Bledsoe, T. Scott, and Kimberly A. Setterlund. "Thriving in ministry: Exploring the support systems and self-care practices of experienced pastors." *The Journal of Family and Community Ministries* 28, no.1 (2015): 48–66.

Blount, Ashley J., Dalena Dillman Taylor, Glenn W. Lambie, and Arami Nika Anwell. "Clinical supervisors' perceptions of wellness: A phenomenological view on supervisee wellness." *The Professional Counselor* 6, no. 4 (2016): 360–74.

Bryant-Davis, Thema, and Eunice C. Wong. "Faith to move mountains: Religious coping, spirituality, and interpersonal trauma recovery." *American Psychologist* 68, no. 8 (2013): 675.

Burns, Bob, Tasha D. Chapman, and Donald C. Guthrie. *Resilient ministry: What pastors told us about surviving and thriving*. Downers Grove: InterVarsity Press, 2012.

Butler, Lisa D., Kelly A. Mercer, Katie McClain-Meeder, Dana M. Horne and Melissa Dudley. "Six domains of self-care: Attending to the whole person." *Journal of Human Behavior in the Social Environment* 29, no. 1 (2019): 107–24.

Carroll, Michael. *Effective supervision for the helping professions*. London: Sage Publications, 2014.

Chandler, Diane J. "The impact of pastors' spiritual practices on burnout." *Journal of Pastoral Care & Counseling* 64, no. 2 (2010): 1–9.

Chircop Coleiro, Angie, Mary Creaner, and Ladislav Timulak. "The good, the bad, and the less than ideal in clinical supervision: A qualitative meta-analysis of supervisee experiences." *Counselling Psychology Quarterly*: (2022) 1–22. DOI: 10.1080/09515070.2021.2023098.

Davys, Allyson, and Liz Beddoe. *Best practice in professional supervision: A guide for the helping pofessions*. London: Jessica Kingsley Publishers, 2020.

Figley, Charles R. "Compassion fatigue: Toward a new understanding of the costs of caring." Pp. 3–28 in *Secondary traumatic stress: Self-care issues for clinicians, researchers, and ednucators,* ed. Beth. H. Stamm. Baltimore: The Sidran Press, 1995.

Foreman, Tamarine. "Wellness, exposure to trauma, and vicarious traumatization: A pilot study." *Journal of Mental Health Counseling* 40, no. 2 (2018): 142–55.

Hanley, Tifani-Crystal Enid. "Compassion Fatigue, Self-Care, and Clergy Members: How Social Workers Can Help." Master's degree thesis, California State University, 2019.

Hawkins, Peter, and Aisling McMahon. *Supervision in the Helping Professions.* London: McGraw Hill, 2020.

Hendron, Jill Anne, Pauline Irving, and Brian Taylor. "The unseen cost: A discussion of the secondary traumatization experience of the clergy." *Pastoral Psychology* 61, no. 2 (2012): 221–31.

Holaday, Margot, Trey Lackey, Michelle Boucher, and Reba Glidewell. "Secondary stress, burnout, and the clergy." *American Journal of Pastoral Counseling* 4, no. 1 (2001): 53–72.

Iosim, Iasmina, Patricia Runcan, Virgil Dan, Bogdan Nadolu, Remus Runcan, and Magdalena Petrescu. "The role of supervision in preventing burnout among professionals working with people in difficulty." *International Journal of Environmental Research and Public Health* 19, no. 1 (2021): 160–75. https://doi.org/10.3390/ijerph19010160.

Jung, Carl G. "Fundamental Questions of Psychotherapy" in *The Collected Works of C. G. Jung*, eds. Herbert Read, Michael Fordham, and Gerhard Adler (Vol. 16). Princeton: Princeton University Press, 1951.

Kelly, Ewan. "Translating theological reflective practice into values based reflection: A report from Scotland." *Reflective Practice: Formation and Supervision in Ministry* 33, no. 1 (2013): 245–56.

Knight, Carolyn, and L. DiAnne Borders. *Trauma-Informed Supervision: Core Components and Unique Dynamics in Varied Practice Contexts*. Oxford: Taylor & Francis Limited, 2021.

Knox, Sarah. "Disclosure—and lack thereof—in individual supervision." *The Clinical Supervisor* 34, no. 2 (2015): 151–63.

Louw, Daniël. "Compassion fatigue: Spiritual exhaustion and the cost of caring in the pastoral ministry. Towards a 'pastoral diagnosis' in caregiving." *HTS: Theological Studies* 71, no. 2 (2015): 1–10.

Maslach, Christina, Susan E. Jackson, and Michael P. Leiter. *Maslach Burnout Inventory*. Lanham, MD: Scarecrow Education, 1997.

McCann, Lisa, and Laurie Anne Pearlman. "Vicarious traumatization: A framework for understanding the psychological effects of working with victims." *Journal of Traumatic Stress* 3, no. 1 (1990): 131–49. https://doi.org/10.1007/BF00975140.

Milne, Derek, and Robert P. Reiser. *Supportive Clinical Supervision: Enhancing Well-being and Reducing Burnout Through Restorative Leadership*. Shoreham by Sea: Pavilion, 2020.

Nikischer, Andrea. "Vicarious trauma inside the academe: Understanding the impact of teaching, researching and writing violence." *Higher Education* 77, no. 5 (2019): 905–16.

Nolte, S. Philip, and Yolanda Dreyer. "The paradox of being a wounded healer: Henri JM Nouwen's contribution to pastoral theology." *HTS Teologiese Studies/ Theological Studies* 66, no. 2 (2010): 1–8. https://doi.org/10.4102/hts.v66i2.861.

Norcross, John C., and Gary R. VandenBos. *Leaving It at the Office: A Guide to Psychotherapist Self-Care*. New York: Guilford Publications, 2018.

Pearlman, Lisa, and Paula MacIan. "Vicarious traumatisation: an empirical study of the effects of trauma work on trauma therapists." *Professional Psychology: Research and Practice* 36 (1995): 558–65.

Rice, Cecil A. "The psychotherapist as 'wounded healer': A modern expression of an ancient tradition." *On Becoming a Psychotherapist: The Personal and Professional Journey* (2011): 165–89.

Scott, Greg, and Rachel Lovell. "The rural pastors initiative: Addressing isolation and burnout in rural ministry." *Pastoral Psychology* 64, no. 1 (2015): 71–97.

Seabrook, Michelle. "'The Golden Question.' Addressing supervisee self-care in clinical supervision." *Counselling and Psychotherapy Research* (2022). https://doi .org/10.1002/capr.12543.

Shrodes, Deanna Doss. "The Prevalence of Unaddressed Trauma in the Lives of Ministerial Leaders and Pastoral Care-Oriented Steps to Greater Spiritual and Emotional Health." Doctoral Thesis, Southeastern University, 2022.

Simpson, Caitlin. "Trauma and Intersectionality in Trauma Informed Ministry." Doctoral Thesis, Bellarmine University, 2021.

Stokoe, Elizabeth. *Talk: The Science of Conversation*. London: Hachette UK, 2018.

Wiggins, Sally. *Discursive Psychology: Theory, Method and Applications*. London: Sage Publications, 2017.

NOTES

1. Ashley J. Blount, Dalena Dillman Taylor, Glenn W. Lambie, and Arami Nika Anwell. "Clinical Supervisors' Perceptions of Wellness: A Phenomenological View on Supervisee Wellness." *The Professional Counselor* 6, no. 4 (2016): 360.

2. Lisa D. Butler, Kelly A. Mercer, Katie McClain-Meeder, Dana M. Horne, and Melissa Dudley. "Six Domains of Self-Care: Attending to the Whole Person." *Journal of Human Behavior in the Social Environment* 29, no. 1 (2019): 107–24.

3. John C. Norcross and Gary R. VandenBos. *Leaving It at the Office: A Guide to Psychotherapist Self-Care.* (New York: Guilford Publications, 2018).

4. Ibid.

5. Butler, Mercer, McClain-Meeder, Horne, and Dudley, "Six Domains of Self-Care," 117.

6. Thema Bryant-Davis and Eunice C. Wong. "Faith to Move Mountains: Religious Coping, Spirituality, and Interpersonal Trauma Recovery." *American Psychologist* 68, no. 8 (2013): 675.

7. Butler, Mercer, McClain-Meeder, Horne, and Dudley, "Six Domains of Self-Care," 117.

8. Bob Burns, Tasha D. Chapman, and Donald C. Guthrie. *Resilient Ministry: What Pastors Told Us About Surviving and Thriving.* (InterVarsity Press, 2012), 61.

9. Ibid.

10. Tamarine Foreman. "Wellness, Exposure to Trauma, and Vicarious Traumatization: A Pilot Study." *Journal of Mental Health Counseling* 40, no. 2 (2018): 142–55.

11. Association for Pastoral Supervision and Education. https://www.pastoralsupervision.org.uk/home/about/definition-and-ethos/ accessed 18 August 2022.

12. Ewan Kelly. "Translating Theological Reflective Practice into Values Based Reflection: A Report from Scotland." *Reflective Practice: Formation and Supervision in Ministry* 33, no. 1 (2013): 245–56.

13. Peter Hawkins and Aisling McMahon. *Supervision in the Helping Professions,* 5th edition (London: McGraw-Hill, 2020).

14. Ibid.

15. Derek Milne and Robert P. Reiser. *Supportive Clinical Supervision: Enhancing Well-Being and Reducing Burnout through Restorative Leadership.* (Shoreham by Sea: Pavilion, 2020).

16. Milne and Reiser, "Supportive Clinical Supervision," 22.

17. Daniel Louw. "Compassion Fatigue: Spiritual Exhaustion and the Cost of Caring in the Pastoral Ministry: Towards a 'pastoral Diagnosis' in Caregiving." *HTS: Theological Studies* 71, no. 2 (2015): 1–10.

18. Tifani-Crystal Enid Hanley. "Compassion Fatigue, Self-Care, and Clergy Members: How Social Workers Can Help." (Master's degree thesis, California State University, 2019).

19. Margot Holaday, Trey Lackey, Michelle Boucher, and Reba Glidewell. "Secondary Stress, Burnout, and the Clergy." *American Journal of Pastoral Counseling* 4, no. 1 (2001): 53–72.

20. Jill Anne Hendron, Pauline Irving, and Brian Taylor. "The Unseen Cost: A Discussion of the Secondary Traumatization Experience of the Clergy." *Pastoral Psychology* 61, no. 2 (2012): 221–31.

21. Burns, Chapman, and Guthrie, "Resilient Ministry."

22. T. Scott Bledsoe and Kimberly A. Setterlund. "Thriving in Ministry: Exploring the Support Systems and Self-Care Practices of Experienced Pastors." *The Journal of Family and Community Ministries* 28, no. 1 (2015): 48–66.

23. Holaday, Lackey, Boucher, and Glidewell. "Secondary Stress, Burnout, and the Clergy." 53–72.

24. Hendron, Irving, and Taylor, "The Unseen Cost," 221–31.

25. Bledsoe and Setterlund, "Thriving in Ministry," 48–66.

26. Greg Scott and Rachel Lovell. "The Rural Pastors Initiative: Addressing Isolation and Burnout in Rural Ministry." *Pastoral Psychology* 64, no. 1 (2015): 71–97.

27. Cecil A. Rice. "The Psychotherapist as 'Wounded Healer': A Modern Expression of an Ancient Tradition." *On Becoming a Psychotherapist: The Personal and Professional Journey* (2011): 165–89.

28. Carl G. Jung. "Fundamental Questions of Psychotherapy" in *The Collected Works of C. G. Jung*, eds. Herbert Read, Michael Fordham, and Gerhard Adler (Vol. 16) (Princeton: Princeton University Press, 1951).

29. Deanna Doss Shrodes. "The Prevalence of Unaddressed Trauma in the Lives of Ministerial Leaders and Pastoral Care-Oriented Steps to Greater Spiritual and Emotional Health." (Doctoral thesis, Southeastern University, 2022).

30. S. Philip Nolte and Yolanda Dreyer. "The Paradox of Being a Wounded Healer: Henri Jm Nouwen's Contribution to Pastoral Theology." *HTS Teologiese Studies/ Theological Studies* 66, no. 2 (2010): 1–8. https://doi.org/10.4102/hts.v66i2.861.

31. Shrodes, "The Prevalence of Unaddressed Trauma."

32. Caitlin Simpson. "Trauma and Intersectionality in Trauma Informed Ministry." (Doctoral Thesis, Bellarmine University, 2021).

33. Lisa I. McCann and Laurie Anne Pearlman. "Vicarious Traumatization: A Framework for Understanding the Psychological Effects of Working with Victims." *Journal of Traumatic Stress* 3, no. 1 (1990): 131–49.

34. Laurie Anne Pearlman, L., and Paula S. MacIan. "Vicarious Traumatisation: An Empirical Study of the Effects of Trauma Work on Trauma Therapists." *Professional Psychology: Research and Practice* 36 (1995): 558–65.

35. Hanley, "Compassion Fatigue, Self-Care, and Clergy Members."

36. Pearlman and MacIan, "Vicarious Traumatisation," 558–65.

37. Andrea Nikischer. "Vicarious Trauma inside the Academe: Understanding the Impact of Teaching, Researching and Writing Violence." *Higher Education* 77, no. 5 (2019): 905–16.

38. Christina Maslach, Susan E. Jackson, and Michael P. Leiter. *Maslach Burnout Inventory.* 3rd Edition (Lanham, MD: Scarecrow Education, 1997).

39. Iasmina Iosim, Patricia Runcan, Virgil Dan, Bogdan Nadolu, Remus Runcan, and Magdalena Petrescu. "The Role of Supervision in Preventing Burnout among Professionals Working with People in Difficulty." *International Journal of Environmental Research and Public Health* 19, no. 1 (2021): 160–75. https://doi.org/10.3390/ijerph19010160.

40. Diane J. Chandler. "The Impact of Pastors' Spiritual Practices on Burnout." *Journal of Pastoral Care & Counseling* 64, no. 2 (2010): 1–9.

41. Charles R. Figley. "Compassion Fatigue: Toward a New Understanding of the Costs of Caring," in *Secondary Traumatic Stress: Self-care Issues for Clinicians, Researchers, and Educators,* ed. Beth H. Stamm (Baltimore: The Sidran Press, 1995): 3–28

42. Louw, "Compassion Fatigue," 1–10.

43. Shrodes, "The Prevalence of Unaddressed Trauma."

44. Carolyn Knight and L. DiAnne Borders. *Trauma-Informed Supervision: Core Components and Unique Dynamics in Varied Practice Contexts.* (Oxford: Taylor & Francis Limited, 2021).

45. Allyson Davys and Liz Beddoe. *Best Practice in Professional Supervision: A Guide for the Helping Professions.* (London: Jessica Kingsley Publishers, 2020).

46. Michelle Seabrook. "'The Golden Question.' Addressing supervisee self-care in clinical supervision." *Counselling and Psychotherapy Research* (2022). https://doi.org/10.1002/capr.12543.

47. Ibid.

48. Sarah Knox. "Disclosure—and Lack Thereof—in Individual Supervision." *The Clinical Supervisor* 34, no. 2 (2015): 151–63.

49. Holaday, Lackey, Boucher, and Glidewell, "Secondary Stress," 53–72.

50. Sally Wiggins. *Discursive Psychology: Theory, Method and Applications*. (London: Sage Publications, 2017).

51. Ibid.

52. Elizabeth Stokoe. *Talk: The Science of Conversation.* (London: Hachette, 2018).

53. Michael Carroll. *Effective Supervision for the Helping Professions.* (London: Sage Publications, 2014).

54. Angie Chircop Coleiro, Mary Creaner and Ladislav Timulak. "The Good, the Bad, and the Less Than Ideal in Clinical Supervision: A Qualitative Meta-Analysis of Supervisee Experiences." *Counselling Psychology Quarterly* (2022): 1–22. DOI: 10.1080/09515070.2021.2023098.

55. Ibid.

56. Carroll, "Effective Supervision for the Helping Professions."

57. Seabrook, "The Golden Question."

Chapter Five

Working with Diversity in Pastoral Supervision

Deanne Gardner

In this chapter, I will be reflecting on pastoral supervision within faith contexts and, specifically, I will be focussing on working with diversity in pastoral supervision. Pastoral supervision is not limited to one setting, but can be offered in various settings, such as clergy based within a variety of Church contexts, chaplains working in various settings, family support workers working with specific communities, or educators working in faith-based schools. Undertaking a small literature search, I note that while working with diversity is an area of discussion in non-faith-based supervision literature, with contributions from writers who range in race, culture, and identity, there is little written about diversity awareness in the faith contexts within the pastoral supervision literature, except for reflecting on culture and diversity outside of the supervisee/supervisor relationship. Emmanuel Lartey,[1] a Black writer in the field, invites counsellors to consider their personal awareness when working with cultural differences, but the supervisory relationship is not explored. Looking further into the working relationship, in terms of having an awareness of the cultural context of the client with whom the supervisee is working, is said to be of importance by both Jane Leach and Michael Paterson[2] and Peter Hawkins and Aisling McMahon.[3] As this issue is highlighted by these writers, in both faith-based and non-faith-based contexts, I will be offering references from the counselling and clinical supervision arena, which I believe are transferable. I will also explore diversity from a biblical context alongside literature from the secular setting. I hope that as pastoral supervisors, we might use some scriptures as our road map when considering how we might work with supervisees who identify as different from us, in whatever way that might be presented in our supervision settings. I am also hoping that in reading this chapter, we might consider what it is that comes up for us individually when we work with difference.

I need to state and clarify my position as a person and a practitioner, as I believe that this will, and does, influence how I write this chapter. I am a Black woman and a practicing Christian from a Pentecostal tradition. I am a psychotherapist and trainer, and I offer both clinical and pastoral supervision. If you ask me what the difference is between the two, in my pastoral supervision practice I would be asking the question, "Where is God in this?" as my pastoral supervision is offered in faith-based contexts. As a Christian who is offering a supervisory space to individuals from faith contexts, I seek to provide pastoral supervision that has a space for theological reflection and which invites the supervisee to reflect on their practice from within, and from, a faith perspective, and to consider what God may be saying and how the Holy Spirit may be directing the process. As a clinical supervisor, I would hold that question for my own personal reflection, as a Christian who considers that I am serving God in all the areas in which I work.

While acknowledging that the love of Christ is central to all interactions and is present in the various contexts in which we find ourselves, what is sometimes overlooked within many supervision and pastoral supervision settings is the importance of diversity awareness and acknowledging our difference and how we might work with it in the supervisory relationship. There is a growing acknowledgement of the need to increase awareness of working with diversity within the counselling and psychotherapy arena.[4] Individuals are encouraged to consider how personal beliefs and values within the counselling/supervisory relationship might influence and impact the relationship and any future personal and professional development. I have observed that diversity training, either as a module or woven throughout counselling and supervision courses, has become a norm rather than an exception in non-faith-based training courses. The training method tends to be a mixture of taught sessions within groups, experiential learning, and personal reflections. It has been interesting to note that while secular supervision courses seek to include diversity training and include areas such as race, disability, gender, ethnicity, class, faith, and spirituality as an element of preparing for working with supervisees, it is difficult to ascertain if pastoral supervision courses include specific diversity awareness as part of their training course. Leach and Paterson[5] propose that cultural awareness, in terms of the client/supervisee/supervisor relationship, is an important factor to hold in mind. However, while there is some invitation to explore parallel processes,[6] the importance of exploring the interpersonal relationship between the supervisor and supervisee in terms of diversity elements of the relationship, is not explored in any depth. I am aware that issues around diversity are quite often taught by trainers who identify in one of the groupings that may come under the 'diversity' umbrella, and I have delivered diversity training or have been asked to add a 'voice' as a Black woman. With that in mind as I write, I am aware that I do not wish to be considered an expert in what I ask us each to consider in this chapter. I know that I might be biased to write about race in the supervisory relationship, and I may well offer some examples from my own experience, but I also hold in mind that diversity includes many elements.

This chapter does not aim to offer a diagnostic or prescribed way of working with diversity. That would negate the need for individuals to take responsibility for personal development and cultivate a sense of personal awareness around working with difference as pastoral supervisors. I will not be setting out a step-by-step approach or provide a list of current terminologies and a meaning for each item. However, I ask you to consider what each term means to you as a way of facilitating your own exploration. I will invite us to pause and do two things; first, to take some time to consider our own values and beliefs that might enter the pastoral supervision space as we work within faith-based settings; and second, to have a conversation with ourselves about our diversity awareness in current supervisory relationships. The aim of this chapter, therefore, will be to consider how we might enhance our pastoral supervision practice by considering who we are when reflecting upon our thoughts about factors such as power and privilege when we are in a relationship with someone who identifies differently from ourselves, be that in terms of race, culture, gender, age, denominational differences, or any other diversities in our pastoral supervision relationships. The practitioner focuses on reflecting upon what they may bring into the room as the supervisor, and on how the unspoken may influence the quality of connections. My hope is that, as pastoral supervisors, we might develop a curiosity that encourages inclusivity in our practice in order that we do not cause our supervisee/s to feel 'othered.'[7]

THE MEANING OF DIVERSITY

It would be easy for me to move quickly into the chapter to consider the ways of how we might enhance our practice when working with diversity without pausing and thinking about what we mean by this term. What is your definition of diversity? How would you identify yourself? The questions that I ask may not be ones that were asked during initial clergy training, or within pastoral supervision training. Diversity could be described as having an awareness and respect for the range of human differences that include, but are not defined by, race, ethnicity, age, gender, sexual orientation, disability, neurodiversity, social class, socioeconomic, spirituality, and religion. Individuals may find that they identify themselves within several of the above-mentioned groups, and interestingly some of those that I have mentioned would not be considered under the 'diversity' umbrella as the 'big 7'—gender, race, class, sexual orientations, disability, religion, and age are usually the categories that are often cited.[8] Kimberlée Crenshaw, a leader in critical race theory, established the term 'intersectionality,' which identifies the convergence of several identities under the diversity umbrella. So, for instance, I am Black—a minority group; I am a woman—a minority group within some settings. I need to wear glasses. So, in some settings, I might be considered as having a disability—another minority group. Therefore, I straddle several intersections in terms of my identity. In pastoral supervision, we might take some time to consider some individuals in scripture who straddled several intersections. I am mindful that my passion for raising awareness of race, ethnicity, and gender socialisation in pastoral supervision may guide my writing. However, I propose that whatever I offer in terms of reflections can be applied across all intersections, and I am aware that you will be reading this chapter from within your own intersection and position.

DO I NEED TO KNOW ABOUT WORKING WITH DIVERSITY?

> A psychotherapeutic process that does not take into account the person's whole life experience, or that denies consideration of their race, culture, gender or social values can only fragment the person.[9]

Is it necessary to consider how we work with diversity? Within most counselling and clinical supervision settings, diversity awareness is considered to be of the utmost importance. It is now incorporated in most training courses, in the majority of places, to prepare practitioners to work with the clients/supervisees with whom they come into contact. From a scriptural context, we may consider pastoral supervision to be a practice that is not new (in that Jesus could be viewed as the first pastoral supervisor). Pastoral supervision, as a practice that is offered to support clergy, chaplains, and those supporting others within a church and faith context, is still relatively new, and many training courses in pastoral supervision are no older than a few decades old. Some, but not all courses, may, for the most part, use an adaptation of a particular model, e.g., the seven-eyed model,[10, 11, 12] and some may not include any diversity element as part of the model. Therefore, it is not a part of the training course.

The 'face' of our churches has changed over the past two decades. Denominations such as Anglican, Methodist, Baptist, and United Reformed churches are now reflecting the communities within which we live, both in the pulpit and the pews. Churches that in the past were composed of predominantly White congregants are now seeing people of colour entering through their doors and, in many cases, staying to become a part of the church community. Churches that were historically made up of predominantly Black congregants from one geographical location are changing, in that there is no longer a homogenous group, but now includes individuals of all races from various countries. Women are now in positions of leadership, and individuals who would not have been asked to undertake pastoral care roles now find themselves supporting others. There is a changing landscape within Church settings regarding people seeking support from pastoral teams, and the diversity in Church leadership teams is observable. There has also been the recognition that clergy, and those offering pastoral support, require and value the support and space to reflect upon the work they undertake, including any issues that have arisen and the impact on them.[13] This has led to a growing need for pastoral supervision from individuals from a range of backgrounds.

Considering recent tensions around race, ethnicity, and gender, intersections and diversity have become regularly used words in our communities. Worldwide events have prompted some difficult conversations within various Church denominations, predominantly around how we respond to and interact with people who are a different colour to ourselves. In 2020, the killing of Black people by White police officers in the United States prompted conversations within Church settings in the UK that culminated in some changes in leadership teams.

Thinking about the question, 'Do I need to know about working with diversity?,' some individuals within the church and pastoral supervision setting may argue that working in faith settings involves everyone being treated equally, and the love of Christ is extended to all. Therefore, there is no need for diversity awareness. However, historically, racism, prejudices, unconscious biases, and discriminatory practices have been present within our Church settings and denying, or not acknowledging, this negates the experiences of individuals who have been on the receiving end of such behaviour. Maintaining a stance of 'we treat everyone the same' may indirectly be saying 'I do not want to invest time or energy in becoming aware of the richness and value of the other,' and it might also send a more profound message regarding a lack of self-awareness. A shared faith does not mean a shared identity, experience, or lack of difference. Lago and Thompson[14] propose that all counselling is cross-cultural, as all the individuals come into the context from differing backgrounds. I offer that all pastoral supervision is cross-cultural, and we each enter the relationship from different backgrounds. There is a risk that in wanting to 'get things right' or 'not wanting to get things wrong,' we neglect the importance of being curious and developing greater awareness. In some cases, we undertake training as a 'check a box' exercise without genuinely opening ourselves to wanting to 'know' the person in the room.

THE SAME AND DIFFERENT

> We are not all the same. We are not all treated the same by everyone we meet. If we are honest with ourselves, we also treat and respond to people differently.[15]

If we are to consider how we work with diversity, we need to ask ourselves the question, 'What do I see?' In my role as a trainer, I have heard students and participants say, 'I do not see colour' or 'I don't see disability or gender.' As a Black woman, I struggle with this statement in terms of my colour; and as a Christian, I struggle with the notion of not being seen. 'I do not see . . .' goes against Genesis 1:31 "*God saw* all that he had made, and it was very good." God saw the amazingly diverse world, including what would be a world filled with people, and He saw it was good. I would add that not seeing someone in terms of their colour is considered as racial colour-blindness[16].

Throughout the Bible, we are made aware of the beauty of diversity. God is descriptive. People are described by gender, colour, age, disability, and socio-location. Jesus offered us descriptions of His disciples. In places where few details are offered about a person, the writer may offer us a name or the gender, location, and status of the character they are speaking of. The richness of the description (even in some cases giving some detail regarding the person's personality), provides us with an image of the person and the quality of the relationship. We see this as an example in the friendship between David and Jonathan.

Why might it be important to hold this in mind as pastoral supervisors? I believe that God wanted us to know that we are made unique and different, and in some ways the same. For those of us who choose not to see, we may miss the person in front of us and diminish the richness of what it is that they bring into the room. Reflecting on the statement, "I do not see . . . ," I wonder if, for those of us who hold to this argument, we ourselves choose not to be seen, or perhaps we do not see ourselves and what it is that we bring into the supervisory relationship. In my experience, upon enquiring what the individual might mean, there is often more to the statement, and it is usually linked with not wanting to define someone by race, gender, or disability only, and ultimately not wanting to cause any discomfort for themselves or others. There is often the wish to meet the whole person apart from the difference presented in the room. Some writers encourage the supervisee to identify and verbalise the differences present in the supervisory relationship from the start, to work through any power differentials that might impede the relationship.[17, 18] Some may argue against this suggestion, believing that there is no necessity to talk about what is visible/not visible.

As I bring myself into the relationship, I am led to consider a question taken from the solution-focused theory, 'What would you like me to know about you'? From a faith context, might there be something that we can learn from the secular supervision setting, or might we use the bible as our road map? As a practitioner, it is something that I note, and for most of the time, verbalise with my supervisees specifically, but not only around colour and what that might mean for us. I found that this was particularly important in 2020, when issues regarding race, power, and privilege were frequently in the news, and churches were reflecting upon how this impacted the treatment and integration of congregants from ethnic backgrounds, and church leaders and members of their leadership teams were seeking pastoral supervision as a place to examine, reflect, and consider their past and current practices.

THE CALL: BIBLICAL EXAMPLE OF DIVERSITY AWARENESS

> Many of us have not seen or understood that diversity is pervasive throughout the Scriptures and that there is a theology of diversity which begins in Genesis and finishes in Revelation.[19]

Considering diversity with a wide-angled lens, interactions between different sets of people are observable in the scriptures: Esther and King Ahasuerus (religious and cultural dissimilarities), David and Jonathan (social class), Ruth and Naomi (age and cultural differences), and the wounded traveller and good Samaritan (socio-location and maybe socioeconomic). As we consider each of these connections, we see differences between the two people. However, they had discovered a way in which to connect that did not dismiss the uniqueness of the other and was not influenced by unconscious biases, power, or privilege. The scriptures state the differences and share the relational aspects of navigating friendships and connections. Reflecting on diversity and pastoral supervision from a biblical perspective, we have an excellent example of Jesus calling the disciples to serve others; they could be considered pastoral carers. The group was from different professions, including fishermen (same but different), a doctor, a tax collector, and a zealot (today Judas may be considered a politician). I imagine that while different, they were similar in that they were followers of Jesus. They were also different in character, personality, and identity. The disciples may have been located in the same region but, reflecting upon their professions, they would probably not have been neighbours. Therefore, each would bring different dialects and customs to the setting. Let us consider Jesus as the pastoral supervisor and the disciples as his supervisees. Jesus (the pastoral supervisor) knew who he was and did not hide that in any way from his disciples (the supervisees) (*presence*). He ensured that they knew who He was (*transparency*) and would ask questions about who they were (*curiosity*), showing an interest. While Jesus spoke with the disciples collectively, He recognised their individuality. Jesus *saw* each person who would then become a disciple.

Working with diversity begins from the initial inquiry that we receive from someone wishing to find out about the services that we might offer. As we consider the 'call' that we might receive from an inquirer who is seeking our services as a pastoral supervisor, can we give some thought to our first interaction? What are we drawn to in the inquiry, or what do we notice? How do we become connected? Do I notice anything that I am avoiding? From the outset, can we be present, transparent, and curious in relation to ourselves and the other? Do I notice an accent, and what is my initial response to hearing the person's name enquiring about accessing pastoral supervision?

PRESENCE AND TRANSPARENCY

Up to this point, I have invited us to consider our understanding of diversity, and I have asked for some exploration of our thoughts about the relevance of diversity to pastoral supervision. I have introduced the idea of diversity within a biblical context and Jesus as our example of the pastoral supervisor. I have alluded to the idea of knowing ourselves as the foundation of working with diversity; by knowing ourselves, I refer to our beliefs, value systems, and worldview that influence our day-to-day interactions. The beginning of many counselling training courses invites the trainee to explore who they are within different contexts. When I have facilitated diversity training courses, this question has raised many issues for participants and has led to some rich discussions. Leach and Paterson discuss various processes that help to develop a good pastoral supervision relationship. Reflecting on the Emmaus Road story (Luke 24: 13–27) of Jesus being present with the disciples, they explore the supervision setting and various elements that the supervisor may attend to in preparing for their work with the supervisee. Leach and Paterson also invite the supervisor to set the scene and ready themselves to be present for their supervisee, who they suggest should be at the centre of the pastoral supervision session.[20] To be both present and transparent, I propose that it is beneficial for us to step back and consider some key areas that may be pertinent to setting the scene, and being present and transparent in the room. I believe that these considerations will be ongoing throughout our practice.

The first part of the process could be exploring who we are. I invite us to consider our family contexts, ideas, and values that were communicated by primary caregivers, and messages that were given by extended family members and the community within which we live towards others who were different to our own families and communities in which we were brought up or currently live. As an example, my parents were immigrants from Jamaica, and through their own experiences of being treated less than others, the spoken and unspoken message they shared with us as children were that we should not trust White people—particularly those in authority— because they would smile at us and possibly stab you in the back at the same time. As I grew up, I held this message in mind, and it impacted on my relationships with White people in authority, until I came to realise that the belief was not actually true for most White people in authority.

I invite us to give some thought that who we are may also be influenced by the faith context and positions that we hold within those settings, and the messages communicated to us from our peers and significant mentors/managers. We may consider the denominations within which we reside to be superior to other Church denominations, and this in turn could lead to us seeing ourselves as more superior to individuals from other Church denominations or vice versa. What might this mean for the supervisory relationship?

Messages within society may influence our value system. Asking ourselves the question 'Who am I?' is essential in increasing our awareness of our internal systems, beliefs, and prejudices that influence our capacity to be transparent with others. It also impacts how I view and interact with others outside and inside the supervisory space. This raised awareness can assist us in acknowledging difference which then communicates that we have seen the 'other' in relation to ourselves. This process may be difficult for some, as thinking about values and beliefs that we may have ingested from significant others, may bring up feelings of shame. This area has been discussed in terms of the shame a White counsellor/supervisor might bring into the supervisory space when working with a client/supervisee who is a different colour to themselves. It might be worth approaching the question with the following sub-questions such as, 'Who am I within my Church, and what informs this?' 'What beliefs and values are held within this faith context, and how might this influence how I work with differences?' 'Are there any messages that I am not aware of that might be impacting how I meet and interact with others in my role as a pastoral supervisor?' 'Can I work towards greater transparency within my relationships where the person is different to me?'

Earlier in this chapter, I mentioned that various pastoral training courses may adopt different models when delivering training programmes. This has been my experience in supervision training courses that do not include a theological element to them. Continuing to reflect on presence and transparency, I would like to take some time to consider some of the modes used in Hawkins and Shohet's seven-eyed model of supervision, which is a model that is adapted and used on some pastoral supervision training courses. I believe that there are two modes in this model that encourage presence, curiosity, and transparency to facilitate a good working relationship when working with diversity. Mode 1 of Hawkins and Shohet's seven-eyed model[21] seeks to explore the relationship between the client and the supervisee and ties in with Mode 5—The supervisor/supervisee relationship. Mode 8 which is used in pastoral supervision training brings a theological component to the model, and perhaps at the commencement of the supervisory relationship, the theological question from Mode 8 could be asked in terms of 'where is Jesus in this relationship?'

Ryde,[22] reflecting on cultural sensitivity in supervision, suggests that each mode might be reconsidered when working with diversity in the supervisory relationship, but considers this from the supervisee's position to the client. Leach and Paterson encourage the supervisor to prepare themselves, but only as far as to get the work in the room. Mode 1 usually encompasses getting the story (client) into the room through various considerations and questions that we will explore.

Preparing the scene for our supervisee and preparing to be present as the supervisor, I propose that we use Mode 1 as our starting point as we consider what we notice about ourselves as we come into the room with our supervisees in terms of identifying differences. The following questions are examples of questions used to focus on the client's experience. Instead of asking these questions about the supervisee/client relationship, I wonder if we might transpose them to the supervisee/supervisor relationship? The questions in italics are alternative questions that we might ask ourselves from the outset as we work with diversity.

1. How do they [client] come into the room? *How do I come into the room to meet my supervisee who may be of a different race/ age/faith context or socio-location to me? How do I bring myself, and what am I bringing into the room?*
2. How do they [client] sit? *How am I positioning myself physically, emotionally, and spiritually in this space in which cultural difference is apparent?*
3. How do they hold [client] themselves? *What am I holding in my body, and how might I visibly present myself?*
4. How do they [client] talk? *How am I speaking? How might I sound in this space where language differences are present?*
5. What might be their [client] perception of you? *What might my supervisee's perception be of me? What might they be thinking about our relationship and me as their supervisor?*

REMAINING CURIOUS—SELF AND OTHERS

The above questions invite us to remain present and transparent for our supervisees by developing a sense of presence in ourselves. Curiosity in pastoral supervision permits us the opportunity to invite our supervisees to share who they are and develop the relationship further, thus creating a base for the exploration of elements that may present themselves within the supervision work. I know that I have valued my supervisor's curiosity, which has permitted me to bring my whole self into the supervision space without leaving out parts that I might perceive might not be accepted.

There are several questions from the above that link into the APSE definition and ethos of pastoral supervision and its code of conduct. One of the eight elements of the definition and ethos are 1. Pastoral supervision seeks to encourage pastoral supervisors to be contextually sensitive: "*pays attention to the particularities of setting, culture and world-view*" (APSE).[23] A section included in the Code of Conduct is: 'Act with due respect for integrity and difference, including sexual orientation, ethnicity, religion, disability or gender' (APSE). I do not know what emerged for you as you read the questions above, but as a Black woman there are several things that stand out for me: How do I bring myself into the room? Can I bring my whole self into the space as a Black woman, holding in mind that some may have certain perceptions of Black women? I wonder how I might use my own language and who has the power in the room.

HEARING THINGS—USE OF LANGUAGE AND POWER

> Language, often the very tool through which we conduct our therapeutic processes, is a complex and ever-changing 'mindset.'[24]

Language and speech, as a form of communication, is and can be very beautiful. The way that we hear and understand words and their meaning, can be, and is, most often influenced by our upbringing and cultural context. The way in which we view people who speak differently to us is also often influenced by the dominant group within which we live. Judgements can be made of someone who speaks differently from us. As supervisors, do we hear the other person in the room and how they relay their story? In terms of working with diversity, it is important to hold in mind that words have different meanings for different people. We may have a shared language, but, from the context of being a Black woman, the meanings that I give to words are different from what they mean to my White supervisor. Pastoral supervisors hold a certain amount of power that they may, or may not, be aware of. Power differentials can become pronounced when we are working with cultural differences or gender differences, and may be more obvious in our speech, accents, and our use of language.

CASE STUDY:

Benni has arranged to meet their supervisee for the first time and reflected on the telephone conversation that had taken place. The prospective supervisee is from a very different denomination from Bennie. They have not met their supervisee but were aware that although the caller spoke English, they spoke with a deep accent indicating someone for whom English may be a second language. Bennie could not quite place the accent. *What are your thoughts?*

The supervisee attends the appointment at the time arranged and arrives wearing leathers (they are a passenger of someone who rides a motorbike). The supervisee is White and looks like they are in their fifties. *What are your thoughts?*

The session commenced, and Benni noticed that the supervisee looked at them intently as they spoke, and the supervisee's responses were somewhat difficult to understand clearly. *What are your thoughts?*

It was only when the session had ended, and the supervisee stood up to leave, that Benni noticed that the supervisee was wearing hearing aids. *What are your thoughts?*

CONCLUSION

Working with diversity commences before we get into the room with our supervisee. The 7 + 1-eyed model invites us to bring the work into the room by setting the scene. Before asking 'what it is that my supervisee might bring into the room?,' in terms of setting the scene we need to ask ourselves 'what am I bringing into the room?' 'Do I want to see my supervisee?' 'Is there anything that might stop me from seeing them in terms of judgements, prejudices, and a sense of power?' It is useful to ask the following questions:

- How do I feel about my supervisee?
- How might I advertise myself as a pastoral supervisor?
- What do I notice when someone comes into the room who looks and sounds very different from me?

- What about my responses to my supervisee who is of a different culture to me?
- What is my supervisor's first impression when they see me, and how will this influence the relationship?

If the secular setting is encouraging training and personal development in the area of diversity awareness, why would the faith settings not also be encouraging these for their leaders? Our very faith highlights diversity and intersections. Ought we not to be the leaders in encouraging open dialogues? There has been a seismic shift and change within our Church settings. While, as a pastoral supervisor, you may not subscribe to any particular governing body that might terminate your membership or take you to task or down a disciplinary route, I believe that as individuals we are called to serve others and 'love our neighbours as ourselves.' We have a moral obligation to work in the best way possible with every person that we meet.

I am aware in this chapter that I might have focused upon issues such as unconscious bias, fragility, overt and covert racism, othering, and many other words that could be used to describe the current doing to [others] and receiving from [others], but I may then have missed an opportunity to start at the very beginning of our journey in working with diversity. It would have offered an easy explanation of terms for me looking in, but not for you looking out.

I close this chapter asking you the reader to take some time to consider what diversity means for you, and how you work with it within faith-based pastoral supervision. A refrain of a song that comes to mind, 'and the creed and the colour and the name won't matter, I'll be there.' Perhaps as pastoral supervisors within faith-based settings, we might seek to extend these words within our pastoral practice as we recognise and value the richness and uniqueness of others with whom we sit alongside in our positions as pastoral supervisors. The group of individuals seeking pastoral supervision is growing ever more diverse, and you may have found yourself working with individuals you may not have worked with before. I know that I certainly have, and I have needed to attend to my own preconceptions to be present for my supervisee.

BIBLIOGRAPHY

Alleyne, Aileene. "Overcoming racism, discrimination and oppression in psychotherapy": Pp. 117–29 in *The Handbook of Transcultural Counselling & Psychotherapy*, ed. Colin Lago. Maidenhead: Open University Press, 2011.

Association of Pastoral Supervision and Education, "*Definition and Ethos*." https://www.pastoralsupervision.org.uk/home/about/definition-and-ethos. (accessed 1 August 2022).

Eddo-Lodge, Reni. *Why I'm No Longer Talking to White People About Race*. London: Bloomsbury Publishing, 2018.

Gubi, Peter Madsen, and Tuntufye A. Mwenisongole. "A pilot evaluation study of pastoral supervision provision in the Moravian Church (British Province)." *Journal of Mental Health, Religion and Culture* 25, no. 2 (2022): 197–206. DOI: 10.1080/13674676.2022.2045924.

Hawkins, Peter, and Aisling McMahon. *Supervision in the Helping Professions*. London: Open University Press, 2020.

Hawkins, Peter, and Robin Shohet. *Supervision in the Helping Professions*. London: Open University Press, 2012.

Hylton, Owen. *Crossing the Divide. A Call to Embrace Diversity*. Nottingham: Inter-Varsity Press, 2009.

Lago, Colin, and Barbara Smith. "Anti-Discriminatory Practice revisited": Pp. 13–22 in *Anti-discriminatory Practice in Counselling and Psychotherapy*, eds. Colin Lago and Barbara Smith. London: Sage Publications, 2010.

———. "Ethical Practice and Best Practice": Pp. 1–12 in *Anti-Discriminatory Practice in Counselling & Psychotherapy*, eds. Colin Lago and Barbara Smith. London: Sage Publications, 2010.

Lago, Colin, and Joyce Thompson. *Race, Culture and Counselling*. Maidenhead: Open University Press, 1996.

Lartey, Emmanuel Y. *In Living Colour: An Intercultural Approach to Pastoral Care and Counselling*. London: Jessica Kingsley Publishers, 2003.

Leach, Jane, and Michael Paterson. *Pastoral Supervision: A Handbook*. London: SCM Press, 2015.

McKenzie-Mavinga, Isha. *The Challenge of Racism in Therapeutic Practice: Engaging with Oppression in Practice and Supervision*. London: Palgrave, 2016.

Moodley, Roy, and Lee Murphy. "Multiple Identities and Anti-Discriminatory Counselling Practice": Pp. 137–48 in *Anti-Discriminatory Practice in Counselling & Psychotherapy*, eds. Colin Lago and Barbara Smith. London: Sage Publications, 2010.

Ryde, Judy. "Culturally Sensitive Supervision": Pp. 142–51 in *The Handbook of Transcultural Counselling & Supervision*, ed. Colin Lago. Maidenhead: Open University Press, 2011.

Seneviratne, Seni. "Race, Culture and Supervision": Pp. 99–114 in *Freedom to Practise: Person-Centred Approaches to Supervision*, eds. Keith Tudor and Mike Worrall. Ross on Wye: PCCS Books, 2004.

Watson, Marlene F. "Supervision in Black and White: Navigating Cross-Racial Interactions": Pp. 43–49 in *Culturally Sensitive Supervision and Training: Diverse Perspectives and Practical Applications*, eds. Kenneth V. Hardy and Toby Bobes. London: Routledge, 2016.

NOTES

1. Emmanuel Y. Lartey, *In Living Colour: An Intercultural Approach to Pastoral Care and Counselling* (London: Jessica Kingsley Publishers, 2003).

2. Jane Leach and Michael Paterson, *Pastoral Supervision: A Handbook* (London: SCM Press, 2015), 23.

3. Peter Hawkins and Aisling McMahon, *Supervision in the Helping Professions* (London: Open University Press, 2020).

4. Colin Lago and Barbara Smith. "Anti-Discriminatory Practice revisited," in *Anti-discriminatory Practice in Counselling and Psychotherapy,* eds. Colin Lago and Barbara Smith (London: Sage Publications, 2010), 13.

5. Leach and Paterson, "Pastoral Supervision," 23.

6. By 'parallel processes,' I mean what similar internal experience might be happening for me and my supervisee, at the same time, during our time together.

7. 'Othering' means to treat a person differently from yourself, usually as less than. For example, Black people are considered as 'other' and treated as suspects. See Reni Eddo-Lodge, *Why I'm No Longer Talking to White People About Race.* (London: Bloomsbury Publishing, 2018).

8. Roy Moodley and Lee Murphy, "Multiple Identities and Anti-Discriminatory Counselling Practice," in *Anti-Discriminatory Practice in Counselling & Psychotherapy,* eds. Colin Lago and Barbara Smith (London: Sage Publications, 2010), 137.

9. Seneviratne, "Race, Culture and Supervision," 105.

10. Hawkins and McMahon, "Supervision in the Helping Professions," 85.

11. Leach and Paterson, "Pastoral Supervision," 86.

12. Judy Ryde, "Culturally Sensitive Supervision," in *The Handbook of Transcultural Counselling & Supervision,* ed. Colin Lago. Maidenhead (Open University Press, 2011), 142–51.

13. Peter M. Gubi and Tuntufye A. Mwenisongole, "A pilot evaluation study of pastoral supervision provision in the Moravian Church (British Province)." *Journal of Mental Health, Religion and Culture* 25, no. 2 (2022): 197–206. DOI: 10.1080/13674676.2022.2045924.

14. Colin Lago and Joyce Thompson, *Race, Culture and Counselling* (Maidenhead: Open University Press, 1996).

15. Owen Hylton, *Crossing the Divide: A Call to Embrace Diversity* (Nottingham: Inter-Varsity Press, 2009), 51.

16. Aileene Alleyne writes, "Failing to notice the client's race and falling prey to the colour-blind syndrome ignores human diversity and uniqueness. The notion that I don't see colour, everyone is a human being in my eyes, is a clear example of race avoidance." See Aileene Alleyne, "Overcoming racism, discrimination and oppression in psychotherapy," in *The Handbook of Transcultural Counselling & Psychotherapy,* ed. Colin Lago. (Maidenhead: Open University Press, 2011), 119.

17. Isha McKenzie-Mavinga, *The Challenge of Racism in Therapeutic Practice: Engaging with Oppression in Practice and Supervision* (London: Palgrave, 2016).

18. Marlene F. Watson, "Supervision in Black and White: Navigating Cross-Racial Interactions," in *Culturally Sensitive Supervision and Training. Diverse Perspectives*

and Practical Applications, eds. Kenneth V, Hardy and Toby Bobes (London: Routledge, 2016), 43.

19. Hylton, "Crossing the Divide," 19.

20. Leach and Paterson, "Pastoral Supervision," 51.

21. Peter Hawkins and Robin Shohet, *Supervision in the Helping Professions* (London: Open University Press, 2012).

22. Ryde, "Culturally Sensitive Supervision," 142–51.

23. Association of Pastoral Supervision and Education, "*Definition and Ethos*." https://www.pastoralsupervision.org.uk/home/about/definition-and-ethos. (accessed 1 August 2022).

24. Colin Lago and Barbara Smith, "Ethical Practice and Best Practice," in *Anti-Discriminatory Practice in Counselling & Psychotherapy,* ed. Colin Lago and Barbara Smith (London: Sage Publications, 2010), 1–12.

Chapter Six

Working with Stuckness in Pastoral Supervision

Sally Bubbers

'Stuckness'? I wonder what this word brings to mind for you? For me, I picture someone in quicksand. It also brings up memories of getting stuck in thick mud that sucked my Wellington boots in, so that it was hard and a bit scary to try and move anywhere. However, my trauma therapist head starts to think about stuckness in a different way: how people are sometimes not able to move physically, mentally, or emotionally because of internal drivers and historic patterns that disable them through PTSD, stress, and flashbacks. Sometimes, this is compounded by external pressure from close relationships or organisational and cultural inhibitors. Strangely, these can be 'known' to us and 'unknown' at the same time. Physical or psychological stuckness is a difficult place to be, particularly if there is no one else around, and you feel alone. It can be scary, worrying, and isolating. People can try and keep busy finding things to distract or pull them away, and it is helpful to be aware that this can also enter the pastoral supervision space.

In this chapter, we (you and I), as pastoral supervisors, will think about how we experience stuckness within the pastoral supervision relationship. We will think about how we might determine who is stuck—the supervisor, the supervisee, or maybe both—and explore what might be impacting the supervisor/supervisee relationship. I hope to offer some new tools by introducing ideas from Internal Family Systems (IFS), drawing on the work of Richard Schwartz as a helpful lens to widen our gaze and find some new ways to open up some space through collaboration and transparency. IFS is a constraint-releasing model, offering a way to identify internal constraints that prevent us from addressing external pressure and stress in an appropriate, nonviolent manner. IFS argues that we all have an internal family that consists of many parts (see below), and I hope that you can start detecting parts in yourself and your supervisees, with compassion and curiosity.[1] Integrating the ideas from IFS into your supervision practice also increases the possibilities for relational collaboration between the supervisor and supervisee.[2]

Stuckness can bring up strong emotions of blame, isolation, helplessness, hopelessness, failure, frustration, irritation, and shame, but the question is, 'who or what is stuck?' Is the stuckness co-created within the pastoral supervision relationship? Has one of us, who is engaged in the process, brought it into the room? Has it spread and affected the other? Are they both being influenced by an external situation? In counselling language, this is talked about as 'transference' and 'countertransference.' Transference is when the supervisee projects feelings and attitudes onto the supervisor from a past relationship or from someone in the present; countertransference is when the supervisor has a strong emotional reaction to the supervisee.

WHAT MIGHT BE THE SUPERVISOR'S ROLE IN THE STUCKNESS?

Have you ever heard yourself saying, 'my supervisee is stuck'? When you feel that a supervisee is stuck, are you able to be curious about where that sense of being trapped, boxed in, or unable to change anything is coming from? If they are stuck in a seemingly intractable situation, and the topic has stretched over a number of sessions, our stuckness can easily turn to frustration. Maybe you feel that they have 'overreacted' to something that has happened. Do you feel confused and judgmental towards them? Do you feel the supervisee has made the situation worse by their actions? Later in this chapter, we will look at some of the dynamics involved in this.

Understanding the parameters and concept of pastoral supervision from the start supports the building of a relational container within the supervision space and can avoid misconceptions and misunderstandings arising. We all carry memories of good and bad previous experiences, some as clear narrative memories and some as implicit memories[3] (held in our bodies) that are below our level of awareness. These determine how we understand and interpret what someone is saying to us, particularly when there is a power imbalance or the supervisee or supervisor do not feel at ease with each other.

In my work with clergy, frequently the 'problem' is related to relational dynamics or the organisational structure of the Church, where someone has lost hope, but we have to bravely find a way to help them dive in and unpack what is going on, in order to explore if there may be a step forward, or to acknowledge that that is not possible.

There are various models that invite us to explore ourselves in connection to the relational world around us: one such is The Johari Window (see Figure 6.1), which is a model of interpersonal awareness that helps us to think about areas we may be blind to or unaware of.[4]

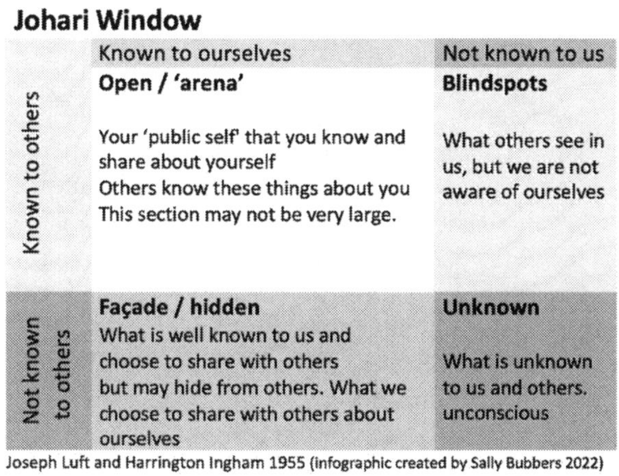

Figure 6.1

As pastoral supervisors, we are not all trained therapists but, from our professional and lived experience, we may notice blind spots in our supervisees that we struggle to find a way to name in a compassionate way, without our reflections sounding judgmental and triggering the supervisees' defences. We will look shortly at how the language of parts may help with this.

Hawkins and Shohet propose in their seven-eyed model of supervision that there are various lenses through which we can view supervision. It is important to hold in mind the process and interactions of the supervisor and supervisee individually and of the relationship between them and around them in their external worlds which include spirituality and belief.[5] I also find it helpful to use the ideas from Internal Family Systems (IFS)[6] to understand what might be going on in myself, the supervisee and the world around us both. Our unique life experiences and beliefs influence our internal world. The systems that surround each of us in the external world will have impacted our development and influence our way of being and functioning in the present. These range from the microculture of our family or close relationships to the macro-culture of our local community, country, and the world, and they will also come into the supervision space. Emma Redfern expands the Hawkins and Shohet model to eight facets through the lens of IFS, adding in 'Self' as the 'game changer,' and offering the containment of the Larger Self,[7] whom I would name as God. I will explain some of the thinking within the IFS model and then look at its relevance and application in pastoral supervision.

WE ALL HAVE PARTS

Richard Schwartz was a family systems therapist who realised that just as each member of a family is a part of a dynamic system that influences how it relates and functions within itself and with the external world, so too we all have parts 'within' us, creating an internal system of parts. He started to integrate systems thinking with a non-pathologising, multiple-part view of the mind, with a belief that we are all created with a core of good, which he calls 'the Self' or 'Self-energy.'[8] How often have you said or heard someone say, 'I went to the meeting intending to be calm and then I just lost it'; or 'A part of me knows that I should not do . . . but I did it'; and 'I cannot make my mind up; one minute I think. . . . and the next minute I think the opposite.' The language of parts used within IFS is not critical to our understanding here: we can call our parts 'parts,' or by the name of their role, or emotion, or body sensation—for example 'our critic,' or 'our fears'—but for ease of reference, I will use the language of parts in this chapter. This model was devised as a therapeutic tool, but it is now also being used to support our understanding of human nature and behavioural dynamics, and it is being integrated into coaching, supervision, education, prisons, mediation, peacekeeping, and more global forms of systems thinking, looking at how groups of people, organisations and even countries relate to each other.

PRINCIPLES

The principles underpinning Schwartz's thinking are:

- we all have an indeterminate number of sub-personalities;
- we all have a core 'Self' that is inherently good and is able to lead the internal system;
- there are 'no bad parts': they all have good intentions for us, each having taken on roles and burdens to help our survival.

I see Self as the essence of us made in the image of God. Self can inhabit solid matter (particle form) and can be experienced in the form of energy (wave). This understanding fits with my belief that God is in all He created. We can understand Self to be our 'God Essence'[9] or our True Self.[10]

Our internal system of parts is often called the Ego, or False Self. Schwartz reframes this into two groups: parts that we exile within our system, and parts that protect us (managers and firefighters) (see Figure 6.2).

Firefighters: Generally, hide out of sight, below conscious awareness until they react to threat or distress. Provide the ultimate defence to protect or distract to stop exile pain. They may use anger, addictions, suicide, or shut down

Managers: They are the first line of protection and proactively run our lives to prevent the exiles from being seen or upset. They can appear to be chaotic or rigid in their approach to life and will use strategies like perfectionism, overwork, caring, illness, exercise, and routine to help us. The world often sees them as us.

Exiles: They are often buried deep in the subconscious holding burdens of pain, and memories, emotions, or behaviours which were either disapproved of by adults, or things we do not want to be seen in the world

Self: Innate qualities at the core of everyone: compassion, curiosity, clarity, creativity, calm, confidence, courage, and connectedness; patience, perspective, persistence, perseverance, and playfulness.

Figure 6.2

As we grow and develop, our parts, in order to help us survive, start to take on roles and burdens so that we can remain in connection with our caregivers and others around us. Parts can become *exiled* within the system because they are vulnerable. They may take on burdens that consist of painful experiences and feelings that the child wishes to forget, or of beliefs and behaviours that are not acceptable to the caregiver. These parts drop into the unconscious and are protected by the *Manager* parts that help maintain 'normal life.' Their role is to proactively run the life of the child and subsequent adult in such a way that the exiles do not become distressed and destabilise the internal system or become seen in the world. Exiles and managers do care about relational breaches. For example, how often have you, as an adult, felt bad as you have heard your mother's voice in your head saying, for example 'take your elbows off the table'? If the proactive managers fail to keep the exiles safe and under control, then the '*Firefighters*' will leap into action. These parts are the ultimate defence of the system. They have no consideration for the physical or relational damage which their actions may cause. They are highly reactive, and their main role is to distract from the pain within the exile, or to draw attention away from a vulnerable part.[11] For example, you may feel bad when you are late for a meeting with your partner and when they tell you they have been waiting over an hour. Instead of saying you are sorry that you lost track of time, your Firefighter responds defensively with, 'I can't remember the last time you were on time.' Or, if you start to feel undermined by a strong-willed person, you may start to become more dogmatic and defensive.

SELF

Self is the innate, core good in each of us. Its qualities are embedded in us. In addition, each part has its own well of Self energy at its core, but this can get quashed by the roles and the burdens that parts take on to help us survive. Schwartz enumerates a number of qualities of Self, which he calls the 8 C's and 5 P's: compassion, curiosity, clarity, creativity, calm, confidence, courage, and connectedness; and patience, perspective, persistence, perseverance, and playfulness. [12]

Our parts are often not aware of Self as we transition into adult life, so parts that have taken on burdens and roles to help us survive in childhood are often left feeling alone with no protection as they try to navigate the adult world. The hope is to become more Self-led, which some may understand as being in our True Self. Self can offer protection, bring harmony, support healing, and facilitate internal attachment repair. When someone is Self-led, they are able to be present with their parts, understanding them and facilitating communication between their parts, with the knowledge that they all have good intentions for us, even if sometimes other parts do not understand or think they are helpful.

THE GOALS OF IFS

The goals of IFS are:

1. To liberate parts from the roles or burdens they have taken on to help us survive, so that they can be free to be who they were designed to be.
2. To help parts regain trust in the 'Self' of the system. Schwartz calls this 'self-leadership,' whereby the Self acts as a healer and attachment figure (or inner parent), offering healing, care, and compassion to all parts. Self is also the executive leader, moderator, and mouthpiece for

the system, so that we do not have to speak '*from*' our wounded or protective parts, but Self can speak '*for*' them.
3. To allow for more harmony in the system.
4. To become more Self-led as we interact with the world. [13]

Some important understandings are that:

1. Any postures, body sensations, thoughts, feelings, emotions, or images can be a part trying to communicate with us nonverbally. [14]
2. Parts are not their burdens, but they are weighed down or constrained by their burdens, or roles and behaviours, that can become extreme if ignored.
3. Burdens squash Self-energy.
4. Noticing and listening to parts, and offering love and respect, helps them differentiate from each other and relax inside. This opens up space for greater awareness and helps develop a relationship with Self, i.e., unblending, allowing more space for Self-energy in the system. [15]

We are all partially blended with parts all the time, but sometimes parts take over and sit in the driver's seat. Unblending is the practice of separating from the part, thus making space for you and Self energy to be there as well. We do this by noticing and getting to know parts with compassionate curiosity, and by building connection and trust in Self, which results in parts organically starting to relax. A trained IFS therapist is able to support the unburdening of parts but, as supervisors, we can help supervisees notice parts and allow the system to re-calibrate itself.

Pastoral supervisees can find contemplative practices hard to settle into because of so many thoughts that intrude. I would suggest that this compassionate approach can support our contemplative and mindful practices, as it takes less effort to turn toward, and acknowledge, parts and their roles from our Self energy (i.e., the God essence within us), and this allows us to feel more connected to God and those around us. Attempting to ignore and push away thoughts that may be coming from parts that already feel ignored and isolated takes a lot of internal energy. Different parts can also become polarised, by which I mean they can often be trying to support the same aim within us but have opposite approaches. By noticing from our Self-energy, we can bring understanding and hopefully a negotiated understanding between the parts.

Sometimes our internal system can seem like a cross between a group of scared children and a battalion of small army units, each of which has taken on a mission, but may not be aware of what the other units have been tasked to do. Burdened parts often do not trust Self, or have a relationship with it, or even know Self exists. Burdened parts can be stuck in time, stoically soldiering on in the way that was needed when they first took on their jobs. Through the lens of IFS, we do not see any of the supervisee's protectors as a problem or a block. We acknowledge the protectors' dedication to duty and the difficult job they have taken on. It can be helpful to acknowledge that it is a part of the supervisee that feels protective, and to be curious about how it is trying to help the supervisee. To be able to integrate the understandings of IFS into your supervision practice, it is helpful for you, as the supervisor, to have a sense of your own parts, and then you will be able to be present to the supervisee and notice their parts from a place of curiosity. What follows is an exercise to help you to start to notice your parts.

An exercise in noticing our parts:

1. Sit quietly and bring 'to mind' a supervisee or person that you experience difficulties with. This is called the trailhead (the path to getting to know a part):
   - Please do not choose the most difficult for this first exploration. If at any stage you feel overwhelmed, ask the part to reduce the level of activation so you can be present with it.
2. Notice what comes up in or around your body?
   - Are there thoughts, sensations, feelings, emotions, or an impulse?
   - Does your body posture change?
   - What happens to your breathing? Does it become quicker, slower, deeper, or shallower?
   - What about your heart rate? Does that change?
3. Can you locate it somewhere in your body, and then acknowledge this as a part of you that is responding to the thought of that person?
4. How do you feel toward this part? Notice your relationship to this part:
   - If you feel open to getting to know it, do you have any qualities of Self energy, like curiosity and compassion? If the answer is 'yes,' continue to step 5 *but*
   - If you feel negatively toward it, there may be another part that either does not like it or may be afraid. Can you ask that part to give you some space, so you can get to know the first one?
   - If it is not able to do that, then this second part becomes the focus of your attention.
   - Go back to step 2 to get to know this second part.

     Are you able to find some separation/differentiation between the part and you? This is called 'unblending.'
5. Do you have any qualities of Self as you are noticing it?
6. What happens as you notice this part? Does the part know who you are that is noticing it?

7. Are you able to be curious about what it is that triggers this part's reaction to that person?
8. Can you ask curious questions until you are able to understand the part?
   - What is the job of this part?
   - When and why did it take the job on? (It may show you an image or memory.)
   - What is its fear if it did not do its job?
   - How is it helping you and can you get a sense of what it is protecting in you?
   - Can you update the part and let it know how many years have gone by since it took the job on and who you are now with your adult and Self energy?
9. Does it make sense to you why the part took this job on?
   - If it does makes sense to you, can you let it know that you can see things from its perspective?
10. What do you notice in your system as you bring that person to mind again?
    - Has anything changed?
11. Thank the parts for talking to you and let them know you will come back.[16]

HOW WE MIGHT START TO USE THE IFS LENS WITHIN OUR PASTORAL SUPERVISION PRACTICE AROUND STUCKNESS

Finding a Way into the Stuckness

In the preflight safety briefing before takeoff on an airplane, they always tell you to put on your oxygen mask first before helping someone else. The same applies to IFS. We need to ensure we are as Self-led as possible, before we engage with our supervisee. This is something we then continually track within ourselves during a session. If we notice that we are stuck, we are likely to be blended with a part, and we can go through the following process to help determine if it is us, the supervisee, or both of us that are stuck. The first place to start is aways with ourselves.[17]

Stop: name that we are feeling stuck as the supervisor and invite the supervisee to pause for a moment to reflect on what is going on in them.

U-Turn: we Turn our attention toward ourselves.

Un-blend: from any parts that are blocking your Self-energy, asking them for some space.
Curiously befriend: your part and ask why it is reacting to the parts or story of your supervisee.
Kindly ask: your part to give you some space and let it know you will come back, while you now turn your attention to your supervisee, and from this calm place support them through the same process.

Stop

When we feel stuck, the first thing that can help is to pause and name that we are 'stuck.' We can be so busy helping the supervisee to look for the answers that we do not notice the elephant in the room. I find it helpful to sit back and reflect on how I am stuck in myself, and then with the supervisee. Am I making implicit assumptions about them, or their situation, that are preventing me from helping them to think outside the box and not forever repeat the pattern they are stuck in? This is like stopping on a walk and putting down the map to orientate to the actual place we find ourselves in if we think we may have taken the wrong path. Sometimes, we can only see the next step by stopping and checking.

U-Turn

Doing a You-Turn. Turning our attention towards ourselves, noticing and naming what is happening in me the supervisor: I ask who (in me) is talking and reacting to the other person?[18] An important skill for the supervisor to hone is that of 'present moment self-reflection and parts detection.' We may then do this in real time during a session with our supervisee, so that we can start to become aware of the influence that our physical human presence can have on the relationship. As humans, we all give off, and pick up, the energy of the emotional field of the other, and we have parts of our brain that scan other people all the time, not only for posture, but also for micro-movements of the face, breathing rate, tone, and pitch of voice. My experience is that this happens even on Zoom (online conferencing). You may think that you are 'sitting' on your feelings, but we are rarely able to hide them from the subconscious observation of someone we are in relationship with. Stephen Porges calls it 'neuroception.'[19] This can have a subtle, implicit impact on the experience of the other, influencing how they react to us and affecting the power balance, which we endeavour to be alert to as a professional practitioner. Could it be possible that you feel frustrated or irritated with the supervisee because you do not like the sensations and feelings their stuckness brings up in you?

Un-blend

We can become so blended with a part that we are not able to access our Self-energy.[20] This can happen for various reasons, but generally if there is a part of us that starts to feel vulnerable, then a Manager will step up to take control. Sometimes, our parts can become polarised with a part in the supervisee, becoming locked into opposing positions. When this happens, we are not able to be fully present with our supervisee in the session in an open, accepting, and creative way. Noticing and naming the parts helps to bring them into our conscious awareness. Once you have located the part in your body, ask yourself, 'how do I feel towards this (part, sensation, emotion)?' This helps to determine how blended it is, and if you are able to bring some curiosity and calm presence to meet the part inside you. But if you are feeling judgmental or negative, there may be more than one part being triggered, and you may be blended with another protector part. So, now you need to notice that new part. Check and see if you have a part trying to contain, or push, the first part away, annoyed because your system does not welcome its presence? If one of your protector parts has been triggered by something, it will not want to soften unless it is sure your Self-energy is there, because it will be protecting something vulnerable within you. Also, parts will not normally stand aside if others' parts are glaring at them with criticism or fear. The parts could be glaring at them either from inside you, or from inside your supervisee. Unblending comes with practice, but just noticing a part can help open space within us. If you can be curious and compassionate, bringing in any of the 8 C's and/or 5 P's (mentioned earlier), which are the qualities of Self, then you have some separation and Self-energy to proceed. From this place, you will be using less energy to suppress the feelings in yourself, and hopefully you will be able to become curious about why your part felt frustrated, irritated, or protective.

Curiously Befriend

Befriend your part, and ask why it is reacting to the parts in your supervisee. Gaining some understanding about your part, and some Self-energy in yourself, opens the option of sitting with the supervisee and being with them from a place of calm curiosity, accepting them and trusting in their organicity. From this place, we can trust that acceptance and space will allow them to find their own way. Congruence in this situation may mean naming the 'elephant in the room,' but also giving them permission *not* to explore it in the 'here and now' if they are still blended and triggered. Giving that permission can help settle triggered parts in them and help their parts to relax. Maybe they have never been given that permission. Parents, teachers, and line managers can be demanding of information.

Kindly Ask

Ask your part to give you some space, and let it know you will come back. Now turn your attention to your supervisee and, from this calm place, support them through the same process. It may be helpful at this point to know that people often do not accept and trust themselves. This can fuel self-criticism, shame, and guilt that locks them into a stuck place. In these situations, the human default reaction is often to look outward at others to blame or to seek answers. Inhabiting our Self-energy, we can offer acceptance and trust of their process, supporting them in finding a way through.

Learning to Reframe

Having experienced it yourself, introducing the language of parts can be a helpful start to integrating IFS into supervision. Being aware of our own parts and noticing when we are blended with protector or exile parts can help us, as supervisors, to gain insight into our internal motivation. If we have practiced unblending, as in the exercise above, then we can practice unblending and speaking for a part of ourselves with others. Having done that, we can then look at reframing our thinking (i.e., to think differently about words, concepts, behaviours, or actions). Reframing can help us to see the supervisee's behaviour through the lens of IFS, which helps us to understand that if the supervisee is defensive, a part is protecting a vulnerability and we need to bring compassion and curiosity into the reflective space. The language and understanding of the IFS systems theory can be used as a lens to support the supervision process, but unless the supervisor has received some training in IFS, then it is advised that the supervisor seeks permission from the supervisee to support the supervisee, only to get to know their protectors and only to acknowledge exiles that the supervisor becomes aware of.

WE CAN START TO REFRAME OUR REACTIONS TO A SUPERVISEE

A part of us might start thinking that our supervisee, Joan, has a problem, but she is stubbornly refusing to seek or accept help. But if we can bring our Self energy with its compassion and curiosity, we can reflect that perhaps it was never safe for Joan to admit vulnerability when she was young, and she had to learn to be self-sufficient as there was no adult to offer support, or it was dangerous for Joan to seek help. We might become curious about the possibility that Joan has a part that is feeling vulnerable and cannot bear to think she has done something wrong, or perhaps the response we gave to her was delivered in a way that triggered her protectors, because the supervisor had a part that felt judgmental.

THE LANGUAGE OF PARTS CAN BE LESS JUDGMENTAL AND SHAMING

> What happens if you reframe critical judgments that you hear as: 'it sounds like a part of you feels that . . . ?' [21]

For example, a supervisee, Bob, may talk about someone telephoning about the reading rota late at night:

> Bob: 'I feel really bad that I shouted at Pam for ringing me late on Tuesday evening to ask about the reading rotas.'

That can be reframed by you as:

> Supervisor: 'So (pause), it sounds like a 'part' of you was angry and shouted at Pam when the phone rang so late at night. And now another part feels bad about that. That makes sense to me (pause). Does that make sense to you?

A part of Bob was angry and shouted at Pam for ringing late, and another part of Bob was critical of this reaction and left him feeling bad. If Bob is still blended with the shamed part, he may feel he is bad per se, and also fear that you think he is bad. The language of parts provides space to recognise that the reactive, critical, and shamed parts involved here are not the whole of the person. And by telling Bob that it makes sense to you that a part would shout in this situation, parts can feel heard by you and Bob, helping to minimise guilt and shame in the process and enhancing the supervisory relationship and the supervisee's awareness. If we find that we, the supervisor, cannot sit with the supervisee and respond from a place of compassion and curiosity, then this is when we need to do a *U-Turn* (you-turn),[22] and check what is coming up in ourselves. Maybe you feel, as the supervisor, that Bob should not have shouted in this situation. So, you have some judgmental thoughts. These judgments can show themselves in our body posture, tone and pitch of voice, and even micro-movements in your face.[23] This is when we need to check inside and notice our parts. If we are able to talk to our parts, we can ask them to give us some space and then reflect on their reactions on our own later or in our own supervision. There is an interesting dynamic that can occur in any relationship, not just between supervisees and supervisors. For example, if I have a Manager part that would prevent my parts from shouting at Pam in that situation, if I am not aware of it being present, Bob may feel that I am critical of his reaction. I may then be confused by his defensiveness and react to that. We can become aware of these parts by noticing our thoughts and physical reactions in the present moment during supervision sessions. To help Bob, I might ask him if he is interested in spending some time noticing his parts and getting to know them. Contracting during the session for this type of exploration is important. We can get in the habit of offering this sort of micro-contracting during a session.[24] Taking time to pause and be curious about what was going on for the triggered part in Bob, we can discover that he was afraid that the phone might wake the children, as they were exhausted and had to be up early in the morning. That Pam had a habit of asking lots of questions late at night, and that Bob has a body memory of a phone call late at night to say someone had died, and he has a protector angry that the exile had been upset. It never ceases to amaze me how helpful it is to speak to the parts directly, and see the compassion that can be generated within someone's system when they see things through the eyes of the parts.

CONTRACTING AND EXPECTATIONS

Are you able to take a moment to reflect on your own experience of supervision in the past? Do you routinely ask new supervisees what experiences of supervision they have had in the past? Seeking permission to explore this in the first few sessions can help support the contracting, but also help prevent relational problems from arising. Exploring expectations can help mitigate implicit destructive relational perceptions that can lead to stuckness in the relationship between you both, supervisor and supervisee. For example, a supervisee, carrying an expectation of supervision from a previous line manager may not understand the independent, confidential, reflective space on offer in pastoral supervision. Even if you have told them that this is the case, the part of our supervisee that had the previous experience may not have heard it. Inviting the supervisee to speak for a previous experience can allow that part to be updated. This can give you a chance to explore fears and negotiate how to work together in order to help reduce the power imbalance. You could invite the supervisee to tell you if they feel uneasy at any point with you. But, in order for them to do that, you need to be in a calm Self-led place where you can receive any feelings nonjudgmentally, pausing and checking with your protectors for any defensiveness in you before you reply.

CONTINUAL CONTRACTING

I tend to lean towards continual contracting in a pastoral supervision session.[25] Having contracted at the start of your work together, you then agree on a focus for each session. Sometimes the reflections can drift, or a supervisee may bring in another topic. I may suspect that there is a part that is distracting away from the initial topic. In this case, I will suggest that we pause for a moment and check to see if this new topic should now become the focus, or whether the supervisee wants to return to the primary focus. If I feel that there may be various parts in play, and I am hearing contradictions, I will again pause the session and ask if they would like to spend a few moments noticing the parts. This form of contracting helps the co-creation of the space.

JUDGMENTS

Judgments are an interesting area, one where it is vital for the pastoral supervisor to explore their own implicit bias, which is based on personal preferences and core beliefs that we have developed over our lifetime, e.g., role, lifestyle, leadership style, theological positions , faith (or none) and spirituality. Ethnicity, heritage, oppression, intersectionality, disability, medical/ psychiatric diagnostic labels, family, culture, economic class, addictions, and coping strategies also need to be taken into account. It is possible for us to implicitly approve, or disapprove, of a course of action that a pastoral supervisee is planning, and we can influence their thinking by the way we react to, encourage, or discourage, thinking in a certain direction by our reflective questions, ponderings, or curiosity, even if we think we are being neutral in the words we may choose to use to reflect back. We do not want to tie ourselves up in knots about this, but it can be a helpful reflection. Supervisees can have self-critical parts that can lead them to become mentally paralysed, which can have a knock-on effect physically and emotionally, resulting in a fear that they may be making the wrong decision or taking a wrong action. This can send them into a very black-and-white world of right and wrong, success or failure, humiliation and shame, resulting in a deep fear that any step could be very dangerous. This sort of paralysing fear can prevent any movement and also quashes creative thinking.

We can ask the supervisee if they would like to get to know the protector, but we must ensure that we are in our self-energy and not speaking from a judgmental or critical part of ourselves.

If the supervisee wishes to explore further, then our first question would be, 'how do you feel towards that part of you?,' then ask what it is afraid would happen if it did not do its job. These questions often give you both a clue about what it is protecting (i.e., the exiled part or vulnerability). This process must always be conducted collaboratively with the supervisee (if at all). So we, as the supervisor, need to be aware of our parts and sit in a place of self-leadership and genuine curiosity, and compassion, with the awareness that underneath each protector lies a vulnerable exile. This is a delicate process, and so we, as supervisors, can help the supervisee to gain insight into their internal motivation. As we unblend and speak for our parts, we can also reframe our thinking with the understanding that we have gained about the vulnerability in the supervisee.

COLLUDING WITH THE SUPERVISEE

Is it possible that you have parts that are colluding with your supervisee to avoid a topic? This is something that we can take to our consultant supervision to explore.

SLOWING DOWN

Slowing down the speed of interaction can help to allow space for inward reflection and to check 'who' is responding. One thing that I try to monitor is the speed of response. When conversation speeds up, and the exchanges become like a tennis final at Wimbledon, neither person is responding in a reflective way. When I become aware of this happening, I will pause and consciously slow my own breathing by extending my 'out' breath to activate my parasympathetic nervous system in order to help regulate myself, and also interactively regulate the supervisee. Then I will say something like, 'can we pause here?,' or 'can we slow down for a moment?' This is also teaching them a skill to use in the world when they are in a tricky meeting or exchange with someone.

OFFERING INSIGHTS AND OBSERVATIONS

As supervisors, we may notice blind spots, or patterns, within the supervisee that fall into quadrants of the Johari Window (see Figure 6.1). The language of parts can help us to name things we have noticed by allowing us to speak *for* our parts and wondering about a *part* of the supervisee. This can have the effect of minimising the observation, helping it to sound less judgmental, with the implication that you know this is not the whole of them. For example:

There is a part of me that is wondering if you might be feeling a little upset about that?

I wonder if a part of you is feeling irritated about that?

PATTERNS OF COMMUNICATION

Stuckness can be perpetuated by patterns of communication that we fall into with a certain person or group of people. I like to try and spot these patterns if they are arising within a supervision relationship and encourage the supervisee to notice patterns in their own internal and external worlds. Our parts can start to anticipate reactions from other people, and then we are primed for the inevitable rerun! If we can spot the predictable pattern and raise it into our consciousness, then there is a chance that the inevitable can be avoided. Parts will be very aware of people they find a problem, or difficult, and they can put us on high alert for a disagreement. When that happens, just seeing the name or telephone number of someone come up on the phone, or thinking about seeing them at a meeting, can leave parts of us feeling threatened or irritated, already anticipating a predictable pattern, and risking a misunderstanding around the intention behind any communication. They may interpret a request for a date, or plan, to be changed as a criticism, or a parishioner asking to travel in the car with them to a meeting (which may not be practical for them), as an inconsiderate invasion of their space. But actually, that person may be asking because they want to spend time with you, or are scared of going to the car park after the meeting on their own. If the supervisee's reaction left the parishioner feeling rejected, that, in turn, primes both systems for the next miscommunication. In my experience, these types of misunderstandings can lead to a great deal of stuckness within relational dynamics, which supervisees bring because of the internal and external systems keeping them stuck. Richard Schwartz has a wonderful saying that people we find difficult are our tor-mentors—they 'mentor' us by showing us the parts that we need to work with.[26]

THE WEATHER HOUSE

These dynamics remind me of an old weather house that my grandmother owned, where the woman came out on a sunny day, and the man on wet days. A part can fly to the front of us and jump in the driving seat, blending with us within milliseconds. Then another can come out and push the first away. What we want is for them to both be in the shelter of the house (our system), with Self at the front speaking for them. We can always make a conscious choice to send a certain part out to the front, but it goes with the support of our Self energy and support of the other parts, not taking over because if is defending vulnerability at all cost.

EMPATHY AND COMPASSION

There is a difference between empathy and compassion. We need an empathic charge to connect with our supervisee's story,[27, 28] but the empathy is normally because a part of us has resonated, and connected, with something in the supervisee's story. If we continue to work from this place, we will wear ourselves out emotionally. If we can shift into compassionate curiosity (i.e., become more Self-led), this is a much more grounded place to work from. It is less exhausting, and we can see more clearly what is our stuff and what is theirs.

OUR SUPERVISOR PARTS

It is possible to become blended with our 'supervisor' part and to be unaware of that. This may be a part that knows all the theory, but if that part becomes blended with us, focusing on process and method, we are not always able to be present with our Self-energy and to notice our parts during a session. Practicing being our own *parts detector*, noticing the relational dynamics, roles, and burdens that our parts carry and detecting them in ourselves and others, allows our settled presence to help a supervisee to feel safer at a deep implicit level.

SOME EXAMPLES OF HOW THIS MIGHT WORK IN PASTORAL SUPERVISION:

Jack

One of my supervisees, Jack, was stuck in his job, unable to move on, and I felt we were stuck in supervision. Jack was a local minister, living and working in the area where he had grown up, and he wanted to move to a new job. But every time he read an advert for a job he was excited to apply for, either he could not bring himself to apply for it or there would be a myriad of reasons why it was the wrong job. Jack was starting to feel confused and quite ashamed about this inability to even apply for the new jobs. This went on for nearly a year and, to be honest, my parts were getting frustrated. I also had a part that was starting to feel quite negative, prior to our meetings, because of this confusing and frustrating stuckness. Notice how I have framed my reaction as a part as well. It was not the whole of me, but it was helpful to notice the negativity in me and acknowledge it. At this point, I decided to bring in the language of parts and the IFS theory that I had begun using in my counselling practice. I started by offering the idea that maybe he had one part that really wanted to move to a new job, and another part that, for some reason, was not happy about that. This intervention helped to open some space inside Jack so that he could identify the critical protector, which was telling him he was a failure and a total disaster. Gradually he was able to identify three parts:

1. a part that wanted him to move and was excited about a new church role;
2. a possible group of protectors that were seemingly against the idea and were preventing the applications from being written, creating lots of negative thinking and distracting Jack from the task;
3. a critical part that was trying to motivate him to take action, but was, in fact, crippling him with shame and accusations of failure.

When I invited Jack to get curious about his parts, he found protectors who believed it would be dangerous and scary to move. Once we met the protectors, we discovered that they had taken their role on when he was a young lad. I suggested that Jack ask the protectors to soften and allow him to see who they were protecting. They were protecting a vulnerable seven-year-old who had been traumatised by the move to that town. Having settled in that town, the seven-year-old and his protectors had prevented any further moves in Jack's life. Four months later, Jack had a new job and was able to move. He learnt to notice when his seven-year-old was nervous or upset, by noticing the body sensations connected to him. Jack learnt to listen to the concerns of the seven-year-old part and then he would settle and, in turn, this allowed the protectors to settle, and Jack could get on with the application and move forward.

Noreen

Noreen was telling me that she was concerned that some of the congregation in her new church did not seem to like her, and she was puzzled by that. She wondered whether perhaps they did not like female clergy? She felt stuck and unsure as to how she should deal with this situation. We paused the session, and I asked her if she would like to take a moment to notice what was coming up as she shared her thoughts. She agreed, and we took a moment to notice what was coming up 'in or around her body.' She identified that she felt uneasy, and was able to locate this sensation of unease in her stomach. As she stayed with that feeling in her stomach for a few moments, a thought came up and she realised that she did not want to engage in conversation with these members of the congregation. Agreeing that this made sense, I invited her to stay with this. As she stayed with the feelings and the thoughts, she realised she had developed a pattern of staying in the vestry after a service in order to avoid them. This meant that she was not available at coffee time to talk to everyone else. This was a big insight, and also helped her to become curious about the parts that were nervous about talking to these people. After reflecting and listening to the parts, Noreen made a connection to an intimidating teacher she had had at school, whom she felt had always disapproved of her. So, actually, she had been trying very hard to please, and her strategy to feel safer was to try and be friends. She became aware that the people were happy to engage in polite conversation, but as soon as her part started to try to be friends, seeking a deeper connection, they started picking holes in things she was doing. Once Noreen made sense of this and was able to let the younger part know that these people were not the scary teacher from the past that she was trying to please and updated the part about the passage of time, things started to settle. I asked if the young part knew it did not have to go to work with her and that her adult could handle her work situation. This was a revelation to Noreen, who was able to notice her behaviour and the parts, and from there start to find a way through the stuckness.

Rozelle

Rozelle was exhausted as we emerged out of the COVID-19 pandemic in Summer 2021. She had been doing four services a day on a Sunday before lockdown, and we worked over quite a few sessions on contacting her parts which could not bear the thought of beginning again in the autumn with four services. During one session, she just wanted to rant about the pressure she was under and the fact that she could not do what they were expecting. After the initial burst from Rozelle's pent-up parts, I needed to consciously slow down my parts and body energy to prevent them getting pulled into her energy. I reflected on what I thought I was hearing:

> Sally: 'Can I check that I am hearing this correctly? There is one part that is feeling really angry that the church is expecting you to pick up everything you were doing before lockdown, and there is also another part that feels you cannot cope with doing that?'
>
> Rozelle: 'Yes.' (The energy in her system immediately started to settle as the parts were heard).
>
> Rozelle: 'But then there is another part that says I should do it, and I do not want to let down the few that come to the 8 a.m. and 6 p.m. services.'

Sally: 'How would it be if we spent a few moments getting to know each of these parts?

Rozelle: 'That would be good.'

Sally: 'Which one would you like to start with?'

After speaking to each of the parts, and bringing the qualities of Self to each in turn, checking how she felt toward each one and building the Self-to-part relationship, Rozelle was able to find some space to see all three parts from an unblended place with Self-energy. This enabled her to think more clearly instead of: a) feeling she was being asked to take on something that was unsustainable; b) feeling like shouting at a church meeting because she did not feel heard; and c) then having her critical part attack her for letting people down and behaving badly. From her place of Self-energy, she was able to feel less boxed in and speak for her parts. She was able to explain to the next meeting from a clear adult part with confidence and clarity, that she did not feel it was sustainable, but that she would be happy to look at a compromise of working on three services a Sunday, maybe alternating the 8 a.m. and 6 p.m. services.

DRAWING IT ALL TOGETHER

So, we now know that when stuckness comes up, there is likely to be more going on under the surface for the supervisee, and/or supervisor, individually, and possibly between them. For protectors, survival trumps everything: their mantra is 'never again.' So, if there are parts experiencing fear or distress, they will react. By noticing and befriending the protectors, we can discover and acknowledge the exiles they are protecting, which can give us a clue to what the core beliefs are driving the internal system.

We can become afraid of change, and it can feel dangerous to become aware of a vulnerability. Our protective system has been doing its job for so long that is has often forgotten why the young parts became exiled, or what burdens they are carrying. The protectors only know that it could be bad to approach something which they fear might explode with emotion and disrupt their current life. It is good to remind yourself, and anyone you are working with, that nothing can overwhelm you if you are in Self energy. Parts are so relieved to be found and listened to and to know that they are no longer on their own, that they generally settle. Often supervisees realise how much effort it has taken to contain large amounts of emotion, or push parts away. In stuck places, we can become too focused on one particular outcome.[29] Sometimes it takes courage to acknowledge that there is currently no external way forward. To have that witnessed and affirmed by the pastoral supervisor can be a relief if the supervisee has been desperately searching for a way forward. In this case, we can try to help them explore how they can find new ways of managing the impact of the situation within themselves.

Parts language often opens up space for exploration and enables you to offer wonderings with the understanding that a part is not the whole of anyone. It enables the supervisee to name feelings and thoughts that they may not feel they want to 'own' as theirs. Framing a feeling, or thought, as a part, provides space and intitiates the unblending process, helping to expand Self energy, presence, and compassion. In supervision, we tend to work only with protectors. You need to have gone through proper training to work with exiles in someone else, but simply noticing the exile can start the healing process as it realises that it is not on its own, that there is a caring adult in the system. Organic unburdening can follow as the part lets go of the stress, burden, or role it has been carrying for many years. This, in turn, allows the protectors to realise that they do not have to work so hard.

We bring who we are to each situation, and if the supervisee has a part triggered by a certain person, so that they are always blended with a protector every time they see them, they will find it very difficult to respond differently. If we can help them notice what is happening, and be more Self-led when they meet that person, they have the possibility of changing the dynamics as they will be operating from a more grounded place. Naming the 'elephant in the room,' accompanied by permission **not** to speak about it if the supervisee does not want to, may be a new experience for them. This can be helpful if you suspect there is an implicit power imbalance.

CONCLUSION

Clergy may become very defensive and vulnerable because of the way their faith, identity as a priest, and vocational calling, are tied up with their role. When we see this in supervision, we can hypothesise that there are vulnerable parts underneath that the system is struggling to contain. Offering compassion from a place of Self-leadership encourages them to see that although they may have hit a tricky patch or a stuck place, there is hope. Young parts, and their protectors, can disempower us in the adult world, but if we can earn their trust, we can speak for them from Self-energy. If, as a supervisor, we are able to lead from our Self, and sit alongside the supervisee with presence, curiosity, and compassion, we do not need any answers; we simply have to enable the supervisee to talk to their parts, and the system will find its own way organically. Even if our supervisees leave our office without the answers they were looking for, if they have made contact with their parts, they can continue to open up space and settle internally as they carry on with their lives.

We have explored how we experience stuckness in pastoral supervision, and we have considered how our supervisees might be stuck, and what may be contributing to that stuckness. We have also thought about how both the supervisor and supervisee will be influenced by their internal beliefs and the implicit bias that they each bring to the session, and by factors in the external world that surround them both individually and in the supervision relationship. I have offered a new way to explore and unpack stuckness in each of them, through the lens of IFS in the supervisee-supervisor relationship, in the supervisee and supervisor, and also in the external world. We can help the supervisee to be curious by listening for parts in their stories, by being the *parts detector* for them.

If you are interested in exploring parts work further, and integrating it into your supervision practice, I would suggest starting with yourself. Notice your parts, name them, and experiment by asking them to step back in your everyday life. We have incredible brains that are able to observe ourselves, and our parts, and also be present to the supervisee at the same time. When you have practised with yourself, you can then try offering it to your supervisees. Internal Family Systems (IFS) allows us to work with external and internal dynamics in a relational way, establishing contact with things that we, the supervisor and supervisee, may not have previously been aware of. It is a compassionate approach that is not aggressive to our systems of parts. It can support the development and growth of the supervisee in their life and ministry, as well as help co-create a safe container for supervision. It can also support congruence within the pastoral supervision setting, by giving us the ability to speak *for* our parts. If the model makes sense to you, it can become the lens through which you see yourself and others in the world. Making more space for Self within the system, and relieving protectors of their energy-sapping roles, opens up more space for God's presence in our lives.

BIBLIOGRAPHY

Fisher, Janina. *Healing Our Fragmented Selves*. New York: Routledge, 2017.

Halpern, Helen. "Supervision and the Johari Window: A Framework for Asking Questions," *Education for Primary Care* 20, no.1 (2009): 10–14. DOI: 10.1080/14739879.2009.11493757

Hawkins, Peter, and Robin Shohet. *Supervision in the Helping Professions.* Maidenhead: Open University Press, 2009.

IFS, Institute. *Internal Family Systems.* https://ifs-institute.com (accessed Sept.3, 2022).

Krouse, Pamela, Lawrence Rosenberg, and Martha Sweezy, "Getting Unstuck": Pp. 10–28 in *Innovations and Elaborations in Internal Family Systems Therapy,* ed. Martha Sweezy and Ellen L. Ziskind. New York: Routledge, 2017.

McGonigal, Kelly. *The Science of Compassion: A Modern Approach to Cultivating Empathy, Love and Connection*. Boulder, CO: Sounds True Audio Book, 2016.

Merton, Thomas. *New Seeds of Contemplation.* New York: New Directions paperback, 1972.

Ogden, Pat, and Janina Fisher. *Sensorimotor Psychotherapy: Interventions for Trauma and Attachment*. New York: W.W. Norton & Company, 2015.

Porges, Stephen. *The Pocket Guide to the Polyvagal Theory: The Transformative Power of Feeling Safe.* New York: W. W. Norton, 2017.

Redfern, Emma E. *Internal Family Systems Therapy: Supervision and Consultation.* New York: Routledge, 2023.

Reed, D., and Ray Wooten, "A model of IFS informed supervision and consultation: Un blending from struggle into Self-Led Clarity:" Pp.14–32 in *Internal Family Systems Therapy: Supervision and Consultation,* ed. Emma E. Redfern (New York: Routledge, 2023).

Riemersma, Jenna. *Altogether You: Experiencing Personal and Spiritual Transformation with Internal Family Systems Therapy.* Marietta, Georgia: Pivotal Press, 2020.

Schwartz, Richard C. *No Bad Parts.* Boulder, Colorado: Sounds True, 2021.

———. IFS Institute. IFS-institute.com (accessed Aug.5, 2022)

Schwartz, Richard C., and Robert R. Falconer. *Many Minds, One Self: Evidence for a Radical Shift in Paradigm.* Oak Park, IL: Trailheads Publications, 2017.

Schwartz, Richard C., and Martha Sweezy. *Internal Family Systems Therapy.* New York: The Guilford Press, 2020.

Singer, Tania, and Olga M. Kilmecki. "Empathy and compassion." *Current Biology* 24, no. 18 (2014): 875–78.

NOTES

1. IFS Institute, Internal Family Systems, ifs-institute.com (accessed Sept.3, 2022)

2. Dan Reed and Ray Wooten, "A model of IFS informed supervision and consultation: Un blending from struggle into Self-Led Clarity," in *Internal Family Systems Therapy: Supervision and Consultation,* ed. Emma E. Redfern (New York: Routledge, 2023), 15.

3. Pat Ogden and Janina Fisher, *Sensorimotor Psychotherapy: Interventions for Trauma and Attachment* (New York: W.W. Norton & Company, 2015), 441.

4. Helen Halpern, "Supervision and the Johari Window: A Framework for Asking Questions," *Education for Primary Care* 20, no. 1 (2009): 10–14. DOI: 10.1080/14739879.2009.11493757.

5. Peter Hawkins and Robin Shohet, *Supervision in the Helping Professions* (Maidenhead: Open University Press, 2009).

6. IFS Institute, Internal Family Systems, ifs-institute.com (accessed Sept.3, 2022).

7. Emma E. Redfern, "In Search of Self," in *Internal Family Systems Therapy: Supervision and Consultation*, ed. Emma E. Redfern (New York: Routledge, 2023), 215.

8. Richard C. Schwartz, *No Bad Parts* (Boulder, CO: Sounds True, 2021), 1

9. Jenna Riemersma, *Altogether You: Experiencing Personal and Spiritual Transformation with Internal Family Systems Therapy* (Marietta, Georgia: Pivotal Press, 2020).

10. Thomas Merton, *New Seeds of Contemplation* (New York: New Directions paperback, 1972).

11. Richard C. Schwartz, IFS Institute, IFS-institute.com (accessed Aug. 5, 2022).

12. Ibid.

13. Schwartz, *No Bad Parts*, 34.

14. Ibid.

15. Richard C. Schwartz and Robert R. Falconer, *Many Minds, One Self: Evidence for a Radical Shift in Paradigm* (Oak Park, IL: Trailheads Publications, 2017), 207.

16. Schwartz, *No Bad Parts*, 23–24.

17. Pamela Krouse, Lawrence Rosenberg, and Martha Sweezy, "Getting Unstuck," in *Innovations and Elaborations in Internal Family Systems Therapy*, ed. Martha Sweezy and Ellen L. Ziskind (New York: Routledge, 2017), 10.

18. Krouse, Rosenberg, and Sweezy, "Getting Unstuck," 12.

19. Stephen Porges, *The Pocket Guide to the Polyvagal Theory: The Transformative Power of Feeling Safe* (New York: W. W. Norton, 2017).

20. Krouse, Rosenberg and Sweezy, "Getting Unstuck," 10.

21. Richard C. Schwartz and Martha Sweezy, *Internal Family Systems Therapy* (New York: The Guilford Press, 2020).

22. Schwartz, *No Bad Parts*.

23. Pat Ogdon and Janina Fisher, *Sensorimotor Psychotherapy: Interventions for Trauma and Attachment* (New York: Norton, 2015).

24. Reed and Wooten, "A model of IFS informed supervision and consultation," 14–32.

25. Ibid.

26. Schwartz, *No Bad Parts*.

27. Tania Singer and Olga M. Kilmecki, "Empathy and compassion," *Current Biology* 24, no. 18 (2014): 875–78.

28. Kelley McGonigal, *The Science of Compassion: A Modern Approach to Cultivating Empathy, Love and Connection* (Boulder, CO: Sounds True, 2016).

29. Janina Fisher, *Healing Our Fragmented Selves* (New York: Routledge, 2017).

Chapter Seven

Developing an Understanding of Trauma in Pastoral Supervision

Sally Bubbers

This chapter offers an introduction to the relationship between neurobiology and behaviour patterns that impact our daily lives. I will offer a brief overview of some concepts that you can draw on in pastoral supervision. You may be drawn to one particular theory, but they all intersect. Did you know that our bodies can remember events without us having conscious memory or words that go with them? Or that when a person becomes distressed or agitated, they have a reduced capacity to think clearly? Have you ever been confused by the reactions of your supervisee that might not seem logical or 'adult' and did not fit with the person you thought you knew? Simple mindful practices that are embedded in contemplative traditions and go back to the Desert Fathers can help bring the 'thinking brain' back online in times of stress. Looking through the lens of neurobiology and using the language of parts, we can find new ways to make sense of confusing behaviour in ourselves and others, supporting better communication and reducing stress levels. Trauma-informed practice also seeks to help us understand ourselves if we are supporting a supervisee who is dealing with a complex relational situation or event, in their parish, or in their private life, because we can pick up some of their stress as we engage with them. This is called 'vicarious trauma.' We can learn to support ourselves by learning to differentiate between our 'stuff' and their 'stuff.' This helps us to be present to our supervisee in a compassionate, curious, and boundaried way, allowing them to feel seen, heard, and understood. They can learn that it is possible to feel calmer and find new ways of becoming reflective.

Christians are charged to 'love one another, as we love ourselves,' but the tricky thing is that we often do not love ourselves. We have parts that criticise and shame us, and then those parts can be judgmental of others as well. I hope that by gaining a basic understanding of trauma and of how it can be present in our daily lives, you may be able to accept yourself and others, since I believe God loves each of us as we are. The challenge is that we need to start with ourselves. This affects who we are as we sit with a supervisee and how we are able to bring curious noticing, attuned acceptance, and compassion to the encounter. For me, this is a lifelong journey. Please take care of yourself as you read this chapter, because you may resonate with some of the information in a new way. I hope that as a supervisor, you will have your own support network in place. What follows is a brief summary of current knowledge and psychological theories that each interweave to help give you a sense of what may be going on in you and your supervisee as you engage in the microcosm of pastoral supervision. I feel I need to say that I do not believe that there is any one theory that fully describes any one of us, because we are all unique individuals.

HOW TRAUMA IS DEFINED

It is easy to think about trauma as a single event, but developmental trauma[1] can result from persistent mis-attunement by a caregiver. Trauma can be defined as anything that is so overwhelming that we are not able to integrate the experience.[2] This will vary according to our age and life experience; we cannot gauge the impact of an event on another person, because we do not know what levels of stress are already in their body or mind.[3] Childhood distress or abuse (developmental trauma) can result from persistent low levels of distress in the child, and parents who are not aware of the needs of the child[4] can have a long-lasting impact on the way an adult is able to be present in the world and in their relationships. The child may experience the caregiver as unpredictable if they are frightening or frightened themselves.[5] Ethnicity, heritage, disability, poor physical and psychological living conditions, displacement, and surrounding cultural insecurity all have an impact. Good attachment comes from knowing that someone accepts you for who you are and that you can rely on them to be there for you.

USING THE LANGUAGE OF PARTS

I explained some of the theory of Internal Family Systems in chapter 6, , but, in brief, Internal Family Systems asserts that at our core we all have Self-energy which is good: I understand this to be the part of us made in the image of God, our God essence,[6] or True Self.[7] We also all have non-pathologized parts that hold good intentions for us, but having taken on roles and burdens to help at some stage in our lives, our parts do not always realise the consequences which their actions may have on us or on those around us. Schwartz[8] divides the parts into two groups. Firstly, parts that become exiled in our system because they hold painful memories and emotions that we could not integrate as children or behaviours that were not acceptable to those around us. These become burdens that the parts carry, but it is important to remember that parts are not their burdens: they have taken on the job of carrying them to help us survive. Secondly, the protective system has two lines of defence. In order to stay in relational connection with our parents or caregivers, we develop managerial parts that proactively run our lives to ensure that the exiles are not seen or upset. If something happens that upsets us, and the managers cannot contain the 'fire' inside, then the firefighters come out. They are the ultimate, reactive backup that have no concept of the relational damage or physical harm they may cause by their actions. They just want to distract attention away from the exile's distress or sense of being overwhelmed. Unfortunately, we often then develop managers that can be critical of us and hold shame about our firefighters, which can affect our self-esteem and confidence and drain our energy, thus leading to stress and exhaustion. Some pieces of the jigsaw we are going to look at include attachment theory, the neurobiological triggering system, and some psychological theories that interweave and overlap to help us understand the impact of trauma on ourselves and our supervisees.

ATTACHMENT THEORY

As we grow, we embody the relational dynamics of the family, or caregivers, that we live with. These ingrained patterns become familiar to us, laying down unconscious patterns that become a 'blueprint of our expectations' in future relationships.[9] These maps[10] of how to navigate the world can fail us when we are challenged and stressed in our adult lives. What is not generally understood is that we can change these by noticing them and updating them about the years which have passed and letting them know that we are now adults and have new ways of navigating life. Because children are vulnerable and physically dependent on parents/caretakers for their survival needs in terms of shelter, food and attuned presence, their thresholds for 'trauma' are different. Turmoil can be generated inside the child as their defence systems are overridden to attach, and they deny their lived reality in order to remain in connection for survival. We cannot define overwhelming or traumatic events in terms of size: the test is the impact on the child, and if that is not acknowledged by an attuned adult, this can cause deep confusion, anguish, and distress.[11] One example of this could be a mother who sends the children into the garden while she washes the kitchen floor. One child may feel that there is a freedom to play, and another child may feel the closed back door cuts her off from her mother, and she feels abandoned and rejected. The important thing is that the experience of the child is not minimised and that repair is offered.

There are four categories of attachment style,[12] which are formed in relationship with parents or caregivers. Before you read the following paragraphs, it is good to remember that secure attachment can be 'earned' in later life, if we find good relationships and 'make sense' of our lives.[13] Some children also experience the support of extended family, neighbours, or teachers who support secure attachment if it is not available at home. We are often a mixture of styles, but we are looking at patterns and generalisations of secure and insecure emotional attachment that can result from developmental trauma.[14]

Secure emotional attachment is when we have caregivers who are able to be attuned and be present to the baby and growing child, who are able to offer 'repair' when the child is upset, and who are consistent enough to allow the child to reliably predict the way the parent is likely to react—i.e., 'good enough' parenting.[15] This results in an adult who is able to calm themselves (autoregulation) and who is able to seek help when they need it (interactive regulation). The secure adult can generally say they feel 'safe' in the world as they navigate different places and relationships. They are autonomous and flexible. The good news is that secure attachment can be 'earned' in adult life, if we did not get it as a child.

Anxious attachment is the legacy of parents who inconsistently meet the needs of the child. The child may become insecure and self-critical and anxious that they will be rejected. This often results in an adult who becomes preoccupied with being in a relationship. They seek approval and reassurance and often feel insecure, worrying about rejection.

Avoidant attachment is found in the adult who did not have parents who were aware of the child's needs and who did not allow themselves to be emotionally available. The child may try and get close to the parent and then get hurt or rejected. So, they end up taking care of themselves. This often results in an adult who can be dismissive of others and who greatly values their independence. They will start forming relationships but then become afraid and mistrustful if they get too close. They can start to devalue the person, or relationship, and detach themselves from getting hurt again.

Disorganised attachment can be found in adults who can seem chaotic or rigid. They may have parts that are adult, responsible, and organised, but they can also become disorganised, disempowered, fearful, and aggressive. This can be very confusing for them and for everyone around them. They have had a tough time in childhood. They had parents who were frightening or frightened, unpredictable, and scary. They may have experienced abuse and had to find ways of surviving in the very different environments of home and school. They may have developed parts of themselves that can operate in different ways and in different situations, in order to survive. They can appear to have a mix of the other attachment styles. Their attempts to seek interactive regulation can seem very needy, and their self-regulation can actually be a shutdown, rather than a calm state. They have the capacity to 'dissociate' parts of themselves, and can appear forgetful and lose time sometimes, as they wander off into daydream states. They can become dysregulated quickly and tend to either shut down or become agitated (fight and flight). Instead of being flexible, they tend to become rigid or chaotic in their lives or have a mixture of both.[16]

Dissociation is a word can be used to describe various experiences. We all have the capacity to dissociate, and we sometimes call it 'daydreaming.' It is a way to leave in our mind because it is too overwhelming or frightening to be where our bodies are, but we cannot physically leave or run away. Sometimes people may not have any memory of an event, or of how they have behaved or spoken in a certain way. People can report that they feel like they are outside their bodies looking down on themselves. This is a normal survival strategy in situations of extreme physical and mental distress.[17]

In pastoral supervision, you may start to spot some of these attachment patterns. This can be helpful information to share with your supervisee if you feel it may support them to gain some emotional space and compassion. For example, they may be struggling to understand a needy parishioner or someone to whom they have given a lot of pastoral support, and now that person has spurned them. It is also helpful to understand these dynamics if supporting a couple who are struggling in their relationship. Some of these attachment patterns may also be evident in your relationship with your supervisee.

ADVERSE CHILDHOOD EXPERIENCES

Research[18] has concluded that there is a strong connection between childhood trauma and our adult health. Adverse childhood experiences are now considered to include childhood experiences in the household, community, and environment. Our understanding of how developmental trauma can affect the developing brain is evolving all the time. For example: the corpus collosum that links the two halves of the brain fails to develop fully if the child is living in a stressful or distressing environment.[19] The child can copy and learn behaviour from those around them. Nurture versus nature is intertwined with attachment theory, adverse childhood experiences, and epigenetics. Epigenetic studies, which emerged from the work of Rachel Yehuda and her team, are trying to discover the link between nurture and nature, and how each affects the other.[20] Two significant research results are that children and grandchildren of Holocaust survivors can fit the criteria for post-traumatic stress disorder because they have lived with traumatised parents. The research has also shown that we can pass down the impact of trauma through three generations (nature), which can unconsciously determine how we experience and respond to future events.[21]

In pastoral supervision, we do not have to go into great depth about the theory mentioned in this chapter. I believe that if we, as pastoral supervisors, are able to support clergy through our acceptance of them, helping them to find ways of noticing their reactions so they can start to respond to events, and normalising behaviours as survival strategies and supporting change, this can help reduce stress and anxiety within them and those they live and work among. In reality, when we are stressed, we tend to have less patience, and this can show itself especially with our loved ones. Ministry invades the clergy home and lives in a way that not many other jobs do. So, if we can support the clergy, we are also hopefully supporting and reducing stress for any children living in the clergy family. Dan Siegel concludes, from his research, that the best protective factor for the children is the sense that the parents have made of their lives. [22]

HOW THE BRAIN AFFECTS OUR DAILY FUNCTIONING

We are going to go on a lightning tour around some of the things that can help us understand the neurobiological drivers in our human bodies. I have found that gaining an overview of this has helped me to have compassion for myself and for my supervisees. Our ways of responding to events can become so ingrained in us that we do not always realise what is happening until our whole system becomes so overwhelmed in the adult world, that parts of us can start causing panic attacks, depressive states, or illness. We have the capacity to remember things in our bodies, and these memories often have no words attached to them. I will explain how they can override the whole system in the section headed 'Triggering System.' The important thing for now, is to understand that this is all about speed of response, so that we can react faster the next time a distressing event occurs. There are various factors that affect how we store information for our survival, and this can determine how we react to future events that are deemed to be life-threatening to us. Remembering bad things in our bodies helps us respond quicker next time we are in danger, so we do not have to think about what to do. Even when we have had good experiences, we tend to remember the bad experiences more. Rick Hanson speaks of how bad, or negative, things stick on as if to Velcro in our brains, and good/positive things tend to slip off as if they were on Teflon.[23]

Triggering System: The brain is divided into two hemispheres but, for ease of reference, I will name all the thinking parts as 'the left brain,' and the emotional and procedural parts that include the limbic system and reptilian brain as 'the right brain':

- *The Left Brain:* working memory, thinking brain including prefrontal cortex:
  - problem solving, analytical, rational, conceptual; coping ability (carries on with daily life regardless of what happens); ability to learn from experience and to tell stories, with verbal and narrative memory; ability to have insights, judgments and draw conclusions.
  - has no direct connection to the amygdala, but the frontal lobes can notice and 'label' body and emotional reactions as 'just memory.' It can send a signal to the limbic system that 'we are safe' rather than in danger, which can "turn off" the amygdala.[24 25]
- *The Right Brain:* survival brain, comprising the limbic system and reptilian brain:
  - the amygdala; the noticing brain (awareness, sensations, movements, curiosity); nonverbal language; emotional and sensory memory.
  - reactive to body sensations, with fearful expectations that a danger *will* happen again; 'on guard' with focus on the past and no concept of time.[26, 27]

The survival system in the brain is hierarchical, so the older reptilian and limbic systems can override, or trump, the more modern complex systems of the thinking brain. Also, communication between the two sides of the brain can be restricted for survival. Thus 80 percent of the messages go up from the reptilian brain, and the executive control of the higher thinking brain is bypassed.

The Limbic System and the Reptilian Brain

The reptilian brain and limbic system work together, largely below our conscious thinking, which allows us to have our higher thinking functions. The reptilian brain learns procedural activities such as making a cup of tea, brushing our teeth, or playing a piece of music on the piano. It also scans for danger and monitors emotions, feelings, and sensations all of the time without us having to use our conscious brain. But this can leave us vulnerable if they are triggering alerts that send us into high arousal or shutdown at things that are not life-threatening. Because they are below our conscious level of awareness, we can feel confused or ashamed of our behaviour, or reactions, because we do not know why we reacted in a certain way. The amygdala is like the smoke detector in the brain, but it has no hotline to communicate to the thinking parts of the brain. If it gets triggered, it has only two choices: either delay pressing the alarm for a few milliseconds to check briefly with

Table 7.1 . Possible dysregulation in the system of the supervisee

Survival tactic	*Activation state*	*Examples*
Homeostasis	In the window of tolerance/ Ventral vagal	Able to self-regulate and seek support. Digest food and make choices. This is where we want to be.
Fight	Sympathetic nervous system	Anger, rage, verbal, and physical violence. Passive-aggressive.
Flight	Sympathetic nervous system	Impulse to run, escape BUT if that is not possible, a person: a) may go into a freeze or flop. b) may dissociate in their minds as the body cannot leave. This ranges from daydreaming to numbing out mentally and actually leaving our bodies. c) may use distractions to numb distress: addictions, work, exercise, drugs, alcohol, or pharmaceutical drugs
Freeze	Sympathetic nervous system	High tension in the body like a rabbit in the headlights. People who use this resource a lot often report symptoms like fibromyalgia.
Food	Sympathetic nervous system	Either eat all the time or limit food. If we view this through the survival lens, if you feel there is imminent life threat, you will not eat as you may need to run at any moment. If you feel there is a perceived threat or a possible shortage of food in the future, you can eat to store fat to use later. This can become an ingrained pattern or habit.
Fawning	Sympathetic nervous system	Wanting to please the people around you, in order to feel safe.
(F) Reproduction	Sympathetic nervous system or dorsal vagal	Either too much—seeking connection without relational depth. or too little—not feeling safe to be that vulnerable.
Fart	Hypo-arousal/dorsal vagal	When we are operating persistently in the DVN the main thing left running is our gut, which can lead to dysregulated gut symptoms and inflammation. This often shows up as Crohn's disease and irritable bowel.
Flop	Hypo-arousal/ dorsal vagal	Collapse, as an animal drops to the ground and feigns death so the predator goes away. People who use this a lot often display symptoms similar to chronic fatigue syndrome and ME.

the left brain via the hippocampus or go straight for the panic alarm via the hypothalamus, thus raising the autonomic nervous system onto high alert. The autonomic nervous system will be expanded on later, but essentially it operates as an accelerator, and brake, on levels of energetic activation in our body. This turns off the parts of the brain that generate and store speech,[28] retuning our hearing for danger[29] and using the procedural responses already programmed in the brain for fight, flight, or freeze/collapse. But the thinking part of our brain can communicate with the activation if it becomes aware of a problem: it can notice, offer support, and calm the whole system.

When we learn to drive a car, we have to practice. We have to focus and use our full brain capacity, but then our reptilian brain and muscle memory take over by remembering the procedural patterns for us. Once we have learnt the procedural process of driving the car, our amygdala (like a smoke detector) monitors for any problems or dangers, thus freeing us to start thinking, as we drive, about what we are going to cook for dinner tonight or say at our next meeting. If the amygdala picks up on a problem, there are the two routes which this information can take through the brain: Route one: If, for example, a child is spotted on the kerb, and there is not deemed to be an immediate threat to our life, the brain takes the time to check the large filing system in the left brain for information. In this case, the alert signal routes through the hippocampus. Messages are now sent to raise this into your consciousness, and you realise that your leg has already started to press the brake and your eyes have orientated to the child. You drive past slowly and all is well. Now your hippocampus can make a story that you survived and that can be stored for the next time. This slows us down so that we can respond, rather than react, to the event. Route two: This happens if someone runs into the road in front of you. In this case, there is an immediate threat to life. There is no time to check with the brain's filing system, so the alarm is sent straight to the hypothalamus. The thinking brain is completely bypassed, and we have no conscious awareness of what is happening. At the same time, two other areas of the brain are bypassed, which generate speech and help us store memory in the form of words, because we do not need them in times of extreme threat. Within millionths of milliseconds, our body has slammed on the brake. At that point, our conscious brain wakes back up to see what has happened. But all we can do at this point is to try and make sense of what has happened. Therefore, people who have had accidents, or felt under extreme psychological threat from another person, are not always able to tell you what happened. They make sense of it later, but often do not have a declarative memory of the actual events. Following traumatic situations or a very difficult meeting, we need to help the supervisee notice that they did survive. This may sound strange, but that information needs to be stored in the thinking brain, otherwise parts can live trapped in the moment of fear, trying to '*fix*' what was '*wrong*' then.'[30]

NOTICING

If someone feels threatened in a relational situation, noticing body sensations and realising you are suddenly feeling anger or fear, will allow the conscious mind to assess the situation for life threat, but it can only do this if it has time. Once the alarm is raised, the prefrontal cortex has been seen to go dark (offline) on brain scans and it can take time to come back online.

Animal defence responses—these include fight/flight, fear/freeze, submit, and cry for help.[31] It can be helpful to notice these as your supervisee is speaking. Our brain sees the world through our own individual, unique perspective. It is alert for any danger that could affect our survival. It can make meaning out of any new experience, but the meaning may be based on implicit bias that is honed from previous experiences, which are embedded deep in our nonverbal trauma logic, and not from a wider perspective possible through the left brain. If we are exhausted or triggered, we are more likely to react to something through the threat/hypothalamus route which bypasses the thinking brain. Inviting your supervisee to pause for a moment before responding can help them take that skill into the workplace.

UNDERSTANDING NONVERBAL BODY MEMORY

The amygdala comes online four weeks before we are born and starts scanning for danger. How can we tell what the amygdala is scanning for?

A Story to Illustrate How the Smell of Coffee Can Become Dangerous

- Act 1: Imagine you are walking past a coffee shop and suddenly you are mugged. Implicit neuroception (our body's radar system for external threats)[32] picked up on: 1) a man in a Day-Glo jacket; 2) there was a particular gray paving stone; 3) the smell of coffee; and 4) it was a sunny day. These four things are now suspect for the amygdala and are to be monitored. Every time your neuroception picks up on any one of them, your autonomic nervous system will go up a notch.
- Act 2: Some years later, you fall and break your leg on: 1) the same gray paving stone; and 2) it was a sunny day; and 3) there was the smell of coffee. Now these features go higher up the watch list.
- Act 3: Some months later, you have an upsetting row with someone you care about, and there is the smell of coffee in the room.

Now the smell of coffee will activate the fear and defence systems in your autonomic nervous system. Every time you are around the smell of coffee, you may notice your heartbeat rise, your breathing rate increase, your body tense a little, and you are more alert to danger. This, in turn, means you are more likely to become dysregulated and less likely to make clear rational decisions.

How Can We Tell What Our Amygdala Is Scanning For?

We can become aware of what the amygdala is scanning for if we start to become curious and notice shifts in our body, the activation levels in our autonomic nervous system, or patterns of negative thinking. Apart from the autonomic nervous system activation that operates out of our awareness, parts of us can become scared of certain situations as well, and they can ramp up the activation of the autonomic nervous system. The thinking brain has no idea what is happening, but it knows there is fear and panic in the system. Signals start flying from gut to brain—the brain is flooded with stress hormones (cortisol, adrenaline)—the heart and lungs speed up—we may have thoughts that this did not go well last time—our body may tense—this changes our voice—we start to feel hot or cold—panicky—other people around us sense we are tense. The mind picks this up and panics as it does not know what the problem is—we become conscious and either start worrying what the problem is or realise that we have already reacted, or are reacting, to the danger. Parts can start running round like headless chickens inside, worried that no one is in control. If we are unaware of our own physical reactions, the first thing we notice may be other people's reactions and think they are being 'off' with us. This can lead to miscommunication and mistrust in both people present as our neuroception triggers both of us. The earlier we can spot these patterns, the quicker we can:

1. notice the activation.
2. name it as a part that has been triggered.
3. try to spot patterns and be curious about what has triggered us.
4. let the part know it is not on its own and we are there noticing it with our Self energy and our adult.
5. extend our out breath slightly to help bring the parasympathetic (calming systems in our body) online.
6. make a story that we survived this time.
7. update the part in terms of time.
8. make a mental note to anticipate a problem with coffee next time we smell it.
9. your amygdala will not remember but gradually as you notice and load information into the left brain, your millisecond reaction can become a response.

What You Might See in Your Supervisee

- What you might see in your supervisee are things like irrational, out-of-character, reactions to something; they are overfocused on a particular topic or person, resulting in them looping round the subject without finding a next step; and, if a way forward is identified, they are unable to put it into action. If they become agitated, anxious, or stressed, they are either unable to hold healthy boundaries with the volume of work that they are doing or become exhausted and overwhelmed at the thought of work.
- They may become disempowered and lose confidence in themselves and their ability, resulting in their feeling threatened by events and communication with certain people.
- Common addictions in clergy are overwork and perfectionism, but when they have pushed themselves as far as they can, their body will try to stop them with physical ailments.
- They say things like:
  - 'I just reacted and did not know why.'
  - 'I just felt I had to get out of the room.'
  - 'I was not able to think of a good reply in the moment.'
  - 'I cannot cope with chairing another meeting.'

Window of Tolerance

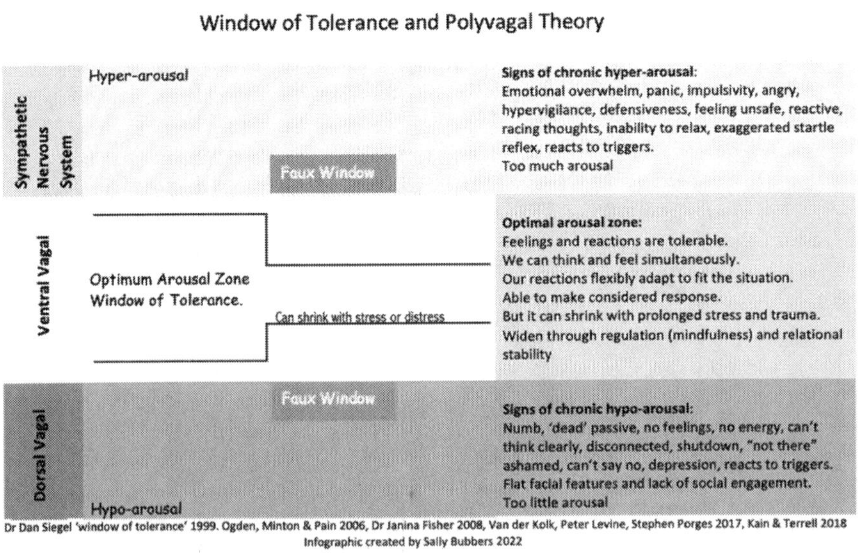

Figure 7.1

We all have a window of tolerance, or optimal arousal zone. Children are born with a small tolerance for distress. We develop our own window, dependent on the level of safety we feel in our bodies, but that can shrink under stress or distress. When our tolerance levels are low, we can get thrown out of it (triggered) quicker and then we do not have such a wide optimal zone to operate in.[33] Kain and Terrell have added to the idea that people who are living with a permanently narrow window of tolerance develop strategies to operate in a 'faux' window of tolerance, which sits just inside the hyper- and hypo-arousal areas. This feels to them like the optimum arousal zone, but they do not know that a greater state of calm is possible.[34] It has been shown that contemplative practices which bring us into the present moment can help widen our window of tolerance.

Stephen Porges, in his paper 'Polyvagal Theory: A Science of Safety,' reflects on how we have come to accept the phrase, 'I think, therefore I am' (Descartes), ignoring our felt sense[35] of body, emotions, and feelings. Porges says that we have to be able to feel ourselves in order to fully exist: 'I feel myself, I exist.' Cues of threat and safety are not under voluntary control, so we need to find ways to monitor them. Feelings of safety form the basis of our ability to navigate the social world. Darwin's belief around the 'survival of the fittest' has led to the cultural veneration of strength and aggression, but we are social mammals who need to learn how to cooperate and co-regulate in proximity to other humans.[36] If we are permanently hypervigilant and expectant of danger at any moment, it does not take much for us to overreact. We have multiple alarm systems within our body and brain that operate like guards at 'look out' posts. The network of sensors that monitor our external world are called by Porges neuroception[37], and they assess for safety, danger or life threat, and the sensory network of our internal world, which he calls interoception—our 'sixth sense.'[38] These systems, which continuously monitor for signs of threat and safely, are not under our voluntary control.[39] Any one of them can set off the alarm systems in our bodies. If we are living with permanently high stress, any additional agitation, worry, or concern can send panic through the system. If we are not able to bring our adult conscious attention to this, we can go into our preprogrammed defence strategies learned in childhood. This happens in milliseconds, turning down our capacity for higher 'logical' thinking. This presents a problem if you are trying to chair a meeting or make complex relational negotiations. Alarm messages can be sent around the system at any level, but if we ignore the early warning signs, we can live in permanent levels of vigilance which reduce our window of tolerance, resulting in any further threat being read as a potential threat to life. This may sound extreme to you, but that is the implicit reality within our physiological and psychological assessment of the danger. We can react instantaneously to danger, but also to lower levels of activation. Blending information from our interoception and neuroception, we observe, and assess, the intentions behind the actions of others, the warmth and prosody of voices around us, and facial expressions. Feelings of safety form the basis of social connection, but our systems were devised to survive in a hostile world where a smell on the wind, or the sound of a snapping twig may be a lion heading toward us.

THE POLYVAGAL THEORY

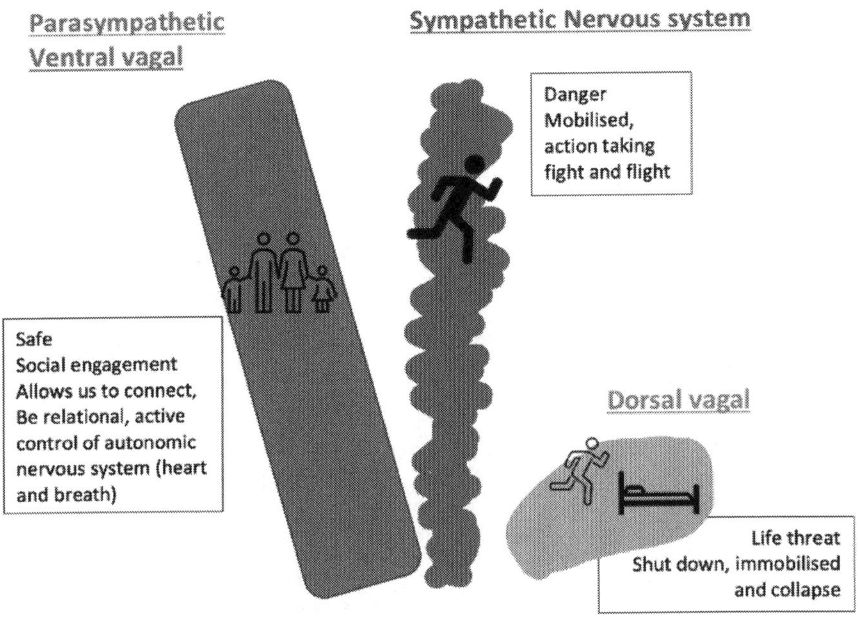

Figure 7.2

The autonomic nervous system is made up of the sympathetic nervous system, which is 400 million years old, and the parasympathetic nervous system. This is made up of the two branches of the vagus nerve, comprising the ventral vagal nerve, which is 200 million years old, and the dorsal vagal nerve, which is 500 million years old. They divide at the diaphragm—the dorsal having control below the diaphragm/gut and ventral vagal above.[40] The ventral is the newest part and is myelinated, which means that signals can move very fast. Eighty percent of the fibres in the vagus nerve travel up from the gut to the brain, while 10 to 20 percent travel down. The ventral vagal nerve can be equated to the optimal arousal zone in the window of tolerance. The sympathetic arousal equates to hyperarousal. This is when people can become highly activated, angry, or compulsively busy. The dorsal vagal nerve equates to hypoarousal of the window of tolerance. A dorsal vagal shutdown can look like someone is depressed. They tend to lose facial tone and signs of social engagement, and the middle ear tenses, which affects hearing. The main thing left running in the body is the gut. People can go into a sort of hibernation. Ventral is a place where we can regulate our internal stability, emotionally and physically, and have control over our breathing and heart rate: we can speed them up, or slow them down, by choice, even while external conditions may be changing.[41] It is sometimes called 'rest and digest,' or 'homeostasis.' We can think clearly because we have our full thinking brain online. We can store memories with language and generate fresh creative thoughts and language. The implications of this for communication is that you will not be able to have a productive, reflective session with a supervisee, and be able to explore creative ways to address a problem, if they are not within their ventral vagal or optimal arousal zone. And you will not be able to support them, or help interactive regulation, if you are not within your ventral vagal or optimal arousal zone as well. This is a challenging reality. We are created with multiple parts, each of which has its own core of self-energy, but, beginning with our life in the womb, we start to face challenges. As we enter the world, children have to find ways to remain in connection to their caregivers or they will die. This can be very challenging if the people you depend on for care, shelter, food, and relational connection are psychologically and/or physically wounding in any way. Dan Siegel talks about the dilemmas of a caregiver being unavailable, frightened, or frightening to a child. When a caregiver is chaotic or rigid, or unpredictable, this is very scary for a child (and the adults around them).[42, 43] Often children have to deny their reality to remain in connection, and they have it denied by others who do not admit any fault.

As pastoral supervisors, we model listening, letting the person feel heard and that we understand their perspective. But are we able to model saying, 'I got that wrong,' and owning our mistakes? Church leaders can feel that they ought to have an answer or view on everything, and consequently find it hard to ask for help, say they do not know, or admit fault. We can model that for them to copy. Validating someone's experience is also very important. Clergy can be disempowered if they learnt to shut down as a child into the dorsal vagal around people whom they found it hard to connect with. We can affirm their experience, and this can help to open space inside them and build trust.

MODERN-DAY STRESS AND NEUROPLASTICITY

Dan Siegel has a saying, "neurons that fire together, wire together."[44] If we continually experience anxiety and autonomic nervous system activation in a certain situation, then the stress and fear circuits can be activated as we mentally ruminate about it or anticipate the situation. The body becomes primed to react faster next time, as the highway of neural messaging becomes well-worn and faster. The reshaping of neural pathways is called 'neuroplasticity' and can be used for negative and positive change in our brain structure.[45] Our bodies do not recognise the difference between the threat of a lion attack, endless mental stress, or the church meeting. They react in the same way, unless we notice that there is a difference. A supervisee may have a visceral feeling that they will not survive the parish meeting, despite their thinking brain knowing that they are unlikely to lose their life. Our systems are designed to react to short-term stress, which, in the case of running away from a lion, would be accompanied by physical exertion to burn off the adrenaline. But in our modern-day life, we live with persistent ongoing stress, while often spending hours doing sedentary administrative tasks on the computer. The first sign that you, or your supervisee, may be going into adrenal fatigue is if you start to wake up tired in the morning and start to feel tired all day long, even after getting a good night's sleep.[46] This can result in the "amplification of numerous inflammatory pathways and increased susceptibility to developing inflammatory diseases, including autoimmune diseases, mood disorders. . . . (and) chronic fatigue syndrome."[47] Noticing rumination, or automatic negative thoughts, provides another way to calm our system. Our brains can fall into these as a persistent habit that drains our energy. Using the skills we have learnt, through mindful contemplative practices, to notice them, helps to calm our whole system. Whenever we notice an automatic negative thought, I would suggest recognising it as a part that is worried about something. Check if the part believes it is true, and if the answer is 'yes,' acknowledge that, and then you can spend a few moments checking if another part of your adult has other information. This can help settle the system and bring the worried part up to date with a realistic assessment of the situation.[48] Environmental situations and complex relational dynamics cannot always be changed, but we can help our supervisees to find ways of *being*, so that the situation does not drain them as much, and they have better emotional boundaries and take less stress into their home.

TRIBAL THINKING

Ken Wilber speaks of how we can progress through various stages of development:[49]

- *Grow up* through the early stages of emotional maturing.
- *Clean up*, doing the shadow work with the legacy of trauma (and I would suggest that some of the burdened parts quash space for our Self energy/ God essence as we are weighed down by old patterns, beliefs, and self-criticism which were laid down so long ago that we do not even notice them). By noticing and honouring the roles these had for our survival we can make space for spiritual growth.
- *Wake up* through spiritual practices like contemplation.
- *Show up* in the world as a more congruent person, who is able to be flexible, adaptable, and a more stable person, so we may make space for our True Self where God can dwell.

Without cleaning up and waking up, humans can get stuck in, or revert, in a crisis to tribal thinking, and utter self-centredness. Actually, these are developmental stages that are connected to group safety and individuation. But again, noticing is the key, and this is another pattern we can notice in ourselves and others. As adults, it can feel safer if we form groups around belief and joint identity. Looking at the wider context of trauma in our society, and the impact on our clergy, the next example may not be relevant to your situation, but the principles can be drawn out and applied. The COVID-19 pandemic generated some level of fear in many people. I heard someone say, 'physiologically, it was like having a sniper on the loose outside your door, and you never knew if anyone you met could be hiding a weapon.' As far as our bodies were concerned, no one could be trusted. There was real fear for our lives. Fear controlled us, and that drove us into our tribal mentality to determine who, and what, was safe, putting our autonomic nervous system on high alert for much of the time. We never knew if it was safe to step outside or bring anything, or anyone, into our homes. Then on top of that, we had the divisions generated around vaccination and mask wearing. This led to scapegoating to help people feel safe and a part of the tribe. In Britain, COVID-19 came on the heels of Brexit, which drove wedges into our society, forming tribal camps, even within families. Once groups of people start to form like this, they can look for subgroups to connect with as well. Then we had the 'Black Lives Matter' and 'Living in Love and Faith,' and the massive reorganisation within many dioceses and local churches. When we look at this though a trauma lens, and add the instability around in the world caused by the political, energy, and food problems as compounded by global climate change, it is hardly surprising that clergy are having to deal with fractured and tribal groups, who are looking for similarity and places of connection and are alert to difference. This leads to people making instant assessments about people and groups. Demarcation lines are drawn up in an instant largely based on implicit bias. As I write, there is a legacy of tribal thinking which I believe has not helped clergy, as they have returned to 'church' after COVID-19 and are hit by the reorganisation which many dioceses are undertaking in the Church of England. Suddenly, the vicar is the enemy, changing old patterns of services because they now have extra churches to cover, or the village church may even be closing. This understanding can help the supervisee not to take it so personally. Many are living with a narrow window of tolerance, and with a legacy of exhaustion which they cannot see how to remedy. Norma Howes, a child forensic psychologist,[50] has a helpful way of alerting you to underlying dysregulation in the system of a supervisee. All of these can be triggered in milliseconds through the triggering system:

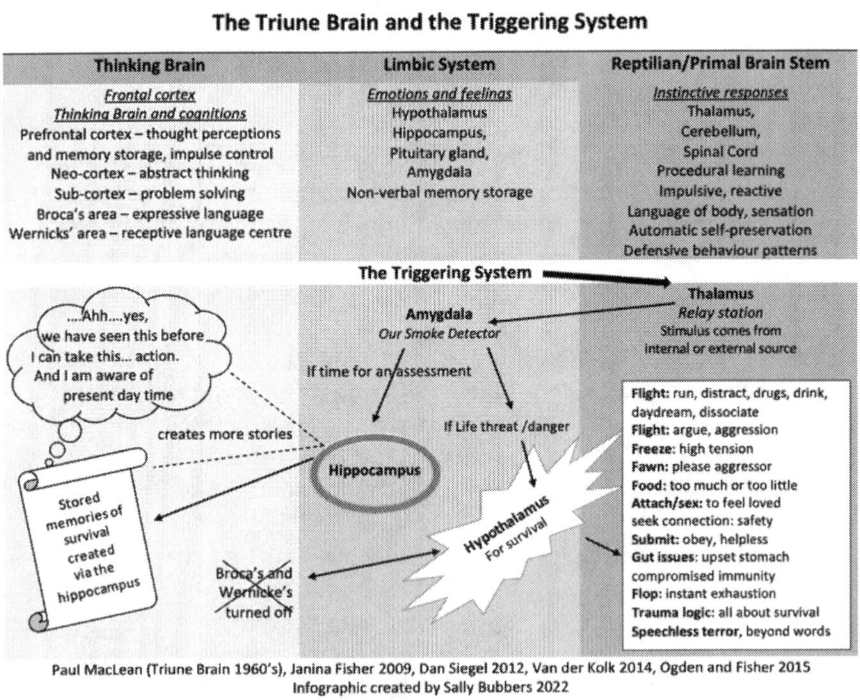

Figure 7.3

I am curious if you are starting to see patterns of behaviour in yourself and your supervisees. Do you have a supervisee who is unable to take action to address an intractable problem, or who is physically afraid of tackling a problem within their Church, but who is not really able to verbalise why? Any solution you explore is not actioned over months, and they may avoid, or fear, going to a meeting. Have they been struck down with exhaustion, or display agitation, or shut down in your sessions?

INTEGRATING THESE UNDERSTANDINGS INTO SUPERVISION

Pause to take in anything positive, however small. Sometimes a supervisee may mention something that went well, but rush past that to the problem they want to reflect on. We all have a negativity bias in our brains to ensure that bad things never happen again. This was very helpful when negative events could be life threatening. Rick Hanson talks about how the negativity bias means that negative experiences stick like Velcro in our memories, while positive things slip off, as if on Teflon.[51] We can change this pattern by pausing to notice the good thing for a few seconds. This helps to redress the balance, helping us to feel more positive about life in general.

George: I think I did a bit better chairing the PCC meeting this month, but the arguments about evensong go on. So, I want to focus on that today.

Supervisor: Would it be OK if we pause a moment? I think I heard you say you did a better job at chairing the PCC meeting.

George: Yes, I did.

Supervisor: Could you say a bit more about that, and how you know you did a bit better?

George: I was not so agitated before the meeting because I did what you suggested and noticed the worry beforehand. Then it just didn't feel so stressful, and when I noticed myself getting agitated, I checked my feet were on the ground, and then I noticed I was slumping in my chair, so I sat up straighter and made my out-breath longer. It really seemed to work. It was still difficult, but I was calmer.

Supervisor: What are you noticing now as you tell me about this?

George: I had not really noticed how well I did.

Supervisor: Can you take that in now?

George: Yes, that feels good.

Supervisor How can you tell it feels good?

George: I can breathe, and there is not the same dread as I think about it.

Supervisor: That feels good to notice. Maybe you can remember that next time as well.

Does it feel OK to shift back to evensong now?

NOTICE HOW THEY 'TELL' THEIR STORY TO YOU

Try and get into the habit of being really curious about the nonverbal story that their body is telling, and see if that fits with the words that are coming out of their mouth:

- Is there a part saying, 'I am OK,' or 'I can handle this,' but maybe their shoulders are drooping.
- Do they start to slump with a sense of being weighed down with the weight of it all?
- Do their hands fidget or form fists? Maybe they feel angry or threatened?
- Do their feet tuck under the chair? Maybe they feel trapped and cannot see a way out?
- Do they cross their arms and look out of the window, possibly defensive or seeking an escape? Sometimes supervisees can feel nervous of what you might be thinking about the way they handled a situation, which is bringing up shame and the self-critic.
- Does the tone, pitch, pace, or volume of their voice change?
- Does their body tense or pull back as they talk?

If we, as supervisors, notice anything about our supervisee that may connect to information in this chapter, we can make a choice about whether to comment or not, but it is good to notice. We have to be very careful not to make the observation sound like a criticism of them. So, this needs to be offered in a tentative and gentle way. Can you be curious about what you are feeling in your body, or emotionally, as you listen? We can use this information to empathise with our supervisee. If we use the language of parts to understand our resonance, often we find there is a part that is emotionally connecting with the supervisee as they speak.

IS THE SUPERVISEE OVERFOCUSED ON A NEGATIVE EVENT?

Overfocusing is part of the freeze response, and people can become obsessed with an individual or subject. You may notice that they become very still, and they have a persistent gaze in one direction, as though they are looking through a restricted tube at the world, as if they are reliving the event or relational breach that they are describing. Because the neurobiological freeze has been triggered, they will also feel more threatened internally than you may expect from looking at the outside, and also the thinking brain will be working with limited capacity. Interventions that can help this situation are to invite them to look at something else and, particularly, to move their neck muscles. This initiates the orientating response which can help break the over focusing.

Boundaries: We often talk about boundaries in terms of under-boundaried people who allow others to push them around, and over-boundaried people who do not let people in. There are also those who have no respect for other people's boundaries and invade psychological and personal space. Personal and work boundaries are often a big issue for clergy. Their work is such a big part of their identity that it can go right to the core of who they are in God. This means that they sometimes develop strategies that override their vulnerability and have strong internal boundaries that prevent them from being truly present and congruent or prevent them from counting the personal cost of their ministry. This only becomes evident when they are no longer able to cope, or their bodies get ill under the strain. The parts that drive them on, with no consideration for their personal well-being, can be hard on other people as well. People who we find 'difficult' are often either over-, or under, -boundaried. Our perception of that can be determined by how they interact with our own boundaries.

Understanding confusing and contradictory behaviour: From my experience of working with people who lived with feelings of being overwhelmed that were too great for them to integrate as a child, their body was endlessly sending up alarm messages, and their brain started ignoring them because they were interfering with the job of getting on with life. I find it easier to understand this in terms of parts. Distressed parts get stuck in time; our protectors find ways of ignoring the distress in order to prioritise survival (connection to the caregiver and getting on with life). It can take a lot of energy to suppress these feelings and fears. If we continue to ignore the distressed parts, they can start to shout louder, and symptoms of anxiety or anger can flare through sympathetic arousal or depression in an effort to shut down. As we grow older, these parts get stuck in time and struggle to transition their strategies into the adult world, often continuing to drive people-pleasing and perfectionism. Other parts develop ways of relating in the adult world, and they often run our lives, and are what the world sees; they determinedly drive us on. Janina Fisher calls them our 'going on with normal life'[52] parts, but they can struggle to keep distress at bay in our personal thoughts and life, as they endeavour to conform to expected and acceptable 'good' behaviour. Parts can be triggered by our autonomic nervous system and also drive levels of activation, or help to calm it. When it comes to understanding confusing behaviour, or entrenched situations, the first question which we need to ask ourselves is, 'how does this behaviour benefit the person?' Is it a way of distracting away from or defending a vulnerability?

Stress—and anxiety—a cognitive strategy to help think things through: It can be helpful to be curious about what is affecting the supervisee, personally, or what they may be experiencing as personal. There is a subtle difference, and it can be helpful to notice. Once the stress and anxiety start, it can continue to loop and fuel automatic negative thoughts, so that then we may wonder what is being driven from internal worry, or what is being driven from external events triggering the internal system. The final question is to ask what they have control or influence over? Often, we do not have control over external events, though we may have some influence. If we cannot influence the external, perhaps we can consider acknowledging that there is nothing that we can do and turn our attention to what we can influence inside ourselves.

Body structure: Body structure has a big impact on how others perceive us, and how we feel inside ourselves. Muscles can lock in memories as the neural feedback from our own structure affects our mood, and the way we are able to interact with other people. As an experiment, try slumping in your chair, as if you have the world on your shoulders. Notice if your face goes flat and see if it is hard to smile. Notice how your energy becomes heavy and slumps down, making it hard to take a full breath. It is also hard to look around from this place, to orientate to a new direction or connect to someone else. Now try saying 'I am happy.' Is that hard? Now sit up, lengthen your spine and let yourself breathe. Move your head and look around you. What do you notice is different in this place? Can you think of something that makes you happy and notice the ability to smile has returned?[53] Our human brains monitor the body structure of others, but unless we consciously notice our own, we are not aware of its silent influence on our mood. When we are in sessions with our supervisees, the body can speak louder than their words.[54] How we notice what other people are saying, is read implicitly and not just through the actual words. They may say, 'I am fine,' but can you notice what is happening in their body? Is there a slight slump in their shoulders, or a body collapse, or does one hand make a fist? The neck may tighten, or they may pull back, or lean forward.

Consequences of dysregulation: Dysregulation will always happen, but what we can help change is the speed at which it happens in our daily lives, and how quickly we can notice and recover. Moving from reacting (which happens in milliseconds) to a chosen response can be learnt. These psychological, physiological, and neurological understandings can be helpful. They enable me to sit with a troubled supervisee with greater compassion; and if a supervisee is confused about their inability to control their reactions, or understand the behaviours of other people, my sharing of some of this information, and thereby normalising the situation, can be settling and bring some calm to their system. In the previous chapter (chapter 6), I explained the concept of Internal Family Systems.[55] From this perspective, you can understand that individual parts of us can press the alarm buttons in our body and mind, as they react to internal thoughts of threat or to external triggers.[56] We can only intervene to support ourselves if we are able to notice some of the 'tells' in our body, which significantly happen outside of our conscious awareness,[57] alerting us that we are leaving, or have left, our ventral vagal or our optimal arousal zone.

Bringing things to mind in the session (present moment mindfulness):[58] We have Mirror Neurons in our brain that can bring things up in our bodies, as if they were happening now. This includes changing our body structure toward a brace, or collapse, or maybe revving up the autonomic nervous system, or feeling we have no energy to go and tackle that problem today. This can be useful to observe in the supervision session and see if you can help the supervisee notice the somatic signs in their system. Once they have noticed them, they can start to do that in the world. If, for example, you rehearse a conversation that the minister is going to have with a church warden, or elder, before you start the practice, invite them to start thinking about the conversation, pause, and ask them to check how they are feeling as they think about doing it, while they are in your office. We can get ourselves very agitated thinking about a conversation. So, by the time we get there, we have already left our optimal zone/ventral vagal, arriving at the meeting with very little calm available and prefrontal cortex to help. I find the language of parts helpful here, because often when we become blended with a fearful or agitated part of us, we feel that is who we are. To reframe that as a part of you which feels nervous about having this conversation, leaves space for other parts that may be able to provide support.

Building resilience: Developmental trauma affects the ability to set boundaries and be interdependent, often learning that self-reliance is the only option. This impacts on the development of the brain and body.

I wonder if you think that I am talking about noticing, curiosity, and mindfulness a lot. These are key to building resilience and starting to widen the window of tolerance and move people into ventral vagal. Following six weeks of mindfulness practice, the amygdala is less reactive, the hypothalamus can grow, and the lining of the brain thickens.[59] It is incredibly powerful. There are now books that offer ways to notice and take in good things,[60] and also tone the vagus nerve, which can support whole-body regulation. Human beings utilize two modes of regulation. These are defined as: 1) *interactive regulation*: the ability to utilize relationships to help if you start to become either shut down or need to calm yourself. Infants are dependent upon interactive regulation to survive and then gradually learn to develop autoregulation; and 2) *autoregulation*: the ability to self-regulate, independent of other people. A healthy regulation in an adult means that they can flexibly use both. Key here is learning the ability to calm ourselves without going into a dorsal vagal shutdown.[61] We can help supervisees widen the gap from reaction to response by:

- Helping supervisees experience both interactive and autoregulation within the supervision relationship, by modelling this for them and helping them notice if they are leaving their window of tolerance, so that they do not become dysregulated or overwhelmed when talking about something that is upsetting them in sessions;
- Widening your window of tolerance via prayerful mindfulness, breath, grounding, rainbow ball;
- Curiously noticing yourself and others;
- Encouraging supervisees to notice what happens in a session as they think about a stressful situation;
- Encouraging them to be curious if they are overfocused on the problem;
- If they are not able to pray for someone, it can be helpful for them to speak blessings over them. This is an act of compassion;
- Practicing pausing, and noticing anything that is good or positive which they may 'gloss' over to get to the problem topic in the session. Help them to take in the good positive by noticing their physical reactions. Ask, 'what happens when you think about that?,' in the hope that they can notice their body structure change, their breath deepen and slow, and their feeling calmer.

WHEN SUPERVISEES ARE STRUGGLING

We all have parts that seek reassurance that our reactions are normal. When people get triggered, they tend to feel they are a failure, are unable to cope and become self-critical and lose confidence. I would invite you to share any of this information that you feel may help normalise their reactions. Here are some examples of how you might introduce some of this information:

- When we get stressed, we can lose our thinking capacity.
- We can get stressed and anxious just thinking about meeting someone, so it can help to practice settling ourselves before we meet them.
- If you notice yourself becoming agitated, it can help to lengthen your out-breath as you exhale—would you like to practice that now and see if you notice any change?
- Sometimes people can have protective parts that come up to protect their vulnerability.
- Our window of tolerance shrinks when we are under stress.
- We can feel very tired if we get overwhelmed: it is called a dorsal vagal shutdown and we can feel very negative and depressed.

Mindfulness/contemplative practices/Focusing Ball: I often hear that the worries and the busy life of clergy intrude in their quiet times. Over time, and in long service, they can become adept at spiritual bypassing[62] with doing, rather than being, because they do not want to sit quietly and be bothered by worry and anxiety. I am a great supporter of contemplative practices. They teach us to settle ourselves, to be able to spend time being present, and listening to God. As we still ourselves, we start to notice body sensations, feelings, emotions and thoughts. I find some of the language of *letting go* or *watching them pass on by* to be unhelpful from a parts perspective, as it can leave parts feeling ignored and pushed away. This can lead to them endlessly interrupting your prayer time as they keep popping up to get your attention. I would encourage the supervisee to notice these as parts. I would suggest that they ask the parts to give them space before they start; then as each thought surfaces, notice it as a part, and check, 'how do I feel toward this part?' If they are not feeling any qualities of Self energy, then maybe that is the work for the quiet time. But, if they can talk with the parts as suggested earlier in this chapter, then they can ask the part to soften, and let it know they will come back later if it needs attention. This allows them to be in your Self Energy, connected with God in that moment. The *Focusing Ball* exercise is described below and grew out of my desire to have a short grounding exercise to offer, which included an introduction to mindfulness and helped widen their 'window of tolerance.' It can be completed in about three minutes, which I find is long enough for people to notice a difference in levels of activation in their bodies, but short enough for them to start integrating it into their daily life. I have found all ages report carrying the balls with them in their pockets or handbags. High levels of activation, which can lead to panic attacks or intrusive worrying thoughts, can be present in supervisees. So, the worksheet below is written for calming, with the longer out-breath to help activate the parasympathetic.

Focusing Ball grounding exercise

Start breathing in and out at your own pace, not forcing anything

Breath in
1
2
3, pause
Breath out
1
2
3
4, pause

Notice where the 'in' breath goes.
if it is high in your chest, gently try and send it a little further down into your belly

The longer out breath calms the body

Start breathing following the instructions on the left

- Hold the ball in your hand and name or count the colours
- **Rate which colour** you are on the ball eg fizzy red, or calm blue?
- Look around you, moving your neck and name 5 things you can **see**
  Come back to you breath
- Name 3 things you can **hear**
  Come back to you breath
- Notice any **tension** in your body and move if you need to
  Come back to you breath
- Name and just notice any **sensation, emotion or feelings**
  Come back to you breath
- Name any **thoughts, words or images** in your head. Acknowledge them and let them know you will come back to them later
  Come back to you breath
- **Check inside** and see if anything has changed
- Now check and see if you feel any closer to the blue ring

Created by Sally Bubbers 2017

Figure 7.4

Moving the head (orienting) helps disrupt a potential freeze. Naming things around them can help introduce the skill of placing 'time and place' on the felt sensation or triggering event. Noticing the body is often a scary adventure for those who have stopped attending to alarm signals which their body has been sending out. Naming feelings, emotions, thoughts, images and words, can help them notice habitual patterns. If the supervisee is unable to go straight to their breath, they can hold the ball and name, or count, the colours. The 'rainbow' practice golf balls can easily be purchased on the internet.

CONCLUSION

I hope that you have gained an understanding of the following: feeling 'safe' is subjective and dependant on a calm autonomic nervous system regulated by the ventral vagal. Feelings of stress and anxiety can fuel threat and defence responses in our bodies, which have learnt to scan for danger in a unique way using information we have accumulated out of our conscious awareness throughout our life. We need to feel safe, allowing our 'social engagement system' to be online, in order to be able to interact socially and cooperate with other humans, and allow others to feel safe around us.[63] Secure adults are able to flexibly use self-regulation and coregulation interactively, when they need to.[64] This in turn allows them to function from a state of calm (ventral vagal, within their window of tolerance or optimal arousal zone) with their higher thinking functions online. When in a state of distress, we are unable to create explicit memories and stories. The experience is only stored via implicit memory, which can leave us confused about what is influencing our thoughts, decision making, feelings, and behaviours. Repair is possible from a place of calm with those around us, and also by creating stories via the hippocampus that make sense of our experience and acknowledge that we have survived.[65] There is much talk about 'resilience' in ministry, but if there is dysregulation in our core being, it will impact, and affect, our ability to socially interact and collaborate with others. Finding new ways of seeing ourselves and others can be challenging, but we can also become exhausted maintaining ways of relating that we developed in childhood; and the act of resisting change, holding our ground and defending our position, can drain us more in the long run.

Common addictions in clergy are overwork and perfectionism, but when they have pushed themselves as far as they can, their body will try to stop them with physical ailments in order to survive. Understanding how our neurobiology can influence our communication and behaviour patterns, which impact how we relate to people, has been helpful within my pastoral supervision practice. This information is relevant to everyone, but it has particularly supported me to find more compassionate ways to be present with my supervisees and helped them to have insights into systemic problems that they may be experiencing in their church, or with a specific individual with whom they are struggling.

BIBLIOGRAPHY

Ackerman, Courtney. "Twenty-Three Amazing Health Benefits of Mindfulness for Body and Brain." *PositivePsychology.com*. https://www.positivepsychology.com (accessed sept.29, 2022).

Amen Clinic. https://www.amenclinics.com/blog/mental-hygiene-is-just-as-important-as-washing-your-hands/ (accessed Aug. 2, 2022).

Cozolino, Louis. *The Neuroscience of Psychotherapy*. New York: W.W. Norton & Company, 2010.

Dana, Deb. *The Polyvagal Theory in Therapy: Engaging the Rhythm of Regulation*. New York: W. W. Norton & Company, 2018.

Felitti, Vincent J., Robert F. Anda, Dale Nordenberg, David F. Williamson, Alison M. Spitz, Valarie Edwards, Mary P. Koss, and James S. Marks. "Relationship of

Childhood Abuse and Household Dysfunction to Many of the Leading Causes of Death in Adults: The Adverse Childhood Experince Study (ACE)." *American Journal of Preventitve Medicine* 14, no. 4 (1998): 245–58.

Fisher, Janina. *Healing our Fragmented Selves*. New York: Routledge, 2017.

Guilliams, Thomas. *Adrenal Fatigue*. https://adrenalfatiguesolution.com/immune-system/ (accessed Aug. 22, 2022).

Hanson, Rick. *Resilient*. London: Ebury Publishing, 2018.

Heller, Diane. "Navigating the Labyrinth of Love: How Attachment Styles Sneak into Adult Relationships." https://dianepooleheller.com/wp-content/uploads/2018/12/Navigating-the-Labyrinth-of-Love.pdf (accessed Aug. 10, 2022).

Howes, Norma. "Trauma and the Body Workshop." Interview by Ffynnon in Wrexham, North Wales on 24 January, 2009.

Kain, Kathy L., and Stephen J. Terrell. *Nurturing Resilience: Helping Clients Move Forward from Developmental Trauma. An Integrative Somatic Approach*. Berkeley: North Atlantic Books, 2018.

Kurtz, Ron. *Body-Centered Psychotherapy: The Hakomi Method*. Mendocina: LifeRhythm, 2015.

Leach, Jane, and Michael Paterson. *Pastoral Supervision: A Handbook*. London: SCM Press, 2015.

Martin, James. *Becoming Who You Are: Insights on the True Self from Thomas Merton and Other Saints*. Mahwah, NJ: Hidden Springs, 2006.

Masters, Robert A. *Spiritual Bypassing: When Spirituality Disconnects Us From What Really Matters*. Berkeley: North Atlantic Books, 2010.

McGilchrist, Iain. *The Master and His Emissary*. London: Yale University Press, 2019.

Ogden, Pat, and Janina Fisher. *Sensorimotor Psychotherapy: Interventions for Trauma and Attachment*. New York: W.W. Norton & Company, 2015.

Porges, Stephen W. *The Pocket Guide to The Polyvagal Theory: The Transformative Power of Feeling Safe*. New York: W.W. Norton & Company, 2017.

———. "Polyvagal Theory: A Science of Safety." https://www.frontiersin.org/articles/10.3389/fnint.2022.871227/full (accessed Aug. 21, 2022).

Porges, Stephen W. *The Polyvagal Theory: Neurophysiological Foundatons of Emotions, Attachment, Communication, and Self-Regulation*. New York: W.W. Norton & Company, 2011.

Riemersma, Jenna. *Altogether You: Experiencing personal and spiritual transformation with Internal Family Systems Therapy*. Marietta, Georgia: Pivotal Press, 2020.

Schwartz, Richard C. *No Bad Parts*. Boulder, Colorado: Sounds True, 2021.

Siegel, Daniel J. *Pocket Guide to Interpersonal Neurobiology: An Integrative Handbook of the Mind*. New York: W.W. Norton & Company, 2012.

Van der Kolk, Bessel. *The Body Keeps The Score: Mind, Brain and the Body in the Transformation of Trauma*. London: Allen Lane, 2014.

Wilber, Ken. "Growing up, Cleaning up, Waking up, Showing up." Interview by Richard Rohr. The Centre for Action and Contemplation's Conspire Conference in Albuquerque, New Mexico in July 2017.

Yehuda, Rachel. "How Parents' Trauma Leaves Biological Traces in Children Adverse experiences can change future generations through epigenetic pathways." https://

www.scientificamerican.com/article/how-parents-rsquo-trauma-leaves-biological-traces-in-children/ (accessed Aug. 22, 2022).

Yehuda, Rachel, Nikolaos P. Daskalakis, Linda M. Bierer, Heather N. Bader, Torsten Klendel, Florian Holsboer and Elisabeth B. Binder. "Holocaust Exposure Induced Intergenerational Effects on FKBP5 Methylation." *Biological Psychiartry* 80, no. 5 (2016): 372–80.

NOTES

1. Daniel J. Siegel, *Pocket Guide to Interpersonal Neurobiology: An Integrative Handbook of the Mind* (New York: W.W. Norton & Company, 2012).
2. Janina Fisher. *Healing Our Fragmented Selves* (New York: Routledge, 2017).
3. Ibid.
4. Seigel, *Pocket Guide to Interpersonal Neurobiology.*
5. Pat Ogden and Janina Fisher. *Sensorimotor Psychotherapy: Interventions for Trauma and Attachment* (New York: W.W. Norton & Company, 2015).
6. Jenna Riemersma, *Altogether You: Experiencing Personal and Spiritual Transformation with Internal Family Systems Therapy* (Marietta, GA: Pivotal Press, 2020).
7. James Martin, *Becoming Who You Are: Insights on the True Self from Thomas Merton and Other Saints* (Mahwah, NJ: Hidden Springs, 2006).
8. Richard C. Schwartz, *No Bad Parts* (Boulder, CO: Sounds True, 2021).
9. Diane Heller, "*Navigating the Labyrinth of Love: How Attachment Styles Sneak into Adult Relationships*." https://dianepooleheller.com/wp-content/uploads/2018/12/Navigating-the-Labyrinth-of-Love.pdf (accessed Aug. 10, 2022).
10. Ron Kurtz, *Body-Centered Psychotherapy, The Hakomi Method* (Mendocina: LifeRhythm, 2015).
11. Fisher, *Healing Our Fragmented Selves.*
12. Seigel, *Pocket Guide to Interpersonal Neurobiology.*
13. Ibid.
14. Fisher, *Healing Our Fragmented Selves.*
15. Louis Cozolino, *The Neuroscience of Psychotherapy* (New York: W.W. Norton & Company, 2010), 146.
16. Seigel, *Pocket Guide to Interpersonal Neurobiology.*
17. Fisher, *Healing Our Fragmented Selves.*
18. Felitti, Vincent J., Robert F. Anda, Dale Nordenberg, David F. Williamson, Alison M. Spitz, Valarie Edwards, Mary P. Koss and James S. Marks. "Relationship of Childhood Abuse and Household Dysfunction to Many of the Leading Causes of Death in Adults: The Adverse Childhood Experince Study (ACE)." *American Journal of Preventative Medicine* 14, no. 4 (1998): 245–58.
19. Ogden and Fisher, "Sensorimotor Psychotherapy," 179.
20. Yehuda, Rachel, Nikolaos P. Daskalakis, Linda M. Bierer, Heather N. Bader, Torsten Klendel, Florian Holsboer and Elisabeth B. Binder. "Holocaust Exposure Induced Intergenerational Effects on FKBP5 Methylation." *Biological Psychiartry* 80, no. 5 (2016): 372–80.

21. Yehuda, Rachel. "How Parents' Trauma Leaves Biological Traces in Children Adverse experiences can change future generations through epigenetic pathways." https://www.scientificamerican.com/article/how-parents-rsquo-trauma-leaves-biological-traces-in-children/ (accessed Aug. 22, 2022).
22. Seigel, *Pocket Guide to Interpersonal Neurobiology.*
23. Rick Hanson, *Resilient* (London: Ebury Publishing, 2018).
24. Fisher, *Healing Our Fragmented Selves.*
25. Seigel, *Pocket Guide to Interpersonal Neurobiology.*
26. Ogden and Fisher, "Sensorimotor Psychotherapy."
27. Seigel, *Pocket Guide to Interpersonal Neurobiology.*
28. Ogden and Fisher, "Sensorimotor Psychotherapy."
29. Stephen W. Porges, *The Pocket Guide to The Polyvagal Theory: The Transformative Power of Feeling Safe* (New York: W.W. Norton & Company, 2017).
30. Fisher, *Healing Our Fragmented Selves.*
31. Ibid.
32. Stephen W. Porges, *The Polyvagal Theory: Neurophysiological Foundatons of Emotions, Attachment, Communication, and Self-Regulation* (New York: W.W. Norton & Company, 2011).
33. Ogden and Fisher, "Sensorimotor Psychotherapy."
34. Kathy L. Kain and Stephen J. Terrell, *Nurturing Resilience: Helping Clients Move Forward from Developmental Trauma. An integrative Somatic Approach* (Berkeley: North Atlantic Books, 2018).
35. Stephen W. Porges, "Polyvagal Theory: A Science of Safety." https://www.frontiersin.org/articles/10.3389/fnint.2022.871227/full (accessed Aug. 21, 2022).
36. Ibid.
37. Porges, *The Pocket Guide to The Polyvagal Theory.*
38. Seigel, *Pocket Guide to Interpersonal Neurobiology.*
39. Porges, "The Polyvagal Theory."
40. Deb Dana, *The Polyvagal Theory in Therapy: Engaging the Rhythm of regulation* (New York: W. W. Norton & Company, 2018).
41. Porges, *The Pocket Guide to The Polyvagal Theory.*
42. Seigel, *Pocket Guide to Interpersonal Neurobiology.*
43. Fisher, "Healing our Fragmented Selves."
44. Seigel, *Pocket Guide to Interpersonal Neurobiology,* 9.2.
45. Ibid.
46. Hanson, "Resilient."
47. Thomas Guilliams, *Adrenal Fatigue.* https://adrenalfatiguesolution.com/immune-system/ (accessed Aug. 22, 2022).
48. Amen Clinic. https://www.amenclinics.com/blog/mental-hygiene-is-just-as-important-as-washing-your-hands/ (accessed Aug. 2, 2022).
49. Ken Wilber, "Growing up, Cleaning up, Waking up, Showing up." Interview by Richard Rohr. The Centre for Action and Contemplation's Conspire Conference in Albuquerque, New Mexico in July 2017.
50. Howes, Norma. "Trauma and the Body Workshop." Interview by Ffynnon in Wrexham, North Wales on 24 January, 2009.

51. Hanson, "Resilient."
52. Fisher, "Healing our Fragmented Selves," 67.
53. Ogden and Fisher, "Sensorimotor Psychotherapy."
54. Bessel Van der Kolk, *The Body Keeps The Score: Mind, Brain and the Body in the Transformation of Trauma* (London: Allen Lane, 2014).
55. Schwartz, "No Bad Parts."
56. Fisher, *Healing Our Fragmented Selves.*
57. Porges, *Pocket Guide to the Polyvagal Theory.*
58. Ogden and Fisher, "Sensorimotor Psychotherapy."
59. Courtney Ackerman, "Twenty-Three Amazing Health Benefits of Mindfulness for Body and Brain." *PositivePsychology.com.* https://www.positivepsychology.com (accessed sept.29, 2022).
60. Hanson, "Resilient."
61. Ogden and Fisher, "Sensorimotor Psychotherapy."
62. Robert A. Masters, *Spiritual Bypassing: When Spirituality Disconnects Us From What Really Matters* (Berkeley: North Atlantic Books, 2010).
63. Porges, "Polyvagal Theory: A Science of Safety."
64. Seigel, *Pocket Guide to Interpersonal Neurobiology.*
65. Ibid.

Chapter Eight

Working with Shame in Pastoral Supervision

Sally Nash

This chapter is about working with shame in pastoral supervision. I might not have used the word 'shame,' but it is what my eight-year-old self experienced when a teacher had the bright idea of working out the average weight of the class by publicly weighing us all. I feigned illness to get out of the classroom. I was scared of being exposed and laughed at for being the heaviest girl in the class. The public, social shame having a much bigger impact on me than the private, moral shame of lying to get out of a situation; I was a child who knew that lying made me a bad person. I still have some mistrust of institutions to this day, and this is not the only incident of feeling shame as a consequence of the actions, or decisions, of those who have power over me in an institutional context.

This incident was so significant in my life that it was the source of choosing shame as a PhD topic for ordination training over forty years later.[1] For me, shame came with being fat. While it may be disputable that I couldn't help being fat at age eight, putting that on an eight-year-old child that it was their fault, feels equally shaming as what the teacher did to me. That was my weak point, and some of the shame we may work with in pastoral supervision can come from characteristics which are less changeable than weight is, including gender, ethnicity, sexuality, disability, and class, for example.

This is my starting point for reflecting on shame in pastoral supervision. Shame doesn't just happen because of things we do. It can be experienced because of things that others do or say to us (or don't do or say too). Shame is contextual; it is relative. What shames me may not shame you, and vice versa. You might have been quite comfortable to be weighed in the classroom that day and have a more positive body image than I do.

As individuals, we all have different degrees of shame-proneness which impacts what we might bring to pastoral supervision, or how shame may impact us as a supervisor. My experience of being shamed at school was an early example of dissonance between my own experience and official statements about what institutions stand for, and how they treat those who are in it. Oppression, which is what I felt, can happen at a personal, cultural or structural level[2] and each of these can cause shame, but how we address this shame may depend on which of these was experienced. Carrying on with the weight theme, personally, when overweight, I experience shame, particularly when faced with being weighed in medical contexts (sometimes for no discernible reason in respect to what I am attending an appointment for). Culturally, I was born in the wrong century. In other times, fat was a sign of wealth. Structurally, there are sometimes weight restrictions imposed on access to medical treatment.

If we are going to work with shame in pastoral supervision, it is vital that we engage with our own experiences. Rustomjee argues that we need an awareness of "our own hidden shame, our guilt, our vulnerabilities, our love, and our hate, so that we can help towards cultivating a culture that can respond with empathy and attunement, rather than abandon with shame."[3] Reflexivity is vital. We need to be aware of our own values, beliefs, experiences, and context and how this might impact our engagement with those who come to us for pastoral supervision. It is also imperative that we are aware of anything that triggers us where our gut response would be to shame someone. One supervisor shared how they observed their own internal reaction and desire to shame another when confronted with a very narcissistic supervisee. Despite knowing that the narcissistic wound is deep-rooted, they experienced themselves as wanting to shame them. Another issue to be aware of is what about us or our setting that may trigger shame in the supervisee (or vice versa). Although it may sound trivial, I can feel shame when having to admit that I would much rather not have a dog or cat in a room. I do not like them. I am afraid of dogs. I can show the scar I got from a bite and would prefer not to be asked, although I know that, for some, it may be experienced as therapeutic. It might also be that our dress, accent, titles, roles, or other attributes that people know of us, may be problematic and, if we get an unexpected response, it might be worth reflecting on this.

In this chapter, I will define shame, explain the typology of shame that emerged in my PhD research, and explore how pastoral supervisors may work with people who are experiencing shame. One of my main purposes in writing this chapter is raising awareness of shame, particularly in relation to engagement with the church and with Christian organizations. It is often hidden or unidentified and is very hard to address if not articulated.

DEFINING SHAME

One of the challenges of writing about shame is that, as Pattison argues, it is a "family of meanings or phenomena, not a single experience or definition."[4] Gilbert[5] notes that a multifaceted approach to shame includes five components:

- social or external cognitive
- internal self-evaluative
- emotional
- behavioural
- physiological

One might observe any, or all, of these dimensions in pastoral supervision.

Despite the complexities in defining shame, it is important to offer an understanding of how I am conceptualising shame in this chapter. A concise definition of shame by the American sociologist Brené Brown, who has done much to bring the concept to wider prominence, sees it as "the intensely painful feeling, or experience of believing that we are flawed and therefore unworthy of acceptance and belonging."[6] A slightly different insight is offered by the Australian theologian, Neil Pembroke, who suggests that, "Shame arises when the self evaluates itself as flawed, defective, inferior. One judges that one has fallen short of a cherished ideal. One perceives a gap between the self as it really is and a desired identity."[7] Both of these definitions imply that shame has an audience—those who cause us to feel flawed, or a construct of an ideal self which we believe we have fallen short of. Shame is not always easy to recognise in ourselves or others, and can be painful to acknowledge and speak about.

Both Brown and Pembroke in their definitions are talking about what is known as 'disgrace shame'—the shame we might experience after something has happened. However, the term shame is not solely used in a negative way. The idea of 'discretion shame' is the sort of shame which may prevent us from acting inappropriately. It is about respect, boundaries, privacy, and moral motivation to act correctly, for example. In this chapter, I am largely focusing on working with disgrace shame, as that is what I have most encountered as an issue.

Disgrace shame can lead to, or potentially manifest as:

- negative feelings such as a fear of abandonment, inferiority, paralysis, helplessness, passivity, exposure;

- negative self-perception such as seeing self as small, diminished, unworthy, defective, or flawed;
- physiological or physical reactions, most commonly blushing, averting your gaze, hiding or withdrawing, covering your face, tears, rage, and hostility, for example.

Differentiating Shame and Guilt

It is possible to feel guilt or shame, or both, over the same incident. Broadly speaking, much of the literature suggests that guilt focuses on what we have done, and shame on who we are. Thus, we can feel shame about who we are while still feeling that we have done nothing wrong. Shame encompasses all of us, guilt encompasses specific actions. Christine Caine puts it this way: "Guilt is about my *do*. Shame is about my *who*."[8] She then goes on to discuss how in Genesis chapter 3, we see Adam and Eve experiencing shame and hiding from God, and then when the conversation begins with God asking if they have done something wrong—guilt. They could have taken responsibility for their actions, but instead they deflected their guilt and embraced shame.[9] Guilt is usually much easier to deal with. We can confess our wrongdoing, seek to put something right if that is necessary or possible, and receive God's forgiveness. It is not that simple with shame. We have to change the way we think about ourselves.

What Do People Experience Shame Over?

If I asked you to complete the sentence, "I feel shame when . . . ," I wonder what you would say? In this section, I am going to explore some of the wide range of things that people experience shame over, as this can help us recognise if shame is present, or help us, at least, to consider the possibility that what we are seeing, or hearing, might be shame.

Pembroke[10] identifies five contexts where shame may be experienced:

- situational shame, occasions or incidents which cause us shame;
- aesthetic shame, which involves falling short of some characteristic relating to appearance or inherited identity shame which includes, class, ethnicity, culture, gender;
- inferiority shame, where you feel like you are lacking or deficient, you are not good enough;
- moral shame, where you feel as if you have done something wrong or violated your values or ethical code for living.

Lewis[11] frames it slightly differently and talks about impropriety, or inappropriateness, such as walking into an occupied toilet. This has similarities to situational shame which might be something like walking into a lamppost as you play on your phone. He also identifies conspicuousness, such as passing wind in a silent part of a meeting or church service, and lack of competence, which can include not being able to pronounce long lists of names in a Bible reading or coping with modern technology. A failure in interpersonal relationships, such as a divorce or estrangement, may also cause shame. Finally, he talks about empathic shame, where you feel shame because of the way a friend or family member is shamed in front of you. Experiencing any of these types of shame can lead us to think, or feel, that we do not belong, or even have someone tell us that is the case.

Embodied Shame

Shame is embodied, and thus may often arise out of how we perceive and experience our bodies. It may also be connected to developmental processes. McNish[12] suggests that infancy and young childhood are associated with the shame of powerlessness; adolescence with bodily changes and potentially unruly sexuality; adulthood with loss, rejection, abandonment, and not being, or getting, what you hoped or expected; old age comes with a decline in physical and mental capacity, and diminution of physical attractiveness. This indicates a life span element to shame for some, and so it is important to be aware of the stage of life that supervisees are in. I broke my shoulder while I was writing this chapter and couldn't drive for six weeks. I had slipped on a piece of slate, and while nobody was to blame for what happened, and I wasn't being careless, it was very hard to ask for help with the many things I couldn't do. I had to resist a reframing of myself as a needy person as that suggests there is something wrong in requiring support from others which is untrue and dissonant with the value of interdependence which is important to me. I don't think anyone shamed me, but I was fortunate and have had stories shared with me of where people have been shamed for not being able to do simple things for themselves. Loss of some of our capacity is often a trigger for shaming. A further example is to be found in writing on disability. Amy Kenny talks of her experience of being shamed (my interpretation) by people who want to fix her disability, commenting that:

> Some of the irony is that my life isn't disastrous or deficient at all. Most days, my disability isn't the worst part of my day or even what I need prayer for. To assume that my disability needs to be erased in order for me to live an abundant life is disturbing, not only because of what it says about me, but also because of what it reveals about people's notions of God.[13]

Shaming can be used by families, communities, cultures, and institutions as a tactic to maintain compliance. It is likely that most of us have some baggage relating to shame that comes from our engagement in one or more of these contexts. Thus, as a supervisor, and with a supervisee, there may be issues from earlier in life which may arise afresh in supervision, or which are helpful to explore as a window into current actions or attitudes. As a teenager, Dom felt he was given a list of things he shouldn't do. If you did one of those things, you were a bad Christian/person. Somehow, the way it was communicated made, for example, having one too many drinks, something to feel shame about, not just guilt. This lingered even when he was a church leader. More broadly, as anthropologist Martha Nussbaum argues, "some people are more marked out for shame than others . . . societies ubiquitously select certain groups and individuals for shaming, marking them off as abnormal and demanding they blush at what, and who, they are."[14] Who these people are will vary depending on context, and churches, as well as societies, mark people out. Richard Dawkins argued that it was immoral not to abort a foetus with Down syndrome,[15] and that it is possible to abort such a foetus at any time during pregnancy[16] is a clear example of a group marked out for structural shaming—in this instance, sometimes the parents as well as the child.

Identity

One of Pembroke's causes of shame was inherited identity.[17] Similarly, C. S. Lewis[18] argues that what we are most ashamed of are those things which we can't help. Perceptions of identity can be contextual and cultural. However, understanding our identity in the light of how we think others perceive us can help us uncover shame. Identity is also about belonging. As Kaufman observes, "the need to belong to something larger than ourselves, to a group, cause or idea, is one principal source of identity. Shame is another principal source of identity."[19] These two elements coalesced for Dan White Jr., a pastor, who in a podcast[20] shares the story of a conversation with his wife, when, on the way to a party, he talked about not wanting to say what his job was as he felt shame over it. This was, in part, because of the number of people he had encountered who had seen, or experienced themselves, abuse from a pastor, as well as abuse he had received from his congregation. He believed that perceptions of what a pastor was, had changed. It is not unknown for male clergy friends to be called a paedophile, sometimes in a jokey manner, because of the disclosures of clergy abuse in a wide range of churches. Female Anglican friends share stories of how they can feel shamed just for being ordained. One of the participants in my doctoral research shared this:

> As a woman clergy person [Church of England], we are constantly talked about as a "problem" or "issue" that has "divided, destroyed and broken the church." At times, it has felt like we were being publicly named and shamed for daring to be female and a priest. I found this difficult, as it resonated with negative experiences of shame in my own life (often a gender issue), so have probably colluded with this by feeling bad about myself and not valuing properly the ministry God has given me to do at times.[21]

Thus, in pastoral supervision, there may be some core identity issues which are shame-based because of issues such as these.

Sometimes the identity issues that we face are because we are not the minister, priest or whatever, we want to be. Morrison argues that we feel shame when experiencing failure regarding our ideals. He writes, "these failures are experienced as defects in the self-as-I-want-to-be (the ideal self, or the ego ideal of traditional psychoanalysis). If our ideals are harsh and exacting, the internalized ego ideal will remain forever unattainable, leading to chronic feelings of shame."[22] Exploring where the ideal self being judged against comes from, may be beneficial.

A RESEARCH-BASED TYPOLOGY OF SHAME AND THE CHURCH

It can be easy to think of shame as something which occurs to us personally or culturally but, as part of my PhD, I developed a six-part typology which went beyond this. We may encounter shame in pastoral supervision in any of these areas. The six categories are: personal, relational, communal, structural, theological, and historical. I will briefly explore each of them below.

Personal Shame

Personal shame relates to shame experienced by an individual as a consequence of their relationship with the church or Christian organization. One issue is that institutions tend to have norms and mores, which are largely unspoken and unwritten, which set the culture of the institution. Most of us will have had a comment similar to, "We don't do it like that here," which, for some of us, is easy to brush off, but for others can cause shame for not fitting in, thus hampering a sense of belonging.

I am at a church where the other licensed clergy cross themselves at the appropriate parts of the liturgy. That is not my tradition, and I choose not to. When I was younger, I would probably have reluctantly conformed, feeling as if I needed to in order to be accepted. In this situation, I would probably have been experiencing shame in my head which was not imposed by others. I would have speculated, wrongly, about what they thought. Sometimes, we can experience personal shame because of negative, or faulty, thought patterns, or transference from other contexts, where those in authority did shame us or expect unwavering conformity to the way it is done here. Reassuring people that it is important to work out what it means to be authentic for them, and to then work that out in context, can be a beneficial way of working with experienced, or potential, shame.

The job of ministry can trigger shame. As Binau suggests, "If we allow ourselves to be defined by what we *do*, rather than what we are called to *be*, shame will be our nearly constant companion as we do ministry in the hectic modern world."[23] This can be exacerbated if you are following a dearly loved minister and your changes in practice can be the subject of significant criticism. Dion found it hard to cope with the constant snide remarks about a lack of pastoral visiting at home by the clergy, which apparently the previous minister used to have as a focus. But he felt his main gifting was as an evangelist and wanted to take every opportunity to engage with people in the community.

Partners of ministers may resonate with one of my research participants who shared how they felt:

> shame for not attending every Sunday morning service; for choosing between children's sport and social activities and being in church; for not being seen to participate fully in the life of the church—attend a home group, help with creche, alpha course, family services . . . ie. . . .not OK just to 'go' to church.

I have also had conversations with ministers who consequently experience shame because their partner or children are not as engaged in church as some congregation members hope for. Some would go so far as to say that they can see themselves as a bad parent or spouse because this is so. Jed found it increasingly difficult to respond to, "Where is Natalie? We miss her" type comments from members of the congregation, when his wife chose to worship elsewhere.

Relational Shame

Relational shame refers to shame that is experienced as a consequence of identification with the people within an institution - particularly, but not exclusively, leaders. This is vicarious shame which may be something that is experienced, but which is difficult to identify and name. In essence, people feel shame because of what someone, whom they associate themselves with (whether known personally or not), does. Some feel relational shame as a consequence of how Christians are perceived outside of the church and see that as a barrier to relationships. The extent to which people feel shame over this may partly depend on their own theology. Thus, one of my research participants commented that, "I feel it because I am identified as 'the church' by people I know, who are not Christians, and it makes it harder for me to have sensible conversations with them, as they think I share church attitudes." "Tainted by association" was another way of putting it. This was particularly true if there had been a negative incident locally, which had become known in the community.

Relational shame can be exacerbated by public pronouncements or scandals. For example, as I write this in July 2022, the television presenter Nicky Campbell has shared about the abuse he experienced at school, commenting that one of the abusers was prominent in the Scripture Union.[24] I feel a sense of shame when those I might associate myself with, such as teachers and priests, are found to have betrayed trust in that way. 1 Corinthians 12 uses the metaphor of the body of Christ. As part of Christ's body, I cannot say that something that another part does, has no impact on me. Verse 26 says, "if one member suffers, all suffer together with it; if one member is honoured, all rejoice together with it."[25] The implication here is that if one member is shamed, all lament together, or all may experience shame together.

Another way in which people may experience relational shame is in explaining things to family and friends who do not share their faith. Thus, someone shared that, "explaining some of the practices of church management to my non-Christian family has made me feel ashamed at times, because I felt embarrassed about my career and felt protective of a career that they disapproved of." Such shame can linger, and I know that I struggled when I gave up teaching in order to join a Christian organization and, in doing so, gave up some of the hopes and expectations that my parents may have had of me.

Communal Shame

Communal shame relates to shame which is experienced at a group or congregational level. In any community, there can be a tendency toward labeling. This may also lead to stigmatizing. I am, in Church of England terms, a self-supporting minister, which means I do not get paid for the work that I do at church. In talking to others in my situation, we do sometimes feel stigmatized as second-rate or second-best. That is, by far, the minority of experiences, but particular groups can feel less in favour, depending on current fashions and policy and, as a middle-aged, middle-class, White woman, I certainly wasn't in a group that was seen as what was needed! I have also experienced it in talking with others who were priests in the inner city or outer estates, where they have encountered others who have inferred their ministry is less significant than someone with a church of ten times the usual Sunday attendance. Chaplains are another group who are sometimes on the receiving end of attempted shaming, when it is inferred that they are failed parish priests or church ministers.[26] It may also be that someone whom you are working with has not thought about this consciously, but brings to supervision an uneasiness that they experience at denominational gatherings when they are talking to particular people, or when they experience a more explicit slight or put down which resulted in shame.

Tensions can appear in leadership teams, particularly when some things go unspoken. One church leader participant in my research observed:

> we assume we all agree that some things are "right" and others "wrong." Some people don't want to reorder the building or be involved in fundraising and banging on about it . . . they can feel shame at not "catching the vision." It is difficult to voice this difference of opinion - especially if you're on the leadership team, as you are seen as not flying the flag.

Role descriptions, expectations, norms, and culture might all lead to dissonance, which might benefit from being explored in pastoral supervision. Related to this is a belief that, "expectations are set high, we need to wear masks just to survive sometimes. We are supposed to be open and transparent but in truth this is so that we reveal ourselves whilst the powerful gain control through knowledge of our openness." Even in a pastoral supervision relationship, some may feel like this, not being fully clear on who the stakeholders are in the pastoral supervision, and how what is shared may have a wider impact.

Structural Shame

Structural shame happens at the organizational or denominational level, or is the sort of shaming which is embedded in the way that the system works. I have lost track of the conversations that I have had with women who had leadership roles in different contexts, but who were only put forward for Associate Ministry in the Church of England (as opposed to overall leadership) because of misunderstandings about ways of being a leader that did not conform to the expectations of others.

Another manifestation of this is in what is being called, "the blokes worth watching"[27] syndrome with the obvious question, what if I am not a bloke? There have been a series of stories of people who do not fit this description for a wide range of reasons, which can apply to both men and women. It sets up a thought pattern that some are more valuable than others, resonant of the novel *Animal Farm*,[28] where equality ended up being framed as 'some are more equal than others.' Thus, there are some contexts where structurally you are not seen as appropriate for, or permitted to, undertake a variety of roles. Another way that this can trigger shame is that in talking about it, you will usually inevitably be critical of leaders, and again that is something which many of us have been told is wrong. This can, however, lead to collusion, which is dangerous.

Theological Shame

Theological shame relates to institutional belief systems and the way in which one's theological beliefs can engender shame. I occasionally hear the question, "are they sound?," which usually means "do they share my theological beliefs?" This can be an issue across theological traditions. One person from my research comments:

> I hold what would be deemed quite liberal views of homosexuality and homosexual practice, contrary to what the leadership and majority of my church believe and teach. I have felt unable to voice my divergent views for fear of being overlooked for playing an active ministry role.

This can lead to feelings of frustration and dissonance, particularly if you believe that God has called you to serve there. Another person framed it in prioritising their understanding of God's perspective: "If I were called upon to perform a gay marriage, I would have to refuse, and I might feel a sense of shame because of how my refusal might be interpreted as being unloving or legalistic. However, my shame before God for doing something which I believed to be in contradiction to core biblical teaching, would be far worse." Depending on whether your theological views coalesce, or not, with your denominational stated position, can influence the situations where shame might be felt.

Historical Shame

Historical shame relates to issues in the past where there is still a residue of what happened, embodied in people or a group. This can happen because of a personal situation where you still feel shame—divorce or imprisonment, for example. But more particularly, it can happen where there has been a shameful occurrence in a church, such as embezzlement, adultery, or abuse, and while no one talks about it, there is clearly an undercurrent or unease over particular situations or suggestions. It can also be seen as buried shame, because no one has helped the congregation process what happened. Such hidden shame has negative consequences. Anderson and Foley note that

> Whether it be by explicit decision, implicit agreement, collusion, or a combination of these, communities sometimes decide never to tell the whole story and to keep some past event hidden at all cost. As a result, the community is stuck in fixed patterns of interaction, roles are rigidly defined, and stories are closely monitored to keep the secret safe.[29]

They go on to argue that secrets tend to be toxic, contribute to eroding trust, and tend to regularize deception. This is the context that some of our supervisees face but may not quickly realise that it is the case. If there are things happening which seem hard to understand, then this might be an issue.

WORDS THAT PEOPLE USE WHICH MAY INDICATE SHAME

While I need to be clear that the use of these, or similar, words is not evidence that the person is experiencing shame, they might be an indication of it. One of the ways that I identified such words was through analysing responses to data in my doctoral research and exploring words which fitted with the typology of shame. If you hear one of these words, or a similar concept, it may sometimes be worth digging deeper and asking someone to unpack, or explain further, their use of that word.

If someone shares that they feel like a nonentity (or similar), that can indicate issues with identity, belonging or connectedness which might indicate issues with perceptions as to who they are, which is causing shame. A feeling of insufficiency might also indicate this and can be particularly pertinent in relation to the demands of ministry and those we minister to. At a deeper level, an observation of being stigmatised can also be an indication of shame. Morrison[30] offers some other words which may indicate shame: insignificant, puny, invisible, irrelevant, miniscule, nothing, pathetic, ridiculous, weak, freak, loser, stupid, dumb, idiotic, there is something wrong with me. Perhaps the most serious of words that relate to an individual's perception of self as disintegrating. This may suggest that there are shame responses or experiences to this state.

Talking about nonconformity and noncompliance may be very healthy and demonstrate a good self-awareness of a response to a situation. However, it might also be triggering a shame response, depending on the context of the response. This can be particularly true if the response is to decrees from leaders at different levels. Feeling 'dissonant' may also indicate similar frustrations, or issues, where values are not shared, for example.

The remaining words are all ones which suggest that something is not working as it should. Being disaffected, disempowered, or dissociative, indicates a potential breakdown in relationship which most likely merits being explored more deeply in pastoral supervision, to see if there are ways in which this might be ameliorated.

ASKING ABOUT SHAME

One of the insights which impacts my practice with regard to shame in pastoral supervision, is Bonhoeffer's[31] discussion on telling the truth. Bonhoeffer argues this: "The question must be asked, whether, and in what way, a person is justified in demanding truthful speech from another."[32] While this may initially sound dissonant in the context of pastoral supervision, where one would hope that truth would be told, Bonhoeffer suggests that truth telling happens within relationships, and power dynamics may need to be taken into account. He suggests that, "where 'the truth is told' without regard for the person to whom it is said, there it has only the appearance of truth, but not its essence."[33] The person who speaks the truth indiscriminately is descried as someone who "violates shame, desecrates the mystery, breaks trust, betrays the community in which he lives, and smiles arrogantly over the havoc he has wrought and over the human weakness that 'can't bear the truth.'"[34] The example that Bonhoeffer cites, is a teacher asking a pupil in front of others if their father comes home drunk. The answer was 'yes,' but saying so would elicit shame in the child and so they deny it, not having the sophistication of language to answer in a truthful way that does not expose his father, or himself, to shame. Bonhoeffer argues that the child behaved in the right way because the higher truth was that the school had no right to intrude into family life in this way. Being clear on what the boundaries are for areas to discuss in pastoral supervision is something to establish early on.

One of the questions I am often asked is, "do you have a family?" It has been asked in a range of both formal and informal situations, and I understand that what they are meaning is, 'do you have children?' I am not childless by choice, and questions such as this trigger shame in me. This may seem like an over-reaction to some, but it is very real for me. Even the initial 'getting to know each other' element of pastoral supervision needs careful planning and reflection in case one triggers a shame reaction. In setting up such a relationship, I might well talk a little about my background, but then ask someone what would they like to tell me about themselves, leaving them to choose what they share.

Rose and Paterson[35] advocate the use of 'wondering' and 'musing' in pastoral supervision, and suggest questions such as

- *I wonder how you got through that awful situation that you have just told me about?*
- *I wonder what supports you from the inside when you experience distress like that?*
- *I wonder who taught you to be . . . ?*
- *If you had a magic wand, I wonder what you would wish for?*[36]

Framing questions in this way allows the supervisee the capacity to respond in the way that they choose, which may, or may not, include sharing dimensions of shame. A completely legitimate response is, "I need to think about that further," and the encounter can move on without it being awkward.

RESPONDING TO SHAME IN PASTORAL SUPERVISION

Perhaps the most important element of our response, is the quality of our presence. Pembroke writes, "The really gifted and graced helper knows, however, that when she allows herself to enter heart and soul into the relationship, it is not so much words or techniques which are healing and renewing, but her very presence."[37] This can be challenging at times. A supervisor shared how, with a very overweight supervisee, they struggled the whole session to focus on what the supervisee was saying, rather than wondering about their weight. There can be many distractions in pastoral supervision, and we need to be aware of those which most impact us, that may mean our presence is not of the quality we would hope to attain. Shame, Pembroke argues, can be exacerbated when what is offered is a defective presence.[38] There are times when I might share something personal which is impacting my capacity to be fully present, such as the day an ambulance is called for my mum, which is a regular, although not frequent, occurrence. It is usually too late to postpone or cancel, but I know that can be a distraction that I need to try to overcome. For a supervisee to understand what this is may be helpful in them realising it is not them you are struggling with.

Alongside presence, the quality of the relationship is significant in working with those who are experiencing shame. One of my focus group participants helped me to see that she was happy to discuss issues with those she knew cared for her but struggled with others who tended to be judgmental without knowing her or seeking to understand her situation. My research suggested that we need to create a safe space, engender confidence in the supervisee, and offer acceptance, affirmation, and assurance to them as an individual. The hope is to help them feel sufficient. This is built on the doctrine of the *imago*

Dei from Genesis 1:27, which Swinton describes as one that "offers hope to the hopeless, comfort to the downhearted and a wholeness to those whose lives have been broken and damaged by fate and circumstances."[39]

From the perspective of a counsellor, Sanderson[40] identifies eight aims of working therapeutically with shame, much of what she suggests has relevance in pastoral supervision also. Her insights are more process-oriented than those which emerged from my research. The key elements, outside of building a safe and secure relationship which builds both trust and relational worth, include: raising awareness of shame, identifying its impact, exploring how to release the shame, building self-acceptance, empathy, and compassion, and building authentic pride. Remembering these elements in our pastoral supervision and in wider ministry can help build a more affirming culture. Particularly helpful can be public recognition, gratitude and affirmation, which may be done in face-to-face contexts, but also on social media.

An alternative way of expressing this is found in the work of Nelson[41] who explores finding freedom from shame in a church context. He argues that people find freedom by naming their shame, identifying the origins of it, sharing it with those you trust in the community, and actively living out of their understanding of God's grace and redemption. This raises an issue that is found in the shame literature: shame that is deeply embedded can more effectively be healed in community, so positive relationships are needed beyond the pastoral supervisor. Winfrey suggests that "experiencing God loving us through other people is one of the prime ways we know God's affirmation of us."[42] She suggests that safe groups may be helpful, but they require good leadership so that confidentiality and mutual respect are engendered. As pastoral supervisors, we may already run groups, but also might want to explore if there are other contexts where a group would be valuable.

Avoidance of Shame

One of the dilemmas in looking at how we might respond to shame in pastoral supervision is that sometimes that is what our supervisee avoids raising. A question to consider is, 'What is our supervisee not saying, and what do they not want to be asked?' That is also pertinent in setting boundaries to the pastoral supervision. Are there any areas that are off-limits for either party to explore or talk about? Some people may want a very work-focused engagement; others a more whole-life approach. One of the reasons that supervisees may seek to avoid addressing areas where shame is involved, is that they may be projecting their own negative judgments about themselves onto the supervisor. As Morrison argues, "assuming that her vision of us will be the same as our own verdict, and that she views us with disdain."[43]

Bypassed Shame

Pastoral supervisors may find it helpful to understand the concept of 'bypassed shame.' Fowler discusses it in the context of therapy (but it can also apply to pastoral supervision), suggesting that it occurs if we respond "to a tender or painful self-disclosure in a way that wounds the patient or fails to attribute importance to what the patient has risked."[44] He goes on to say, drawing on the work of Helen Block Lewis,[45] one of the classic shame theorists, that this can lead to silence or hesitant speech. This is because the person who was not heard has feelings of anger at the response: guilt about the anger, and depression and shame as the anger is turned on self because it seems wrong to feel anger at the person trying to help. The initial failing to hear is attributed to what the patient shared, evoking unaddressed or bypassed shame in the listener.[46]

TOOLS AND STRATEGIES FOR ADDRESSING SHAME

There are a range of tools and strategies which can be helpful in addressing shame, which might be used in pastoral supervision, but also more widely.

Exploring Theology

One of the tools for responding to shame is helping people to explore theological perspectives which help them understand their shame from a different perspective. I mentioned the *imago Dei* above, but there are other useful insights from the Genesis creation narratives. Middleton suggests that we can see God in Genesis 1, "as a mother giving life to her children, she blesses them and then shares the parental risk of letting them grow, develop and try out their power."[47] When Adam and Eve do exercise their power and find themselves naked, experiencing shame and hiding from God, then the response is one of compassion. God neither leaves the couple to clothe themselves, nor demands that they remain naked. God clothes them, showing mercy, forgiveness, and sensitivity toward their shame. Understanding this is a much more helpful focus than that which emphasises their being banished from the garden or talks about the "fall," which is not a term found in Genesis, the rest of the Hebrew Bible, or in Jewish literature.[48]

Perhaps the most common theological rationale in relation to overcoming our shame is understanding the meaning of the life of Jesus. McNish[49] suggests that Jesus embraced the shame archetype through his life, death, and resurrection. He chose not to engage in the sort of defences are often used, such as rage, denial, scapegoating, depression, withdrawal, blaming, and so on. In confronting shame, Jesus models being able to reconcile who we are, despite shameful experiences, and offers acceptance and belonging. As well as that, Jesus offers us a positive example in the way he approached his ministry. Savage argues that:

> Across the range of Jesus' interactions, we see him on the warpath against all that degrades human dignity and spiritual value. With flexibility and insight, he takes the initiative against the social structures, deceptions, defences, learned helplessness, negative thoughts and patterns and paralysing fears that imprison us. He models an interpersonal style through which he insists on knowing the other, and on being known.[50]

With shame, there are wider issues as to how the church treats and responds to people, and raising awareness of the ways that are inadvertent, or even deliberate, of how shaming impacts people can be valuable in seeking to becoming a less-shaming church. This applies to both what ministers say to their congregations, and what individuals say to the minister and equivalents.

Unhealthy Images of God

Helping people identify their unhealthy images of God can be an integral part of the journey of overcoming shame. Watson helpfully summarises some of the main ways in which people who are experiencing shame, have an unhealthy image of God:

> Often the person living with unhealthy shame sees God as the accuser, not the healer. God is not the one who can restore but is the silent judge in the background, glaring with a disapproving shake of the head. God is not the one who listens; he is removed and uninterested in the plight of people. The eyes of God are either burning into the vulnerable soul or turned away in disgust. . . . Worm theology is very prevalent in the minds of shamed people.[51]

Sometimes it is only when we spend time exploring some of our default thoughts or reactions that we realise we have internalised some unhealthy patterns of thinking.

Gazing on the Face of Christ

Rodin's statue of Eve[52] is hiding her face. This is a common response to shame. The practice of gazing upon the face of Jesus is found in several key texts on shame.[53] You cannot look at the face of God if you are hiding your own face. This is one biblical exemplar for believing God's face to be important. When someone wants a blessing rather than taking the bread and wine at the Eucharist, my normal practice is to pray the Aaronic blessing found in Numbers 6:24–26: "The Lord bless you and keep you; the Lord make his face shine on you and be gracious to you; the Lord turn his face toward you and give you peace."[54] I might also pray this in pastoral supervision, if we have agreed to pray. Goodliff suggests that rituals, such as the peace and the Eucharist, "shapes a habitus of facing. Above all it orientates us to the face of Christ"[55] Stockitt[56] suggests that gazing upon Christ's face can be both empowering and healing, rather than withdrawing from God's face and experiencing shame, sin and guilt. Pattison[57] emphasises the importance of what he calls the *visio Dei,* emphasising the importance of the face. One suggestion is that icons, or images, of Jesus might be used as an alternative to an absolution, offering people the space to gaze upon the face of Christ. There are a range of cultural issues in choosing an appropriate image to use in this way. Stockitt thus suggests that "the mutuality of Christ gazing upon us in love and us reciprocating that gaze is an image of redemption and restoration."[58] There are resonances too with attachment theory,[59] and while it is beyond the scope of this chapter to explore this topic, it may be an issue to consider in the light of shame which emerges in pastoral supervision.

Liturgy

Our identity as Christians is, in part, shaped by liturgy.[60] If we are praying or using any liturgy in pastoral supervision, we may want to consider what is understood by what we choose and what is said. I am from a tradition where extempore prayer is common, but I have worked with colleagues who always use a book. The words and the theological assumptions within them can either help ameliorate shame or exacerbate it. One possibility is to speak affirmations over people, drawing on appropriate biblical concepts, for example:

- Jesus clothes you with beauty, removing the ashes of shame you've worn for the sin committed against you (or sin you have committed if this is appropriate).[61]
- God will rejoice over you. You will rest in God's love; God will sing and be joyful about you.[62]
- God says, you are my beloved child, I am pleased with you.[63]

My usual practice would be to ask God for a particular verse or passage to use in this way.

This prayer (adapted slightly) was written for my book[64] by Gemma Willis and, although originally crafted for children, the simple language can be helpful, and you can contextualise the "when they tell me" phrase:

When they tell me I'm not good enough
I am more because you say I am, God
When they tell me I'll never make it
I am more because you say I am, God
When they tell me I'm unwanted
I am more because you say I am, God
When they tell me I'm dirty and worthless
I am more because you say I am, God
Help me, Jesus, to see myself as you see me and to be a bringer of worth, value and peace to those you love. Amen.

Being mindful about choice is key to liturgy not exacerbating the problem.

Creative Activities

As those made in the image of a creator God, engaging in creative activities can open us up to God. The term "creative repair" is used by Holmes[65] to describe the process of engaging in such activities in pastoral contexts. Different types of writing[66] can be useful for exploring shame. Therapeutic journal writing might be an activity to recommend as it helps us explore things which perhaps have been "previously unknown, unspeakable, or unacknowledged."[67] It might be you ask a supervisee to bring such writing to a session. Sometimes it can be helpful to begin with an existing piece of writing and develop that for those who find a blank page difficult. This is an excerpt from one such example, by Mark Berry, which reflects on extracts from Psalm 139:

In the night my spirit wakes and taunts me,
The voices that tell me I can do no good, that I have no value,
That remind me of my failings, of my weakness, of my splinters and shards.
The faces that stare with eyes which condemn and dismiss me,
That look with disdain and judgement, that punctures my faith.
The sneers and comparisons, the taunts and the jokes.
Deep into my shame I have shrunk.[68]

Art-based activities may be appropriate too. Inviting a supervisee to play with colour on a sheet of paper and seeing what emerges (oil pastels work particularly well), is a tool I have used at times in pastoral supervision. Colour can get beyond the cognitive into the affective domain with some people. Art journaling may be appropriate too,[69] along with a range of other activities that are designed to help people explore their thoughts.[70]

CONCLUSION

Shame will very rarely have a short-term fix. It is something which can require significant exploration and processing, and this will often be more effective if the words, actions, and attitudes of the wider community are congruent with the work that a pastoral supervisor does. This is not always possible, but the development of safe spaces in small groups where the sort of shame-based issues which arise in pastoral supervision can be raised, is immensely valuable but can be rare. Knowing how others experience shame, and seeing how they have come through it, can be liberating.

In this chapter, I have sought to raise awareness of shame and how it might be encountered and/or identified in pastoral supervision and suggest ways of addressing and ameliorating it. However, it remains the case that shame is a culturally constructed, contextual experience with many complexities. After many years of studying and working with shame, I have concluded that the most significant response that I can make is to offer an affirming presence as I journey with them.

BIBLIOGRAPHY

Anderson, Herbert and Edward Foley. *Mighty Stories, Dangerous Rituals.* San Francisco: Jossey Bass, 2001.

Binau, Brad A. "Administrative Ministry: A Link Between Shame and Stress." *Trinity Seminary Review* 27, no. 2 (2006): 99–106.

Bonhoeffer, Dietrich. *Dietrich Bonhoeffer Works Vol 16: Conspiracy and Imprisonment: 1940–1945*. Minneapolis: Fortress Press, 2006.

Brown, Brené. *I Thought It Was Just Me (but It Isn't)*. New York: Gotham Books, 2007.

Caine, Christine. *Unashamed.* Grand Rapids: Zondervan, 2016.

Davis Nelson, Heather. *Unashamed*. Wheaton: Crossway, 2016.

Down's Syndrome Association. "Where We Stand." Down's Syndrome Association, https://www.downs-syndrome.org.uk/about-dsa/who-we-are/where-we-stand/. (Accessed 5 July, 2022).

Fowler, James W. "Shame: Toward a practical theological understanding." *Christian Century* 25, no. 8 (1993): 816–19.

Gilbert, Paul. "Body shame: A biopsychosocial conceptualisation and overview, with treatment implications." Pp. 3–54 in *Body Shame Conceptualisation, Research and Treatment*, eds. Paul Gilbert and Jeremy Miles. Hove: Routledge, 2002.

Goodliff, Paul. *With Unveiled Face: A Pastoral and Theological Exploration of Shame*. London: Darton, Longman & Todd, 2005.

Hawkins, Katherine. "Richard Dawkins: 'Immoral' not to abort Down's foetuses." BBC News, August 21, 2014, https://www.bbc.co.uk/news/blogs-ouch-28879659. (Accessed July 5, 2022).

Holmes, Anne, C. "'Choose your Companions from the Best.'" *Practical Theology* 4, no. 1 (2011): 67–81.

Kaufman, Gershen. *Shame: The Power of Caring* (Cambridge MA: Schenckman Publishing, 1985).

Kenny, Amy. *My Body Is Not a Prayer Request.* Grand Rapids, MI: Brazos Press, 2022.

Lewis, Clive S. *Till We Have Faces: A Myth Retold.* London: HarperOne, 2017.

Lewis, Helen Block. *Shame and Guilt in Neurosis.* New York: International Universities Press, 1971.

Lewis, Michael. *Shame: The Exposed Self.* New York: The Free Press, 1995.

McNish, Jill. "Shame's Revelatory and Transformative Potential, and Its Use and Misuse by the Church's Pastoral Ministry." *Pastoral Psychology* 6, no. 2 (2003): 3–22.

Middleton, Richard J. *The Liberating Image: The Imago Dei in Genesis 1.* Grand Rapids, MI: Brazos Press, 2005.

Mooney, Carol G. *Theories of Attachment.* St. Paul: Redleaf Press, 2010.

Morrison, Andrew P. *The Culture of Shame.* New York: Ballantine Books, 1996.

Nash, Paul, and Sally Nash. *Tools for Reflective Ministry.* London: SPCK, 2009.

Nash, Sally. "Landscapes of Shame in the Church: A Typology to Inform Ministerial Praxis." Birmingham: Unpublished PhD, University of Birmingham, 2015.

———. *Shame and the Church: Exploring and Transforming Practice.* London: SCM Press, 2020.

New Revised Standard Version. *The Bible.* Cambridge: Cambridge University Press, 1989.

Nussbaum, Martha. *Hiding from Humanity.* Princeton: Princeton University Press, 2004.

Orwell, George. *Animal Farm.* London: Secker & Warburg, 1945.

PA Media. "BBC Presenter Nicky Campbell says he as victim of abuse at school in the 1970s." *The Guardian*, July 27, 2022, https://www.theguardian.com/society/2022/jul/27/bbc-presenter-nicky-campbell-says-he-was-victim-of-abuse-at-school-in-1970s. (Accessed July 27, 2022).

Paterson, Michael, and Jessica Rose. *Enriching Ministry.* London: SCM Press, 2014.

Pattison, Stephen. *Shame, Therapy and Theology.* Cambridge: Cambridge University Press, 2000.

———. *Saving Face: Enfacement, Shame, Theology.* Farnham: Ashgate, 2013.

Pembroke, Neil. *The Art of Listening: Dialogue, Shame and Pastoral Care.* Edinburgh: Continuum, 2002.

Pembroke, Neil. *Pastoral Care in Worship.* London: T&T Clark, 2010.

Rustomjee, Sabar. "The solitude and agony of unbearable shame." *Group Analysis* 42, no.2 (2009): 143–55.

Sanderson, Christiane. *Counselling Skills for Working with Shame.* London: Jessica Kingsley Publishers, 2015.

Savage, Sara. "Healing Encounters Psychological Perspectives on Jesus' Healing." Pp 44–61 in *Jesus and Psychology*, ed. Fraser Watts. London: Darton, Longman & Todd, 2007.

Scrivener, Glen. "Evangelical Futures BWWS—the 'blokes worth watching' conveyor belt," Evangelicals Now, July 2022, https://www.e-n.org.uk/2022/07/features/evangelical-futures-bwws-the-blokes-worth-watching-conveyor-belt/0ff5f/#.YrQ6VEuHnVg.twitter. (Accessed July 27, 2022).

Soneff, Sharon. *Art Journals and Creative Healing: Restoring the Spirit Through Self-Expression*. Beverley: Quarry Books, 2011.

Stockitt, Robin. *Restoring the Shamed: Towards a Theology of Shame*. Eugene: Cascade Books, 2012.

Swinton, John. *From Bedlam to Shalom*. New York: Peter Lang, 2002.

Threlfall Thomas, Miranda, and Mark Newitt. *Being a Chaplain*. London: SPCK, 2011.

Thompson, Kate. *Therapeutic Journal Writing*. London: Jessica Kingsley Publishers, 2011.

Thompson, Neil. *Anti-Discriminatory Practice*. London: Red Globe Press, 2020.

Walton, Heather. *Not Eden: Spiritual Life Writing for the World*. London: SCM, 2015.

Watson, John. *Shame*. Cambridge: Grove Books, 2005.

White Jr., Dan. "A Pastor ripped apart by our divided country." *New York Times*, July 21, 2022, https://www.nytimes.com/2022/07/21/opinion/a-pastor-burned-out-by-our-divided-country.html (accessed 22 August, 2022).

Winfrey, Rebecca. *The Cross and Shame*. Cambridge: Grove Books, 2019.

NOTES

1. Sally Nash, "Landscapes of Shame in the Church: A Typology to Inform Ministerial Praxis" (Birmingham University, unpublished PhD, 2015).

2. PCS Model developed by Neil Thompson, *Anti-Discriminatory Practice*, 7th ed (London: Red Globe Press, 2020).

3. Sabar Rustomjee, "The Solitude and Agony of Unbearable Shame," *Group Analysis* 42, no. 2 (2009): 154.

4. Stephen Pattison, *Shame, Therapy and Theology* (Cambridge: Cambridge University Press, 2000), 3.

5. Paul Gilbert, "Body shame: A biopsychosocial conceptualisation and overview, with treatment implications," in *Body Shame Conceptualisation, Research and Treatment*, eds. Paul Gilbert and Jeremy Miles (Hove: Routledge, 2002), 3–54.

6. Brené Brown, *I Thought It Was Just Me (but It Isn't)* (New York: Gotham Books, 2007), 5.

7. Neil Pembroke, *The Art of Listening: Dialogue, Shame and Pastoral Care* (Edinburgh: Continuum, 2002), 142.

8. Christine Caine, *Unashamed* (Grand Rapids: Zondervan, 2016), 37.

9. Caine, "Unashamed," 37–38.

10. Neil Pembroke, *Pastoral Care in Worship* (London: T&T Clark, 2010), 26–29.

11. Michael Lewis, *Shame: The Exposed Self* (New York: The Free Press, 1995), 16.

12. Jill McNish, "Shame's Revelatory and Transformative Potential, and Its Use and Misuse by the Church's Pastoral Ministry," *Pastoral Psychology* 6, no. 2 (2003): 7.

13. Amy Kenny, *My Body Is Not a Prayer Request* (Grand Rapids: Brazos Press, 2022), 5.

14. Martha Nussbaum, *Hiding from Humanity* (Princeton: Princeton University Press, 2004), 174.

15. Katherine Hawkins, "Richard Dawkins: 'Immoral' not to abort Down's foetuses," BBC News, August 21, 2014, https://www.bbc.co.uk/news/blogs-ouch-28879659. (Accessed July 5, 2022).

16. Down's Syndrome Association, "Where We Stand," Down's Syndrome Association, https://www.downs-syndrome.org.uk/about-dsa/who-we-are/where-we-stand/. (Accessed July 5, 2022).

17. Pembroke, "Pastoral Care in Worship."

18. In C. S. Lewis, *Till We Have Faces: A Myth Retold* (London: HarperOne, 2017).

19. Gershen Kaufman, *Shame: The Power of Caring* (Cambridge MA: Schenckman Publishing, 1985), vii.

20. Dan White Jr, "A Pastor ripped apart by our divided country," *New York Times*, July 21, 2022, https://www.nytimes.com/2022/07/21/opinion/a-pastor-burned-out-by-our-divided-country.html. (Accessed August 22, 2022).

21. All similar unattributed quotations are from the empirical research that was part of my PhD.

22. Andrew P. Morrison, *A Culture of Shame* (New York: Ballantine Books, 1996), 73.

23. Brad A. Binau, "Administrative Ministry: A Link Between Shame and Stress," *Trinity Seminary Review* 27, no. 2 (2006): 102.

24. PA Media, "BBC Presenter Nicky Campbell says he as victim of abuse at school in the 1970s," *The Guardian*, July 27, 2022, https://www.theguardian.com/society/2022/jul/27/bbc-presenter-nicky-campbell-says-he-was-victim-of-abuse-at-school-in-1970s. (Accessed July 27, 2022).

25. New Revised Standard Version, *The Bible* (Cambridge: Cambridge University Press, 1989).

26. See Miranda Threlfall Thomas and Mark Newitt, eds., *Being a Chaplain* (London: SPCK, 2011) to support this idea, where among other things chaplains have been described as less skilled or betraying a vocation.

27. Glen Scrivener, "Evangelical Futures BWWS—the 'blokes worth watching' conveyor belt," Evangelicals Now, July 2022, https://www.e-n.org.uk/2022/07/features/evangelical-futures-bwws-the-blokes-worth-watching-conveyor-belt/0ff5f/#.YrQ6VEuHnVg.twitter. (Accessed July 27, 2022).

28. George Orwell, *Animal Farm* (London: Secker & Warburg, 1945).

29. Herbert Anderson and Edward Foley, *Mighty Stories, Dangerous Rituals* (San Francisco: Jossey Bass, 2001).

30. Morrison, *A Culture of Shame.*

31. Dietrich Bonhoeffer, *Dietrich Bonhoeffer Works Vol 16: Conspiracy and Imprisonment: 1940–1945*. (Minneapolis: Fortress Press, 2006), 601–8.

32. Ibid., 601.

33. Ibid., 602.

34. Ibid., 602.

35. Michael Paterson and Jessica Rose, *Enriching Ministry* (London: SCM, 2014), 222.

36. Paterson and Rose, *Enriching Ministry*, 222.

37. Pembroke, *The Art of Listening*, 75.

38. Ibid., 140.

39. John Swinton, *From Bedlam to Shalom* (New York: Peter Lang, 2000), 32.

40. Christiane Sanderson, *Counselling Skills for Working with Shame* (London: Jessica Kingsley, 2015), 171.

41. Heather Davis Nelson, *Unashamed* (Wheaton: Crossway, 2016), 170.

42. Rebecca Winfrey, *The Cross and Shame* (Cambridge: Grove Books, 2019), 22.

43. Morrison, *A Culture of Shame*, 119.

44. James W. Fowler, "Shame: Toward a practical theological understanding," *Christian Century* 25, no. 8 (1993): 817.

45. Helen Block Lewis, *Shame and Guilt in Neurosis* (New York: International Universities Press, 1971).

46. Fowler, "Shame," 417.

47. Richard J. Middleton, *The Liberating Image: The Imago Dei in Genesis 1* (Grand Rapids, MI: Brazos Press, 2005), 294.

48. There is a fuller discussion of this in Sally Nash, *Shame and the Church: Exploring and Transforming Practice* (London: SCM, 2020), 23–27.

49. McNish, "Shame's Revelatory and Transformative Potential," 19.

50. Savage, Sara. "Healing Encounters Psychological Perspectives on Jesus' Healing." Pp. 44–61 in *Jesus and Psychology*, ed. Fraser Watts (London: Darton, Longman and Todd, 2007).

51. John Watson, *Shame* (Cambridge: Grove Books, 2005), 6–7.

52. You can see the image here: https://www.metmuseum.org/art/collection/search/191804 (accessed 25 August 2022).

53. See, for example, Paul Goodliff, *With Unveiled Face: A Pastoral and Theological Exploration of Shame* (London, Darton, Longman & Todd, 2005); Stephen Pattison, *Saving Face: Enfacement, Shame, Theology* (Farnham: Ashgate, 2013); Neil Pembroke, *Pastoral Care in Worship* (London: T&T Clark, 2010); Robin Stockitt, *Restoring the Shamed: Towards a Theology of Shame* (Eugene: Cascade Books, 2012).

54. New International Version

55. Goodliff, *With Unveiled Face*, 99.

56. Stockitt, *Restoring the Shamed.*

57. Pattison, *Saving Face.*

58. Stockitt, *Restoring the Shamed,* 153.

59. See, for example, Carol G. Mooney, *Theories of Attachment* (St Paul: Redleaf Press, 2010).

60. I discuss this in detail in chapter 6 of my book *Shame and the Church.*

61. Drawing on Isaiah 61:3.

62. Based on Zephaniah 3:17.

63. Drawing on Matthew 3:17.

64. Found in Nash, *Shame and the Church*, 104.

65. Anne C. Holmes, "'Choose your Companions from the Best.'" *Practical Theology* 4, no. 1 (2011): 67–81.

66. See, for example, Heather Walton, *Not Eden: Spiritual Life Writing for the World* (London: SCM, 2015), for a range of different sorts of writing.

67. Kate Thompson, *Therapeutic Journal Writing* (London: Jessica Kingsley Publishers, 2011), 67.

68. Found in Nash, *Shame and the Church*, 117–18.

69. Sharon Soneff, *Art Journals and Creative Healing: Restoring the Spirit Through Self-Expression*. (Beverley: Quarry Books, 2011) is a useful text.

70. See Paul Nash and Sally Nash, *Tools for Reflective Ministry* (London: SPCK, 2009) for a wide range of different ways to engage in reflection as well as an introduction to theological reflection.

Chapter Nine

Some Implications of Culture and Religion for Pastoral Supervision

Tuntufye Anangisye Mwenisongole

Pastoral supervision is a new phenomenon in Tanzania, as is counselling. There are very few professional counsellors or pastoral supervisors.[1] Pastoral supervision is an important discipline which needs to be understood and applied to support effective pastoral ministry. Yet, in many ways, pastoral supervision is something which is done informally, in one way or another, without following any recognized principles and procedures. David Steere defines pastoral supervision as

> an extended relationship in which supervisor and supervisee agree to meet at regular intervals for systemic reflection upon the concrete practice of pastoral care in which supervisees are engaged in order to focus all available resources on each supervisee's personal growth in the pastoral role.[2]

Pastoral supervision, then, aims at making sure that people, groups, or organizations are working to the standards and principles that ultimately create harmony and peace, and progress and development.

This chapter argues that pastoral ministry needs professional supervisors who are sensitive to understanding the context of the workplace, in order to make supervision applicable and effective. It discusses some of the issues that are found in the context of Tanzania, based on my personal experience, and will also explore religion and culture in Tanzania.

PASTORAL SUPERVISION IN TANZANIA

I have been a pastor in Tanzania for more than twenty years. I have worked in different contexts and environments. I have worked with children, youth, students, pastors, and laypeople in different places, such as schools, congregations, colleges, and other institutions. I have experienced many things in my pastoral ministry. There have been different challenges of life—personal and even common ones. These challenges include financial crisis, bad/misleading teachings, management and leadership, ethics, faiths, gender issues, and traditional and cultural issues. These are just some of the areas which need to be considered when it comes to pastoral supervision. Pastoral supervision in Tanzania is not formally practiced. Yet, the church and communities at large need to open up to such discipline because of the complexity of the world we are living in.

The Environment of Tanzania

Tanzania gained its independence in 1961 from Britain. The religion and culture of Tanzania have been influenced by various factors, including the Arabic influence in most of the coastal regions in Tanzania, and mostly in its islands of Zanzibar (Pemba and Unguja). The British influence, through colonialism in Africa, has affected many people's lives and in different spheres of life such as education, culture, and social life. Tanzania is dominated mainly by two religions, Christianity and Islam, which are also influences from outside of Africa. Other religions found in Tanzania are African traditional religion, Hinduism, Bahaism, and others. All these factors need to be taken into consideration in pastoral supervision in the context of Tanzania.

One of the biggest factors which has united the Tanzanian people, and which is very important to note in this subject of pastoral supervision, is language. Language is such an important factor when it comes to relationship and communication. Tanzania has more than 120 ethnic groups with different dialects and tribes, which could cause a lot of challenges and conflicts such as civil wars and disputes. These challenges are obvious in some neighboring countries. Fortunately, the case has been different for Tanzania because of one common language which is popular and dominant throughout Tanzania. 'Kiswahili' is a language which is used in many different areas of life. Kiswahili became the national language of Tanzania. English is a second language used in an academic sphere. Therefore, the Kiswahili language in Tanzania can be very proper and useful in the intervention of pastoral supervision in different contexts of work because when people speak one common language, it becomes easy for them to understand one another. Hence, having a common language unites people in a way which is effective.

Personal Experiences

Through my experience and work as a pastor and lecturer at Teofilo Kisanji University (TEKU), I have come to realize that most of the issues or challenges facing the church, and other institutions, are the mentality of stereotype and some destructive cultures and traditions. These are the things that people do most of the time without even thinking about why they are doing them the way they have been.

Religion and Culture in Tanzania

In Tanzania, religion plays a big role in the development and identity of people and their daily activities in different workplaces. The population of Tanzania includes Christians (about 63 percent), and Moslems (about 34 percent). Five percent hold other beliefs.[3] Throughout the history of Tanzania, these people from different faiths have been living side by side without much friction. They have been living a life of cooperation in terms of holidays, ceremonies, disasters, and political issues regardless of their differences in faiths, gender, and ethnicity.[4] Despite the harmony that is prevalent in Tanzania, still people have been going through some conflicts and misunderstandings among themselves, which is normal to any kind of society or people who are not the same.[5] However, the government of Tanzania does not rely on any religious beliefs, but respects individual choices and freedom for whatever a person decides to believe in, without any interference from the government.

The cultural life of people in Tanzania is very much interwoven in tribal ways of life, which is a tradition from the ancestors thatis passed on from one generation to another. Some traditions and cultures of the Tanzanian people are common to many ethnic groups, especially from all who are known as Bantus. Other types of people in Tanzania are people from Nilotic and Cushtic origins.[6] So, although Tanzania has more than 120 ethnic tribes, Kiswahili has become a unifying language which is spoken throughout the country. Kiswahili has helped the country avoid unnecessary conflicts which can be caused by tribal differences. Hence, language plays a great role as a unifying factor for the development of the nation and its people.

Other aspects regarding the issues of tradition and culture are such as clothing, music, arts, and food. All of these things impact the ways people relate to one another and how they grow and develop. Culture and tradition become important in understanding an individual, or an institution, because of what they are used to doing and their ways of living their lives. Hence, pastoral supervision needs to consider such issues of religion and culture for the welfare of the institution and individuals, or even groups, which need to grow and develop.

THE WHOLE SPECTRUM OF PASTORAL SUPERVISION

The whole idea of pastoral supervision in Tanzania is a new phenomenon. One needs to understand, or observe, the work of pastoral supervision in a wider perspective of religion and culture in Tanzania. Pastoral supervision should be understood in a wider picture of supervision in a working environment in a different setting from a religious and secular world, from individual people to institutions or organizations. *The Dictionary of Pastoral Care and Counseling* defines pastoral supervision as a "dimension of the overall ministry of the religious community carried out by a pastor who offers both administrative oversight and a pastoral relationship to one or more persons engaged in developing ministerial competency and identity through actual ministerial practice."[7] Hence, supervision is done in a working place where one or some individuals are capable of working as overseers to monitor and manage the dilemma which can happen in a working place. Such people are capable of establishing a heathy relationship among workers in view of their similarities and differences, norms, and values of the workplace.

The term pastoral supervision should be first understood before proceeding to the function of pastoral supervision. Historically, the term was mainly used by those in clinical pastoral education; but in this postmodern time, we need to understand pastoral supervision from a wider perspective which goes beyond in every area of life. Pastoral supervision should be considered in a picture of Jesus Christ as a good shepherd, who is the overseer of his sheep. It is the ministry of the whole church to supervise her people in a relationship that is meaningful and responsible. Therefore, pastoral supervision should be defined and understood clearly in biblical and theological terms, especially in postmodern times. I personally like the following definition which is defined as:

> A broad space to talk about whatever is happening in ministry, sensitive to God's voice and the spiritual that effects transition and transformation, resulting in the minister having . . . enhanced self-awareness, ministering competence, theological understanding and Christian commitment.[8]

Hence, pastoral supervision, according to the above assertion, should be Christ-centered for the growth and development of faith in a Christian life. I understand this statement through the eyes of contextual theology in the

African soil, where one needs to understand the Bible in the context of people in Tanzania, which is inculturation as some African scholars have termed it.[9]

THE ROLE OF PASTORAL SUPERVISION

The purpose of pastoral supervision in a Christian church can be described in three main points. The first is enhancing the professional functioning of the more junior person(s). The second is monitoring the quality of professional services offered to the client(s) that she, he, or they, see(s). The third is serving as a gatekeeper of those who are to enter the particular profession. At the core of the pastoral supervision process, is the relationship which needs to be considered for the purpose of building a strong web among people in a pastoral ministry. Hence, pastoral supervision allows a sacred space of relationship, transformation, and insights which leads to growth and change. An open and sacred space allows a supervisor and supervisee to explore the client's experiences and stories of relationships, which are composed of a mixture of connections and disconnections. We, in our pastoral contexts and our ministry, should be recognizing, valuing, and engaging differences, honoring the reality of each person's interiority and personal stories. We need to have more awareness of ourselves as supervisors, self-knowledge, motivation, etc. The purpose of all supervision of pastoral psychotherapy is to achieve a "demonstrable increase in professional competence," growth that consists of "ascertainable increase in clinical, theoretical and administrative expertise and appropriate use of self," which can refer "to a whole range of skills having to do with the ability to know and employ one's own strengths and vulnerabilities to the benefit of the psychotherapy one is doing with others."[10] Reflecting on these purposes of pastoral supervision, the pastoral ministry in Tanzania should recognize the importance of pastoral supervision in a broader sense and make it more formal and practical. Hence, the awareness and understanding of people's beliefs, traditions, and cultures will help to build up strong connections and relationships among pastoral ministers in the whole process of pastoral supervision.

RELIGION AND SUPERVISION IN TANZANIA

The concept of religion in Tanzania is not a new phenomenon. Tanzania and its people, through their tribal and ethnic groups, have been believing in, and practicing, religion in different ways for a long time. African traditional religion has been practiced even before the Arabs and the Europeans came to Africa to colonize it. I will not go into details about the history of African traditional religion and its performance, but I will try to share something that Christian pastoral ministry can learn and apply in pastoral supervision. Christianity in Tanzania has been affected by European/Western Christianity and by African traditional religion. The lives of people in Tanzanian communities do not exist in isolation; they have been living in communities and in villages. When Christianity came through the missionaries from Europe, it came also with some baggage of European cultures and traditions, which has affected African lives in one way or an other. Also, the African traditional religion has affected Christianity with its beliefs, which caused some African people to live a syncretistic life. Therefore, living a Christian life in the midst of all these needs, pastoral supervision is a way of reflecting, monitoring, and balancing life for human well-being and wholeness.

CULTURE AND SUPERVISION IN TANZANIA

Being alert and attentive to the culture of the people in the context of pastoral supervision is very serious and important. One needs to understand the challenges and complexities of culture to be effective in pastoral supervision. Culture should be understood in this way:

> Culture includes the entire symbolic environment. Culture defines reality: what is, what should be, what can be. It provides focus and meaning. It selects out of the myriad of events and interactions in the world those we pay attention to. Culture tells us what is important; what causes what and how events beyond our lives relate to us. Culture gives us values and standards of value. What we may distinguish analytically (and at our peril) as fact, value and goal is existentially integrated in culture—in identifications, expectations and demands of individual persons.[11]

Pastoral supervision in Tanzania is obviously influenced by African culture and tradition. You cannot talk about Christianity in Africa without the influence of culture and tradition. Culture and tradition play an important role in whatever we speak and do. Culture and tradition come in various ways which we need to know and discuss and see its place in pastoral supervision. Hence, when one talks about culture and tradition, he/she means the way people live and act in terms of clothing, music, language, food, arts, etc.

The way people in Tanzania value and understand things might differ from other places—even within the same country from one region to another, or from one tribe to the other. For example, in a community from Nyakyusa and Ndali tribes and some other tribes in the Mbeya region of Tanzania, during mourning of a deceased person, women will not be allowed to sit on the chairs or sofas until some certain times. They are only allowed to sit down on the mats inside the house. Therefore, one needs to understand this type of culture before doing anything. However, it is very important to understand that some of the things people behave or do from day to day, are being done unconsciously, even without understanding the value or meaning of them. Attention to the wider cultural issues is very crucial:

> Reflecting on the ways that Western culture affects the embodiment of the body of Christ in our own time and place is one of the ways pastoral supervisors can prepare for the work of supervision and stay alert to these dimensions of the context in which supervisees are working and we ourselves are supervising.[12]

Attention to the cultural complexities will help supervisors to really understand the stories behind the supervisees in more respectful and effective ways. It will show that the supervisors are respecting and opening up a sacred and safe space for the opportunity of growth and development of individuals in a supervisory relationship.

CHALLENGES OF PASTORAL SUPERVISION

In the next sections, I will share some challenges in pastoral ministry which, through my experiences and what I have observed, need to be discussed and understood for the betterment of pastoral supervision in the context of Tanzania. These challenges are what I personally think could be evaluated and applied to keep, and strengthen, pastoral supervision in Tanzania. There might be other challenges which could also be relevant for the whole spectrum of pastoral supervision, but what I will come up with is what I believe, for the time being, will be relevant and applicable. Therefore, what follows are the challenges that I have observed in the pastoral ministry, which I hope will help to inform and be applied to pastoral supervision in Tanzania.

Governance and Administration

Pastoral ministry needs to be governed and administered properly. The pastors of the Moravian Church in Tanzania go to colleges and universities for short, or longer, periods of theological or biblical training, where they study various courses in areas of biblical, practical, historical, and systematic theology, including liberal arts subjects such as psychology, sociology, development studies, computer skills, philosophy, etc. It is through all these courses that pastors are expected to learn about all issues relating to leadership and administration. Through my experience and observation, I still see challenges in leadership within the Moravian church in Tanzania. There have been challenges and conflicts in various provinces of the Moravian church and other Christian churches. The main cause of all these conflicts, is in my view attachment to personal interests, selfishness, evil desires, and pride. This has happened even within the provinces of the Moravian Church in Tanzania, where I personally have also been a leader. Because of some selfish behavior of some leaders, they can move someone out of the position that they hold. Moreover, there is poor leadership and incompetence among these leaders.[13] Whatever they learn from their colleges or universities is not implemented in the proper way; instead, they use their status for selfish desires and fame. Hence, proper mindset and education are needed to be able to learn good skills and ethical issues for effective administration.

Economic Stability (Poverty)

Tanzania is one of the developing countries in the world. The economic situation of the country and its people is not stable. Most people still live under the poverty line, which is a dollar per day. The church in Tanzania is not an island; it lives and sails in the same boat. The ministers of the Moravian Church in Tanzania even live in a greater instability because the salaries they receive are under the minimum wage of the Tanzanian government. The churches are also struggling to pay their pastors reasonable wages. Pastors in villages are even worse off when it comes to their economic status. What makes them survive is because most of these pastors in villages are involved in agriculture, where they can farm different types of crops such as maize, beans, banana, tea, coffee, rice, wheat, and others. They also keep animals such as cows, chicken, goats, pigs, and others. These activities help them to be able to survive and keep up with other needs within the family; but still, this is a big challenge to most African people as well as the church itself.[14]

Pastoral supervision will only be relevant and applicable if pastors are assured of their life today and tomorrow. The uncertainty of life makes pastoral ministry very difficult and uncomfortable, and even tempting. If pastors lack some of the things which are basics to their life, then they will obviously be tempted to a lot of things. The commitment for the work will not be very effective and efficient. The interpersonal relationship with their colleagues and members of congregations will be challenged. Hence, pastoral ministry is challenged to open up more, and open discussions on how to go about economic issues in the Moravian Church; and this can be done through pastoral supervision where financial issues can also be shared. Hence, the church has a role to play on how to sustain pastoral ministry in all contexts.

Interpersonal Relationship

Pastoral supervision is all about relationship. But this relationship is a process which needs to be learned, experienced, practiced, and implemented in proper ways. The challenge that I have seen is how pastors relate to one another. Pastors of the Moravian Church need to learn how to relate to oneself and others, which needs to be cultivated and practiced. Some of the pastors are very much isolated, selfish, disconnected, and proud. This can be caused by ignorance, pride, or intention. That is why pastoral supervision needs to be encouraged in order to explore these issues whereby these could be solved and understood in positive ways. Hence, the issues of interpersonal relationships need to be explored and implemented for the betterment of pastoral ministry.

In Tanzania, pastoral ministry is being challenged when it comes to interpersonal relationship. I have observed and experienced, among pastors, that some are missing the understanding and skills of how to relate to one another, caused by not only ignorance, pride, and selfishness, but also by other psychological issues, such as low self-esteem.[15] Conflicts, fights, and divisions are happening because of the lack of healthy relationships. Interdependence in relationships is healthy, which needs commitment and love of one another. John 13:34–35 says, "So now I am giving you a new commandment: Love each other. Just as I have loved you, you should love each other. Your love for one another will prove to the world that you are my disciples." The scripture again clearly and practically speaks about that love, by saying,

> Dear brothers and sisters, if another believer is overcome by some sin, you who are godly should gently and humbly help that person back onto the right path. And be careful not to fall into the same temptation yourself. Share each other's burdens, and in this way obey the law of Christ. If you think you are too important to help someone, you are only fooling yourself. You are not that important. Pay careful attention to your own work, for then you will get the satisfaction of a job well done, and you won't need to compare yourself to anyone else. For we are each responsible for our own conduct. (Galatians 6: 1–5)

Pastoral supervision needs to consider the spiritual and theological understanding and the maturity of a person in order to relate to one another in a healthy relationship, as Paul speaks to the Christians in Galatia. Each one of us has burdens to carry that are bigger than our strength. We each need someone to carry the burdens with.

Misleading Theologies/Faiths

Religion and faith are very sensitive, and also are very powerful influences in the lives of people. People have been naturally born religious. It means that deep within human beings, there is a sense or thirst—a longing for seeking something bigger than themselves. There is a spiritual longingness in the void in the life of people. Christianity follows the Holy Scripture as the basis for life. Christianity, despite the Bible being followed, does not stand by itself. In it, and through it, there are also customs and traditions from various backgrounds and contexts. To understand the Bible, and to have a proper interpretation of it, one needs divine guidance and revelation, proper theological training, and various experiences from the world.[16] Hence, proper training and understanding of the scripture are needed in pastoral ministry.

Christianity in Africa, and specifically in Tanzania, is growing. Churches are being planted everywhere in cities and villages. The splitting of churches into sects, denominations—even cults—is happening everywhere in Tanzania. The reasons for the breakout of churches, or sects, are the misunderstandings from one another, differences, and conflicts in beliefs and concepts from the Bible. But the other reason for the churches, or denomination, splitting, is because of selfish desires for fame and for the love of money, power, and authority. Therefore, the church needs more skills and principles on how to properly govern the church.

The challenge I have experienced from these blooming churches and denominations, which affect Christendom, is their misleading theologies. These misleading theologies affect pastoral ministry directly, and especially pastoral supervision done in the context of relationship and understanding among pastors. Pastors of some of these churches have been teaching and preaching a prosperity gospel, which misleads Christians to live a life of seeking wealth, health, and fame in improper ways, such as expecting miracles through laying on of hands from ministers such as apostles and prophets, or by supplying them with water, oil, soil, salt, etc. as means for the blessings and successful life, whereby, if used, one is able to own a car, house, or any other property. This is supposed to be a shortcut for being a wealthy person, which is contrary to the principles of the Bible and of life in general. The Bible calls for people to work hard, despite prayers and other things which are being used by some ministers. The Bible clearly says, "See to it that no one takes you captive through hollow and deceptive philosophy, which depends on human tradition and the basic principles of this world rather than on Christ" (Colossians 2:8). Therefore, the church needs to be vigilant in teaching proper and relevant contextual theology and not those misleading theologies, which are "inconsistent, misrepresents, or challenges the sovereignty of God as incarnated in Jesus Christ and revealed by the Holy Spirit."[17]

Traditions and Cultural Stereotype

The people in the Moravian Church, and Christians in Tanzania, are living amid customs and traditions passed from generation to generation. Some of these customs and traditions in our Tanzanian cultures are very important, but others are very destructive and have no value—so, need not to be passed on. Customs and traditions affect people in the way they relate to one another, from one person to the other, or from one culture to another culture. It is very important for theological scholars and Christian ministers to understand and be very critical about these traditions or customs. Holding to bad customs and traditions creates enmity and conflicts among people. Even when it comes to pastoral supervision, customs and traditions affect the whole process of relationship and growth into spiritual development and maturity. Hence, pastors need to be aware of what really surrounds the people whom they serve, to better serve them without generalization.

Some of the cultural stereotypes that I have observed and experienced among pastors I have worked with, are such as not being open to, or transparent about, some issues, such as talking or discussing about sex and other things related to sex education. The other issue pastors need to be open and transparent about is about gender equality. Some people and ministers, arguing from the Bible, think it is biblical to undermine women because they interpret the Bible as asserting that God created human beings differently. These patriarchal communities still exist in Tanzania, and their beliefs need to be examined and understood in order to create gender justice.

There is a problem, or a challenge, of cultural stereotyping in pastoral ministry in Tanzania. I suggest that pastoral supervision needs to check the worldview through the lens of African people, in the way they see life. Africans view the world in a traditional, communal way, while Western people view the world in an individualistic way. The philosophy of African *ubuntu* is, 'I am because we are, and we are because I am.' Therefore, in Africa, when one is hurting, the whole community hurts. Sharing the pain is for the whole society, as well as sharing the joy. It is pointed out that "pastoral care or ministry would be more relevant in our present world if multicultural strategy is considered a priority. . . . this can only be possible if Westerners are ready to dance with other cultures. This demands humility and simplicity of mind to learn the dancing steps of other cultures."[18]

Ethnicity

Ethnicity and tribalism are also social challenges. Tanzania is just like other African countries in that it contains several ethnic groups. Naturally, and psychologically, people tend to like people of their own kind. But, since the fall of Adam, human beings are living in sin of pride and selfishness. Ethnicity and tribalism have caused hatred, division, and conflicts. Segregation among people happened because of divisions. Ethnicity is a major factor in religion, government, and politics. Nwaigbo states that, "Ethnicity constitutes great challenges to Christian leadership in Nigeria. Ethnicity is challenging, and to some extent threatening. We are aware of the sharp criticism and fierce opposition, which are being triggered off by decisions of leaders in favor of one ethnic group at the expense of the others."[19] This is what is happening to most African countries. One needs to be aware of this challenge of ethnicity and tribalism, and understand it in the context of pastoral ministry in Africa. To make pastoral supervision effective in Tanzania, one needs to pay attention to the dilemma of ethnicity. Therefore, Christian leadership needs to address the issue with an open eye and mind, in the service of ethnicity. Christian service is a broader one which goes beyond race, age, gender, and ethnicity. Hence, pastoral supervision is one of the very crucial professions that needs to understand and critically apply psychological, as well as theological, understanding.

Pastoral Moral Ethics

One of the things which I have experienced among pastors in the Moravian Church, and other churches in Tanzania, is the whole issue of ethics. It is one of the big challenges, among pastors, of how to deal with ethical issues. When I talk about ethics or moral behaviour of pastors, I mean how someone is dealing with issues of money discipline, sexual relationship, use of drugs and/or alcohol, and other moral issues. Some pastors have been engaged, and involved themselves, in these issues and would need some help, which most of the time they do not get. Pastors are expected to serve as a role model of faithfulness, truth, honesty, and chastity.[20]

> If someone aspires to be an elder, he desires an honorable position. So, an elder must be a man whose life is above reproach. He must be faithful to his wife. He must exercise self-control, live wisely, and have a good reputation. He must enjoy having guests in his home, and he must be able to teach. He must not be a heavy drinker or be violent. He must be gentle, not quarrelsome, and not love money. He must manage his own family well, having children who respect and obey him. For if a man cannot manage his own household, how can he take care of God's church? An elder must not be a new believer, because he might become proud, and the devil would cause him to fall. Also, people outside the church must speak well of him so that he will not be disgraced and fall into the devil's trap. (1 Timothy 3:1–7)

More knowledge, transparency, and education are needed in this area of how one should control and deal with issues relating to the moral life of a pastor. Pastoral ministry needs to be governed by acceptable standards, and in a proper and reputable professional way. Pastors need to understand that they too need other helping professionals to help them in their professional journey. It is sometimes challenging to accept and acknowledge that a pastor can also pastor him/herself. Otherwise, there must be someone to counsel or supervise a pastor. Hence, pastoral supervision is very crucial here. Some special people need to be trained to become pastoral supervisors in order to make sure that there are sometimes gatherings of pastors where they can talk and share their issues relating to their work, and even talk about issues relating to moral ethical issues.

I have experienced that some pastors get into trouble in matters relating to sexual relationships with their congregational members. The way this is handled, sometimes, is not good for the people involved, or for the congregation, or even for the whole church. Instead of dealing with it in a professional way, it is done in a way that is very embarrassing, not only for pastors, but also for the whole church and community. People will just talk back and publish, and even shame, the pastor without proper means or ways that are more just, empowering, and enriching. Even the media, such as newspapers or other social media, when it comes to issues like that which concern the ministers of God, report it on a front page of their media. Hence, pastoral supervisors, who are professionals, can help in creating an environment that is more confidential and proper and which builds a healthy relationship by understanding the context of the situation and the people around the issue, discussing in detail the pros and cons of the issue.

Education

The history of education in Tanzania is very complex because of its historical background. Tanzania has passed through different educational systems which need to be understood, explored, and properly applied in the context of its people. Historically, Tanzania has been applying traditional ways of educating its people, but it has also gone through involvement with the slave trade done by the Arabs and others. Then they acquired the Western education system during colonialism and after colonialism, whereby Tanzania was colonized by Germany and then by Britain. Even after independence, what I have observed is that the educational system of Tanzania still faces several challenges in order to be relevant to its people.[21] Understanding the education system in Tanzania is very important for pastoral ministry, because theological training has also been affected by the same system, with all its legacies. In this view, pastoral ministry, as well as pastoral supervision in Tanzania, must understand and interpret the learning process according to the contexts of the people, in order to change thinking and behavior into something that is more acceptable and relevant.

SOME EXAMPLES OF CULTURE AND RELIGION THAT FACILITATE PASTORAL SUPERVISION

Language

Tanzania is very fortunate to have a common language which is spoken throughout the country. Kiswahili is almost spoken by all people in Tanzania, despite it not being the first language to most people. Tanzania has about 120 ethnic groups which speak different tribal languages; most of them are known as Bantu languages. Kiswahili, as a common language to Tanzania, has become a unifying factor, where tribalism and ethnic differences are discouraged. Kiswahili is used as the appropriate tool in facilitating unity and motivating socioeconomic integration in the Great Lakes region.[22] Historically, we have learned from other African countries where tribalism has taken over, and where there have been conflicts and wars because of that. A good example of some African countries which have been in conflict because of tribalism are Kenya, Uganda, Rwanda, Nigeria, Burundi, and others. When people speak one common language, it is very easy to understand one another and to live a life of peace and harmony. In Tanzania, Kiswahili is used in almost every area of life, such as schools, businesses, offices, religious gatherings and in everyday conversations. Pastoral ministry is done in the same context, where theological education is basically transmitted in Kiswahili and English as a second language, or a foreign, language. This makes even pastoral supervision more accessible and understandable. Hence, during pastoral supervision, conversation or sessions can become more easy, and fluent because of this commonality in language.

Music

One of the things which the Moravian Church in Tanzania can be proud of, when it comes to culture and traditions which have been passed on from one generation to another, is how music has influenced its people's life. Church music has been very popular to most members of the Moravian Church since its beginning. This church music comes in different styles and forms, where pastoral ministry is being ministered in one way or another, whether it is for evangelism, or for healing ministry, for preaching, and so forth. Music can become one of the instruments or ways of how we can also communicate and understand one another. Music creates an open space for another form of communication and relationship among Christians. Music can be used in pastoral care and supervision as one of the media which is very powerful and effective. It is pointed out that using various musical images and experiences provides a metaphor for increasing understanding of the pastoral supervision process within the pastoral ministry.[23] Hence, music is an important tool for communication and growth of a total person to maturity.

Culture

It is very important to understand that Christians in Tanzania are coming, and living, from different cultures and traditions. Pastoral supervision needs to consider this phenomenon of culture and tradition because the awareness of this will facilitate the relationship of the ministers, if it is to be handled carefully. Some cultures are not good for the development of Christian ministry in Tanzania. Some of the things, or cultures, which need to be changed and forgotten are the way people communicate to one another. What I have observed of some people, especially pastors, is how they deal with issues. Ward asserts that culture plays a significant role in pastoral supervision in clinical pastoral education. She "emphasizes the boundaries between the supervisee's culture and supervisor' culture in order that appropriate dialogue may take place as pastoral counselling skills are learned."[24] Therefore, the culture of people plays a big role in pastoral ministry, in understanding the human behavior, and in thinking.

Religion

It is pointed out that, "religion plays an important and influential role in every culture known."[25] Christianity is one of the major religions in Tanzania. The main other religions that exist in Tanzania are Islam and African traditional religion. Under Christianity, we have different denominations which also have different beliefs. In Tanzania, the main Christian denominations to be found are: Roman Catholic, Lutheran, Anglican, Moravian, African Inland Church, the Baptist Church, and others which are known as mainline churches. There are also Pentecostal and Assemblies of God churches, Seventh-day Adventists, Jehovah's Witnesses, and others. It is not my intention to discuss about these denominations here, but I want to discuss about the relationship which has been existing in Tanzania without much conflict, which is one of the strengths of Tanzania in maintaining peace among people of different faiths. This is important to be aware of, and sensitive to, when working with people of different faiths. Pastoral supervision will be effective if this understanding is taken into consideration.

Other general essential features of pastoral supervision are:

i. Pastoral supervision is an educational procedure which needs to be learned and developed;
ii. Pastoral supervision needs a qualified professional supervisor who has been involved in training and practice;
iii. Pastoral supervision is a professional practice. So, it needs commitment.
iv. Pastoral supervision involves contract between a supervisor and supervisee for better understanding of this professional work.
v. The pastoral supervision role should be professionally appropriate.
vi. Pastoral supervision should be done in the presence of other professionals.[26]

These important roles or principles can help to enrich pastoral supervision in various contexts of pastoral work.

EFFECTIVE METHODS AND APPROACHES OF PASTORAL SUPERVISION IN TANZANIA

Throughout this chapter, the discussion has been about my experience and observation on behaviours and thinking of how people live and relate to one another. The American Psychological Association writes that, "Cognitive behavioral therapy is a form of psychological treatment that has been demonstrated to be effective for a range of problems. . . . CBT leads to significant improvement in functioning and quality of life. . . . [It] has been demonstrated to be as effective as, or more effective than, other forms of psychological therapy or psychiatric medications."[27] Pastoral ministry in Tanzania needs to change their thinking and behaviour from all other misconceptions of culture and tradition which are not good. This reminds me of the biblical texts which direct us to change our mindsets from the old self, or the old human being who is full of evil. This text is from the book of Romans 12:2 which says, "Don't copy the behavior and customs of this world, but let God transform you into a new person by changing the way you think. Then you will learn to know God's will for you, which is good and pleasing and perfect." Therefore, "pastoral supervision is all about 'wisdom' and grace."

Since supervision is an act or instance of directing, managing, or oversight, it is about mentoring, coaching, managing, examining, and overseeing. These are done in different styles and forms, which need innovation and creativity by using and applying arts, music, and drama, in collaborative and corrective feedback, between the supervisor and supervisee. Hence, the thinking and behavior must be changed for the growth and development of an individual person. This can well be understood and applied by people who live in the African cultural context—especially in villages. Some African tribes are busy with grazing animals such as cows, goats, and sheep. When grazing such animals, one needs to be sensitive with the context of the types of animals he has, and the context of where the grazing is taking place, to make sure that the animals are safe and are fed well. This can be seen in the most pastoralist tribes in Tanzania such as Wasukuma, Wamasai, Wagogo, and other tribes. What is happening in the process of leading the animals, feeding, and protecting them, takes some expertise, experience, courage, and strength to overcome all challenges that can happen in the wilderness, to make sure that animals are safe in all areas. I personally can testify to this, because I used to take care of my grandparents' animals in the village where we had also to take other animals from our neighbors, because we took it in turn for each family to look after the animals each week. The flocks were therefore big, and sometimes it was very difficult to control a big flock with many animals. Therefore, you needed extra skills and help from using dogs; and sometimes you had to climb to the top of the big tree to make sure you have a good overview and oversight of all the animals, so that they don't graze on people's crops. Looking out for wild animals which can come against the animals, e.g., hyenas, which were so prevalent in my village, was also part of the task. This example from my personal experience reminds me of the biblical texts such as Ezekiel 34, Psalm 23, or the Gospel of John Ch. 10, where we can learn about the bad and good shepherds. These biblical texts are so important to learn about pastoral supervision in the context of Tanzania because they are so relevant and effective. A good shepherd does not look out only for him/herself but looks out also for the interests of other members or supervisees. A good shepherd will make sure that there is enough food to feed all the members of the family. He/she will make sure there is enough strong protection and security. In general, a good shepherd will make sure that all the physical and spiritual needs of the flock are being met.

CONCLUSION

This chapter has argued that pastoral ministry needs professional supervisors who will be sensitive in understanding the context of the working place, to make pastoral supervision applicable and effective. Pastoral supervision is an important ministry and profession in the Moravian Church in Tanzania, and the church in general. In engaging with this professional ministry, one needs to pay attention to the cultural context and the religion of the people, according to the principles of pastoral supervision. Challenges to pastoral supervision are inescapable and need to be facilitated with awareness, sensitivity and treated with serious consideration for the betterment of this profession. To be more practical, and to build more effective relationships into a pastoral ministry, one needs to follow the methods and models that are relevant to the context of the people that one is working with. Relationships are the key to pastoral supervision in any working environment. More studies and research need to be done into pastoral supervision in the context of Tanzania. The church should embrace this ministry because of the postmodern challenges that the church is going through.

BIBLIOGRAPHY

Agbiji, Obaji M., and Ignatius Swart. "Christian religious leadership and the challenge of sustainable transformational development in post-military Nigeria: Towards a reappraisal." *KOERS–Bulletin for Christian Scholarship* 80, no. 1. (2015): 1–13.

American Psychological Association. What Is Cognitive Behavioral Therapy? (2017). www.apa.org/ptsd-guideline/patients-and-families/cognitive-bihavioral.pdf (Accessed on 22 August 2022).

Aten, Jamie, and Barbara Hernandez. "Addressing Religion in Clinical Supervision: A Model," *Psychotherapy: Theory, Research, Practice, Training* 41, no. 2 (2004): 152–60.

Broughton, Geoff. "What is 'pastoral' about supervision? A Christological proposal." *St. Mark's Review*, no. 254 (December 2020): 9–22.

Eale, Bosela E., and Ngige J. Njoroge. *Addressing Contextual Misleading Theologies in Africa Today*. Minneapolis: Augsburg Fortress Publishers, 2020.

Gahnström, Carl Sebastian Laurentius. "Ethnicity, Religion and Politics in Tanzania: The 2010 General Elections and Mwanza Region." University of Helsinki, master's thesis, 2012.

Hoover, Edwin A. "Pastoral supervision as an Interpersonal experience," *Journal of Pastoral Care and Counseling* 31, no. 3 (1977). https://doi.org/10.1177/002234097703100304.

Hunter, Rodney J. *Dictionary of Pastoral Care and Counseling*. Nashville: Abingdon Press, 1990.

Kishe, Ann M. "Kiswahili as vehicle of unity and dvelopment in the Great Lakes Region," *Language, Culture and Curriculum* 16, no. 2 (2003): 218–30.

Leach, Jane, and Michael Paterson. *Pastoral Supervision: A Handbook*. London: SCM Press, 2015.

Makula, Ngetelile K. "Peace-Building between Christians and Muslims in Tanzania," in *Conceptualizing Christian-Muslim Relations in Tanzania*, ed. Elia Shabani Mligo. Iringa: Gredo Enterprises, 2022.

Mbwette, Tolly S. A., Edward T. T. Bagandanshwa, and Cosmas B. Mnyanyi, "Counselling at the workplace in Tanzania: What can distance education do?" *Huria: Journal of the Open University of Tanzania* 13, no. 2 (2012): 220–29. www.ajol.info/index.php/huria/article/view/110816 (accessed August 24, 2022).

Milne, Derek L. *Evidence-Based CBT Supervision: Principles and Practice*. Hoboken: John Wiley & Sons Ltd, 2018.

Mlyuka, Daud Raphael. "The Impact and Influence of Global Socio-Economy on the Clerical Ministy in the Evangelical Lutheran Church in Tanzania (ELCT)." Master of Global Studies, Stavanger University, 2009.

Nche, George C., Lawrence, N. Okwuosa, and Chinyere T. Nwaoga, "Revisiting the concept of inculturation in a modern Africa: A reflection on salient issues," *HTS Theological Studies* 72 no. 1 (2016): 1–6. http://dx.doi.org/10.4102/hts.v72i1.3015.

Nwaigbo, Ferdinand. "The task of Christian church leadership and the new challenges of ethnicity in West African Sub-region," *Global Journal of Humanities* 3, nos. 1 & 2 (2004): 85–92.

Oderinde, Olatundun Abosede. "Ethical misconduct among Nigerian church leaders in the context of 1 Timothy 3: 1–7." *Research on Humanities and Social Sciences* 4, no. 17 (2014): 27–32.

Ogbuanu, J. N. "The problem of cultural stereotyping in the pastoral care of a suicidal person," *Acta Theologica* 34, no. 1 (2014): 127–44. DOI: http://dx.doi.org/10.4314/actat.v34i1.8.

Pohly, Kenneth. *Transforming the Rough Places: The Ministry of Supervision*. Eugene: Wipf & Stock, 2016.

Richardson, Harvey. "A musical metaphor for pastoral supervision," *Practical Theology* 2, no. 3 (2009): 373–86. DOI: 10.1558/prth.v2i3.373.

Simtala, Joseph. "Examining the Weaknesses of Christianity in Penetrating to Muslim Dominated Areas in Tanzania": Pp. 21–35 in *Conceptualizing Christian-Muslim Relations in Tanzania*, ed. Elia Shabani Mligo. Iringa: Gredo Enterprises, 2022.

Steere, David A. *The Supervision of Pastoral Care*. Eugene: Wipf & Stock, 2002.

Tanzania 2021 International Religious Freedom Report. http://www.state.gov/wp-content/uploads/2022/05/TANZANIA-2021-INTERNATIONAL-RELIGIOUS-FREEDOM-REPORT.pdf (accessed August 26, 2022).

Wandela, Eugenia L. "Tanzania Post-Colonial Educational System and Perspectives on Secondary Science Education, Pedagogy, and Curriculum: A Qualitative Study." Doctor of Education, DePaul University, 2014.

Ward, Edwina. "Similarities and differences in cross-cultural in pastoral supervision." *Journal of Theology for Southern Africa* 116 (July 2003): 51–64.

NOTES

1. Tolly S. A. Mbwette, Edward T. T. Bagandanshwa, and Cosmas B. Mnyanyi, "Counselling at the workplace in Tanzania: What can distance education do?" *Huria: Journal of the Open University of Tanzania* 13, no. 2 (2012): 220–29. www.ajol.info/index.php/huria/article/view/110816 (accessed August 24, 2022).

2. David A. Steere, *The Supervision of Pastoral Care* (Eugene: Wipf & Stock, 2002).

3. Tanzania 2021 International Religious Freedom Report. http://www.state.gov/wp-content/uploads/2022/05/TANZANIA-2021-INTERNATIONAL-RELIGIOUS-FREEDOM-REPORT.pdf (accessed August 26, 2022).

4. Ngetelile K. Makula, "Peace-Building between Christians and Muslims in Tanzania," in *Conceptualizing Christian-Muslim Relations in Tanzania*, ed. Elia Shabani Mligo (Iringa: Gredo Enterprises, 2022), 21–35.

5. Joseph Simtala, "Examining the Weaknesses of Christianity in Penetrating to Muslim Dominated Areas in Tanzania," in *Conceptualizing Christian-Muslim Relations in Tanzania*, ed. Elia Shabani Mligo (Iringa: Gredo Enterprises, 2022), 47–59.

6. Carl Sebastian Laurentius Gahnström, "Ethnicity, Religion and Politics in Tanzania: The 2010 General Elections and Mwanza Region, "(University of Helsinki, master's thesis, 2012).

7. Rodney J. Hunter, *Dictionary of Pastoral Care and Counseling* (Nashville: Abingdon Press, 1990), 1239.

8. Geoff Broughton, "What is 'pastoral' about supervision? A Christological proposal." *St Mark's Review*, no. 254 (December 2020): 9–22.

9. George C. Nche, Lawrence, N. Okwuosa, and Chinyere T. Nwaoga, "Revisiting the concept of inculturation in a modern Africa: A reflection on salient issues," *HTS Theological Studies* 72 no. 1 (2016): 1–6

10. Kenneth Pohly. *Transforming the Rough Places: The Ministry of Supervision* (Eugene: Wipf & Stock, 2016), 49.

11. Jane Leach and Michael Paterson, *Pastoral Supervision: A Handbook* (London: SCM Press, 2015), 191.

12. Leach and Paterson, *Pastoral Supervision*, 195.

13. Obaji M. Agbiji and Ignatius Swart, "Christian religious leadership and the challenge of sustainable transformational development in post-military Nigeria: Towards a reappraisal" *KOERS–Bulletin for Christian Scholarship* 80, no. 1. (2015): 1–13.

14. Daud Raphael Mlyuka, "The Impact and Influence of Global Socio-Economy on the Clerical Ministy in the Evangelical Lutheran Church in Tanzania (ELCT)" (Master of Global Studies, Stavanger University, 2009).

15. Edwin A. Hoover, "Pastoral Supervision as an interpersonal experience," *Journal of Pastoral Care and Counseling* 31, no. 3 (1977). https://doi.org/10.1177/002234097703100304.

16. Bosela E. Eale and Ngige J. Njoroge, *Addressing Contextual Misleading Theologies in Africa Today* (Minneapolis: Augsburg Fortress Publishers, 2020).

17. Ibid.

18. J. N. Ogbuanu, "The problem of cultural stereotyping in the pastoral care of a suicidal rerson," *Acta Theologica* 34, no. 1 (2014): 127–44. DOI: http://dx.doi.org/10.4314/actat.v34i1.8.

19. Ferdinand Nwaigbo, "The task of Christian church leadership and the new challenges of ethnicity in West African sub-region," *Global Journal of Humanities* 3, nos. 1 & 2 (2004): 85–92.

20. Olatundun Abosede Oderinde, "Ethical Misconduct among Nigerian Church Leaders in the Context of 1 Timothy 3: 1–7." *Research on Humanities and Social Sciences* 4, no. 17 (2014): 27–32.

21. Eugenia L. Wandela, "Tanzania Post-Colonial Educational System and Perspectives on Secondary Science Education, Pedagogy, and Curriculum: A Qualitative Study." (Doctor of Education, DePaul University, 2014).

22. Ann M. Kishe, "Kiswahili as vehicle of unity and development in the Great Lakes Region," *Language, Culture and Curriculum* 16, no. 2 (2003): 218–30.

23. Harvey Richardson, "A musical metaphor for pastoral supervision," *Practical Theology* 2, no. 3 (2009): 373–86.

24. Edwina Ward, "Similarities and differences in cross-cultural in pastoral supervision." *Journal of Theology for Southern Africa* 116 (July 2003): 51–64.

25. Jamie Aten and Barbara Hernandez, "Addressing Religion in Clinical Supervision: A Model," *Psychotherapy: Theory, Research, Practice, Training* 41, no. 2 (2004): 152–60.

26. Rodney J. Hunter, *Dictionary of Pastoral Care and Counseling* (Nashville: Abingdon Press, 1990).

27. American Psychological Association, What Is Cognitive Behavioral Therapy? (2017). www.apa.org/ptsd-guideline/patients-and-families/cognitive-bihavioral.pdf (Accessed on 22 August 2022).

Chapter Ten

Pastoral Supervision for Clergy Spouses

Deanne Gardner

"Ministry is, at times, emotionally, physically and spiritually draining and exhausting; the reality may be that it is this most of the time, depending on our age and situation."[1] The clergyperson is often called by God into a vocation of service to others. These 'others' include members of their immediate congregation, the community in which they live, and, in some cases, others outside of their close location, including offering support to individuals nationally and internationally. Clergy are shepherds and, in most cases, the 'flock' that they shepherd are diverse in age, character, ability, ethnic background, and needs. The clergyperson can find him/herself undertaking many roles, dependent upon, but not exclusively because of, the denomination to which they belong. For instance, within the Pentecostal Church that I belong to, along with being a spiritual guide and guiding people through their walk of faith, pastors can often find themselves taking on the role of a social worker, a counsellor (not a spiritual counsellor), an advocate, a mentor, a first responder (responding to all emergency situations that emerge), a teacher, and a mediator. Alongside the spiritual, emotional, and mental support that is offered, I have known some pastors who have used some of their practical abilities and talents, and their role has included cooking, building work, decorating, and IT skills, as they undertake their calling and service to others. The list that I have offered is not exhaustive, and all of these things may be happening simultaneously when serving others in a congregation. People rarely wait in line when they have a need (the woman in the New Testament story, who pressed forward to touch Jesus in the crowd comes to mind), and while serving others in these ways is at times rewarding, ministry can be draining on many levels. Alongside the multiple tasks undertaken by the clergy, it is also worth considering the availability of the clergyperson. Some will work long hours and may adopt an 'on-call' position, feeling that their calling means that they need to be available to those who need them for twenty-four hours a day, seven days a week. With the support that clergy offer to others, it has been recognised that the impact upon the clergyperson can be greatly detrimental on many levels and, in some instances, the effects can be long-lasting. Words such as 'compassion fatigue,' 'burnout,' 'vicarious traumatisation,' and 'disillusionment' have come into everyday conversation, particularly post-pandemic, and self-care and access to resources such as pastoral supervision can be a means of reducing the impact and effects of the demanding role undertaken by clergy.[2]

Earlier, I mentioned the multiple roles that clergypersons might undertake in their everyday tasks. For each of these roles, individuals who work within semi-equivalent jobs such as social work would be offered, and expected to access, regular supervision as a way of supporting the individual in their jobs. Supervision, pastoral supervision, and reflective practice spaces for individuals who are working in helping professions are now offered more widely as a means of supporting those who are alongside those who need help physically, emotionally, and mentally. Our clergy have an added element to the support that is offered to others, and that is that they meet the spiritual needs of individuals in their remit. Some individuals in particular denominations may ask what, if any, support is available to their clergy? Up until recently, regular, structured support for the clergyperson has been sparse in most denominations. Pastoral supervision is still relatively new as a means of support, and it is described as—'a regular space that is offered by a pastoral supervisor to a supervisee to discuss the supervisee's practice.'[3]

Some readers may ask what any of the above has to do with the title of this chapter? I have deliberately opened this chapter with a reflection on the multiple roles and the demands made on the clergyperson, as I believe that it is pertinent to what I will be exploring in terms of the experiences of clergy spouses who are often impacted by the work that their husband/wife undertakes. In this chapter, I will be exploring the position held by the clergy spouse, the possible impact of the calling by virtue of being married to a clergy person, and any relevance or value of accessing pastoral supervision. I will also attempt to explore what pastoral supervision might look like when working with clergy spouses, and also explore issues that we might need to be aware of when working with this group of supervisees. I will touch on, to a small degree, issues around diversity awareness and the use and meaning of language, such as boundaries and confidentiality, holding in mind that working with clergy spouses might be different to the current way in which we work as pastoral supervisors who are working directly with a clergyperson or the individual who is directly employed in the helping profession.

As the author of this chapter, I like to identify my position as a way of being transparent. I am writing from both an insider (that of supervisee) and an outsider (that of supervisor) perspective. I am the wife of a credentialed minister within a Pentecostal church, and I have supported my husband through the highs and lows of pastoring a church. I am a qualified psychotherapist, a clinical supervisor, and a pastoral supervisor. My motivation for writing this chapter stems from having experiences in my position as the pastor's wife where I was often asked to offer the equivalent of counselling support to individuals of our congregation, in the same way that I would as a psychotherapist, but without having access to any external support in the way I would in my position as a psychotherapist. Having conducted a study into the emotional demands made on clergy wives,[4] the findings of the study identified that the provision of pastoral supervision was worth some consideration for those who supported their clergy spouses, and I have included some excerpts from the participants of the study in this chapter, which I hope will allow us to hear the voices of those who may seek out our support. The indented quotations in italics are the voices of participants from my research, although I have given each a pseudonym to protect their identity. My use of the term 'clergyperson' throughout this chapter will refer to a pastor or vicar. I have sat in several induction services of church ministers, and their spouses have stood beside them during the process of the induction ceremony as a way of showing open support and solidarity. I have also noted that during these services, the spouse is usually asked to join the clergy husband or wife, and I often wonder what standing alongside the clergyperson means for the individual and if they would feel comfortable declining the request? Within the Pentecostal tradition, standing alongside the individual who will be taking up the position of the pastor communicates many messages to the congregation.

THE TWO-PERSON VOCATION

> I felt like he was the leader, and I was just coming along with him. It's almost like the Trump and Melania duo . . . She just came with the package. (Carol)

The role of the clergyperson is unique, in that it is a vocation and, for the most part, a calling by God. It encompasses many roles simultaneously, and it is a position that may include the clergy spouse if the clergyperson is married. The spouse may be included, either implicitly or explicitly, in the clergyperson's vocation, and this may even include the spouse being told that they are not expected to be actively involved in their spouse's vocation, but they are expected to be visible.[5] Very few individuals enter a profession needing to give any thought to the inclusion of their spouse and the possible impact of their job on their spouse and family, and there are not many professions that include the spouse at all. However, the call into ministry, and the clergy vocation, has historically been one such setting and is similar to couples for whom one or other of the spouses is in politics, or who hold a senior position in one of the armed forces.[6] Papanek[7] devised the term 'two-person career,' which is described as the inducting of a wife into her husband's career, although she is not officially employed by her husband's organisation; thus, in the situation of the clergy wife, making her an unpaid voluntary partner/curate. It is interesting to note that support for the clergyperson is usually offered from the clergy wife to her husband who is the vicar/pastor, rather than the clergy husband to his wife who is the vicar/pastor.[8] Historically, many Church traditions, particularly Black-led churches, have held an expectation that the clergy wife will take an active part alongside her husband. Research and literature report that the role of husbands of the clergywoman is sparse, with Murphy-Geiss[9] and Drumm, Cooper, Seifert, McBride, Sedlacek[10] being some of the few studies that showed that there appeared to be a different set of expectations for male and female clergy spouses.

Carol, in the above participant quotation, identifies the position that some clergy spouses may feel that they hold, that of being alongside their clergy husband/wife as part of a package. When considering the helping position that the clergyperson undertakes, and the two-person career element of the married clergy couple, it is interesting to note two things:

1. The vocation of the clergyperson could be considered to be included in the helping professions arena. However, the employing organisations of most helping professionals who have spouses or partners, would not expect the spouse to be involved in their employee's employment.
2. The visible role undertaken by clergy, including individual interactions and 'on-stage' activities, is akin to a celebrity-like position and, in some cases, lifestyle.[11, 12] It has been likened to a 'goldfish bowl' existence in that the clergyperson and their family are constantly observed by the congregation and community.[13] Such a position can bring with it demands that come with being visible, and in which the spouse and family members of the minister are involuntary associates. This is very different to that of spouses of professionals within other helping professions; for instance, we would not see, or know, the spouse or family members of the chief of police, or the head of social services.

We can see here that being married to a clergyperson may bring with it a layer that forms a complicated base before we consider what may be added to that base for each individual. I would like to propose that this complex base is present regardless of the cultural context or denominational setting. The differences might be what is then layered onto this; by that, I mean some specific cultural elements that differentiate the experience, such as gender and any unique expectations of the roles undertaken by males and females within the majority culture in which the clergy couple is based. Without any further consideration, these two elements are food for thought in terms of pastoral supervision support that might be offered to the clergy spouse in a two-person career/vocation by virtue of being married to the vicar.

THE POSITION, ROLE, AND TITLE

> As the wife of the church pastor, I think my first role is that I support my husband, because if we don't support the gentleman, then he can't do his best because he's not getting any support for himself. (Elaine)

The life of the clergy spouse is rarely spoken of in terms of the day-to-day demands, intricacies, and nuances. In some settings, the spouse could be considered as the 'silent partner,' whether that be by choice or through pressure. Studies that offer the voices of the clergy spouse are rare. Is it that we do not want to hear the stories of those who support individuals who support others in their vocational calling? Earlier, we looked at some of the tasks undertaken by the clergyperson. I would like us to consider this now from the position of the clergy spouse. The quote from Elaine (above) reflects the position taken by a wife of a clergyman. Clergy spouses often have their own calling to serve in a certain area of church ministry and, alongside this, they may find themselves being responsible for doing a plethora of multiple roles as they seek to support their clergy husband or wife and, in some cases, the congregation. The support offered can be on many levels, including emotional, spiritual, mental, and physical, and although it may not be clear at any point what type of support is being offered, we can see from Elaine's quote above, that support is offered as a way of filling a gap for something that may not always be offered from an organisational perspective. What I mean by that is that it may be that spouses who support their clergy wife or husband might do so on two levels: the first from the position of supporting a spouse as we might do in any couple relationship; and the second from the position, that I mentioned earlier, of meeting a need for support that is not offered from the church setting. I am drawn back to the importance of offering support and what it might look like, and the position from which it might be offered. As a pastoral supervisor, I would be curious to know where the clergy spouse positioned his/herself in terms of location in the clergyperson's vocation and the offering of support, whether that be from an integral ministerial position,[14] or as a spouse of the wife or husband. Some participants within my research placed themselves comfortably alongside their husbands in terms of serving and supporting others. Other participants found that members of the congregation wanted to position the wife next to her husband, and the wife did not necessarily wish to support her husband from that position. This is something we will consider later when exploring the value of pastoral supervision.

I feel that it is important to note that the clergy spouse may, at times, be offering support in various ways to members of the congregation alongside supporting the pastor/vicar. When we consider the relationship between the clergyperson and their spouse, it would not be unreasonable to imagine that the relationship may be very different from the experiences of many married couples who are involved in a helping profession, even those couples who are employed in the same profession, such as the husband and wife being employed in health care or teaching. The vocational calling of the clergyperson is different from the vocational calling of an individual who feels drawn toward working in a helping profession. So, the spouse of the clergyperson, while in most cases having a personal faith walk, may sense the same vocational calling to serve in a church leadership partnership. Some participants that I spoke with in my research shared that their spouse was not a clergyperson when they had first married, but since being married, their spouse had experienced a calling to serve God as a leader of a congregation. Considering further the unique clergy couple experience in comparison to other couples who may be in the limelight, such as politicians or high-ranking officers in the forces, clergy spouses often receive little, or no, preparation or training regarding what to expect when in the position of being clergy spouse of the clergy person. This may risk the individual undertaking unintended roles before they are able to settle into the church in which their husband or wife has been inducted. Earlier, I mentioned the goldfish bowl existence of being watched by others. With many 'eyes' watching, there is the risk of the clergy couple experiencing projections from those on the outside and, for some couples, there is a sensing of an expectation to present a perfect marriage and relationship in line with the way that others expect of Christian marriages.

> It isn't as though you've applied for this position, and you know what's expected as you would do if you applied for a job. You'd have an idea of what job you're going for wouldn't you? And you'd have read through the job description, and you'd say, 'Oh yes, I can manage that. Yes, I can do that. Oh, but I might need training there.' So, you'd know your strengths, you'd know your weaknesses. (Hannah)

Having considered the position of the clergy spouse alongside the clergyperson, we will now look at another element that, in many cases, forms the base in terms of having the title of clergy spouse. While the above quotation from Hannah is not a general reflection of every clergy spouse, it does capture the thoughts in terms of a role and job description in connection to being married to a church minister. For some spouses, there is a title that is placed onto them, and with it comes a projection of how members of the congregation, community, or church institute determine the role to be, based upon the title. The role of clergy spouses is often ambiguous and is commonly directed by external agents such as the congregation, the community, the church as an institution, and finally by the spouse themselves. Finch[15] writes about the unclear job descriptions experienced by clergy wives, which in some ways mirrors the above comment made by Hannah, almost forty years later. As I contemplate my own experience as the wife of a pastor within my denomination that uses the term the "first lady" to identify the wife of the pastor, the wife was expected to be at least visible and, at most, active within the "ladies" ministry. Some individuals might question the necessity of job roles for someone who is not called into the same vocation as their spouse, and they may have some difficulty with this if working with spouses who are based in certain denominations, or with spouses who hold a particular mindset regarding what the call to serve others looks like.

Titles and roles may play a major part in terms of the meaning, expectations and demands experienced by clergy spouses. The context within which we may find ourselves can inform the role and attitude of being an 'aid' to the shepherd. It could be assumed that spouses are happy to be identified as the clergy wife/husband or, within some Pentecostal and Evangelical settings, as the "first lady" (or whatever the male equivalent might be). The title may help the individual, and others in the congregation, to know that they are invested in their spouse's ministry and calling. They may also use the title to create and define their own role and position. On the other hand, some individuals may struggle with a title or with an identity that is placed upon them, seeing it as prescriptive and restrictive, and in my experience, this is not dependent upon the denominational context. It may be that some individuals feel that they lose a sense of themselves and their personal identity if they are considered to be a part of their clergy husband/wife's ministry. The title, or position, and the role are interlinked, and one feeds into the other; depending upon the denomination, the role is more visible and the title grander. Why is this relevant to this chapter? Both can be considered important to hold in mind as something that is woven into the framework that I spoke of earlier, and it may define how involved or uninvolved a supervisee may become in their spouse's ministry, and the level of impact that this might have on the clergy spouse. Having the position of being the clergy spouse may bring with it some unspoken expectations that may need to be managed in a way that had not been planned for, and a conversation regarding appropriate support appears to be important considering our earlier reflections on the two-person career.

MULTIPLICITY OF ROLES

Earlier, I suggested that in their calling, the clergyperson undertakes multiple roles simultaneously and, in some circumstances, we can find clergy spouses themselves undertaking multilayered roles as they support the clergyperson. An image of an open hand supporting another open hand comes to mind. The clergyperson is often likened to a shepherd, and we see that some shepherds have aides to help them look after the flock. For those clergy who are married, the congregation and community (flock) might consider the clergy's wife/husband as that aide, in whatever form that might be, and could expect that a certain role is performed. For instance, the 'role' might range from making cups of tea after the morning service or fixing the plumbing problem in the washrooms, to co-pastoring alongside the clergyperson, and being available and on-call alongside the clergyperson, taking on the role of 'first responder.'

Looking at how a title might impact the roles that are undertaken, I would like to bring in some of the findings from my research, in which wives of pastors spoke specifically, and at length, about the intricate nature of the title and the role. The position that clergy spouses occupied would often lead to them juggling roles, leading them to experience emotional demands. The multiplicity of roles included elements such as being a listener for their clergy husband and being a listener for members of the congregation. Listening to others would often include hearing some personal and traumatic experiences for which *they* had no support. Some spouses might hold a dual parental role due to the clergyperson not being available to be involved in family events and parental duties. There was an element of people-pleasing that was based upon some theological beliefs and also the age of the congregant, e.g., older members were more vocal in terms of what they expected from the clergy spouse, and they often based this upon a cultural or theologically held view of what the spouse of the clergyperson ought to be doing. In trying to please a congregation and the organisation, and in some cases, the clergyperson and themselves, some clergy spouses saw 'wearing a mask' as one of their roles in order to undertake other difficult roles that were incongruent with who they were, or where they considered their calling to be. Reflecting on both my work with clergy spouses and the research that I undertook, the pressure to be, or not be, a particular way in relation to the clergyperson's calling and position, is similar across denominations. Some expectations, in terms of roles were gender-based in that it appeared that more might be expected from clergy wives than from clergy husbands, and it is interesting to note a lack of voice in terms of the thoughts from clergy husbands in the published research.[16]

IS IT ALL ABOUT EXTERNAL EXPECTATIONS?

> I had an internal expectation as well, because that's what I'd seen people doing—so you follow on, don't you? . . . and I think it's overwhelming, the whole thing, if you stop and look at it. (Maureen)

I am mindful that the reader of this chapter may want to question the impact of the expectations that the clergy spouse may experience from various groups of people under the umbrella of the denomination to which they belong, and where the spouse might be positioned within this. It would be easy to assume that the role was defined by external sources. However, there may be another level of expectation and demand that could be overlooked, and that is one that may come from the clergy spouse themselves. The above quote from Maureen reflects this in what is shared by the participant. The tapestry of the role of the clergy spouse can include what the spouse deems to be necessary for developing, and holding, the role, and might include: spiritual expectations—how they feel they ought to portray themselves as a Christian; physical expectations—including how they would like to portray themselves by way of serving others; emotional expectations—including how they permit themselves to experience life events; and intellectual expectations - including how they present themselves if/when asked to communicate and interact with different groups in the congregation and community. While a job description is not provided, we can see that, for some of the clergy spouses who might contact us for pastoral supervision, the role may be self-defined and, to some degree, based on how they may have observed others undertaking the role, alongside what they perceive is expected from others. In the sense of becoming overwhelmed, this may come from having observed many other clergy spouses and making some comparisons in terms of their own competence. As mentioned earlier, it may be worth considering that there could be a gender element linked to this depending upon the context of the church tradition, and the clergy husband's experience is equally important as clergy wives. In fact, as I reflect on this, I wonder if there could be a risk that there might be a lack of definition, or identity, for the clergy husband, as there is often not a pre-prescribed role to assimilate. We might wonder if internal expectations are more difficult to work with than those that come from external sources, and this could be a question for exploration within pastoral supervision.

For some clergy spouses, even before the spiritual, emotional, physical and intellectual expectations form a part of the tapestry, the internal and external expectations of whether or not to attend the same church as their husband or wife who holds the position of priest/pastor, will carry with it its own unique challenges. This final area is one that may be a realistic consideration within all traditions, but could be a thought that spouses from all traditions might contemplate at one point or other during the appointment of the clergyperson to whom they are married.

SERVING GOD, SERVING OTHERS

> I just said, 'God, I'll do what you want me to do, and I'll take this as my learning. I'm just going to serve You as You've given me the opportunity.' (Patricia)

I am aware that the reader could assume that clergy spouses are not in an independent position to serve and enjoy their call to service. While often not called to co-pastor a church or into joint leadership, the clergy spouse may experience times when they are called upon to use their talents and giftings within the church which their spouse is overseeing. Serving and sharing are done with pleasure, and there can be a real joy when spouses are able to minister in areas to which they feel that they a naturally gifted. There is a sacrificial giving to the service of God within the marriage, and whatever that might include within the couple relationship as a clergy couple. The above quote from Patricia demonstrates freedom in the position and role held, and it is part of working for the service of God's work. Giving some consideration to the vocation to which the clergyperson is called, and the respect that is offered to the calling and gifts that are used, it seems prudent to hold in mind that each person who is called to faith, and who serves within a certain area, may consider the specific area that they are drawn to, to be a vocation. With this in mind, offering the same level of support that is offered to the clergyperson, to the clergy spouse, is crucial. However, what if the clergyperson is not accessing any support? Might it then be that the clergy spouse would not be expected, or permitted, to access support for themselves? My experience as a pastoral supervisor has been that the spouse of a clergyperson—generally a wife—may seek to access pastoral supervision and later encourage the clergyperson (usually male) to consider accessing pastoral supervision.

IMPACT OF UNDERTAKING A CARING ROLE

This chapter began with a reflection on the clergyperson's experiences of undertaking their vocation. It included similarities to that of other helping professions and some of the risks that the clergyperson is exposed to when undertaking multiple caring roles, such as burnout and experiencing secondary trauma through listening to, and being alongside, others in their traumatic experiences. I felt that it was important to have this as an overview, particularly as we moved into the notion of the two-person vocation that some clergy spouses, by virtue of being married to the clergyperson, may embark on, including carrying out ambiguous roles, through either personal expectations or the expectations of others. Very little has been written about the emotional demands and impact of being married to a clergy person. While I have offered a few roles that may be performed by a few clergy spouses, this is in no way exhaustive. While the clergy spouse seeks to support the clergyperson, alongside certain groups within the congregation, family, and possibly members of the community—both spiritually, emotionally, and physically—what might be the impact of offering such support, and where might they seek support?

> I have to confess it can be emotionally draining sometimes, and not just emotionally, but physically. (Sheila)

Being alongside the clergyperson in this unique relationship can be rewarding and overwhelming at the same time. While serving others is undertaken with joy and enthusiasm, the impact of accompanying others during their most difficult life journeys can be draining.[17] The church setting is a place that some individuals may turn to as the first port of call for support when faced with a crisis.[18] In my counselling room, I am able to prepare myself for what a client may bring into the session, but as the wife of a man undertaking pastoral duties in a church setting whom I seek to support, I do not know what I might be confronted with, or who I might be asked to offer support to, and in what way.

As the clergy couple is exposed to the impact of people work, it is important to consider the possible impact of such work upon clergy spouses. Participants in my study shared that as they sought to offer physical, emotional, and spiritual support to individuals, including their spouses, they experienced an impact on their own mental, emotional, and physical health. They spoke of ways that they sought to manage the impact in each of these areas, such as pushing down difficult emotions, journaling, giving up roles, and praying. Alongside navigating the emotional and physical aspects of ministry, many were managing being constantly 'on show' to others, alongside having limited times of not being available to others. The term 'tertiary vicarious traumatisation' is used by McCann and Pearlman[19] to describe the impact of being alongside an individual who has experienced secondary trauma. I would like to suggest that for some clergy spouses, this might be an experience that they have as they support their husband or wife in ministry, regardless of whether they take a hands-on role or stay in the background. To give an example, I consider that the impact on some ministers of being present at very difficult church council meetings that may leave them with very painful emotions to process, and the impact that this may have on spouses who observe and may absorb the pain that is experienced by their spouse, although they themselves would not have attended the meeting, to be tertiary vicarious traumatisation.

IS THERE A PLACE FOR PASTORAL SUPERVISION FOR CLERGY SPOUSES?

Clergy spouses may find themselves in the role of the listener and, to some degree, to be the informal pastoral supervisor to their clergy husband or wife, particularly in circumstances where no other access to support is available to the clergyperson. This brings about a difficult dual relationship, or dual context situation, and can put a strain on the relationship. The spouse will know the people involved, the setting and background, and will find themselves emotionally linked to what is being shared by the clergyperson. It is impossible to be neutral and offer support in a way that does not come at a personal cost. The position of the clergy spouse is unique and can be considered peculiar in that there is not an overall structure, outline, or template to be adopted for being the spouse of a clergyperson. Some clergy spouses take an integral position within the couple relationship, with regards to the calling and vocation of the clergyperson, while others do not consider themselves as an integral part of their spouse's calling, and neither do they choose to, nor is there an expectation in their church tradition for them to be involved.

Having reflected on the calling and vocation of the clergyperson, and some of the experiences of the clergy spouse in terms of direct, or indirect, impact, I believe that in both situations, there is justification for the provision of pastoral supervision. At points through this chapter, I have included elements for consideration as pastoral supervisors. Being alongside an individual whose vocation permeates the home setting—e.g., phone calls at various times of the day, appointments that threaten to interrupt family time and the couple relationship, navigating implicit and explicit expectations—cannot but have an impact. The spouse of the clergyperson might be likened in some ways to that of being a carer, and we could ask 'who cares for the carer'? As pastoral supervisors who offer a reflective space to those working directly with individuals within church settings, such as vicars and pastors, the notion of offering pastoral supervision to a group of individuals who do not hold the position of the clergyperson, but who are nonetheless impacted by the work of their spouses, may be a very new notion. Interestingly, when asked what the participants in my research might want, pastoral supervision was identified as one of the four forms of support!

WHAT MIGHT PASTORAL SUPERVISION LOOK LIKE WHEN WORKING WITH SPOUSES?

> I don't know if it's too much to ask for regular supervision. I mean, once every six months would be a bit ridiculous, but once a quarter at least. I think it would be good. I think to call you. To sit down and to be real. You know, "how are things going with your role? How are things going in your marriage? How are things?" (Yvonne)

Reflecting on the unique individual person, and the variety of positions and mindsets that clergy spouses may sit with, there is no one-size-fits-all approach when working with clergy spouses in terms of what might be needed in the pastoral supervision space. The main requirement is the offer of a space, and a place, that allows the individual to be real, and our own personal awareness and ability to ask the clergy spouse questions that are not asked in other spaces. As pastoral supervisors, we may adopt a standard way of working with individuals, such as clergy or chaplains, that may need to be adapted if working with the spouse of a clergyperson. I believe that there are factors to bear in mind when working with the spouses of clergy that may be unique to working with this group. It is important for pastoral supervisors to consider the area of confidentiality and what this means for clergy spouses who have not signed a confidentiality agreement, but who, nonetheless, are expected to keep things confidential.[20] Some spouses may feel silenced, and this is important to hold in mind in our responses, so as not to cause the supervisee to feel judged if they wish to share something within the supervision space. Another factor might be that of 'boundaries,' and how this is perceived, particularly if this has been an issue within the church context, or conversely is not an issue, although what is being shared may cause us to believe that it might be an issue due to our personal values. I am drawn here to some ethnic contexts and the collective element that would be important to hold in mind. Other wider factors to consider are areas such as the cultural context. Do we need to have an awareness of how gender or ethnic backgrounds might impact the experience of clergy spouses? The denominational setting: is there any value in knowing something of the background of the denomination to which the clergy spouse belongs? It also helps to have an awareness of any preconceived judgments that we bring into the supervision space, with regard to clergy spouses, and our views regarding the positions, roles, and titles that are held or undertaken.

There are times when the supervision space might merge, or cross over, into counselling, and this may well parallel the merging spaces that the spouse experiences outside of the pastoral supervision space. Understanding that it is a different space, and that the pastoral supervision space is valuable, particularly for issues that are situationally based, and that a separate counselling space may be beneficial, is worth some consideration. The clergy spouse, who is seeking pastoral supervision, might not want to go into a different space, but may wish to bring the context of what they want to discuss alongside the impact (emotional element) that the context has had on them. We may have a clergy spouse who wishes to discuss the challenges of not being committed to be involved in their clergy spouse's vocation and service within the church, and conversely, we may have a spouse who is expected to be involved. Each of these situations needs to be given the same space, attention, understanding, and unconditional response. It is essential to offer parity in what is offered to each supervisee, regardless of whether or not you hold a view that is different from that of the clergy spouse, remembering that the pastoral supervision space might be the only space in which the clergy spouse can be themselves and speak candidly.

In chapter 5 I wrote about diversity awareness in pastoral supervision, and I have mentioned it again in this chapter as I believe that it is important to hold in mind our values and beliefs that we bring into the pastoral supervision setting. I also asked us, as supervisors, to consider how we might hold diversity awareness in our practice when working with different groups of people. We may hold views about clergy families, spouses, and clergy children and in our personal reflections, so, it would be helpful for us to be aware of where our values, or views, might have originated from in order to ensure that we are sensitive to working with this diverse group.

I mentioned earlier that some of the participants in my research identified pastoral supervision as a possible source of support. They did not say what they might want from pastoral supervision or from the supervision space, and none of the participants had had access to pastoral supervision at the time of the study. Moving forward, it might be that through our inclusive publicity material, we could state explicitly who is able to access the supervision space, and what we offer as pastoral supervisors, so that clergy spouses feel comfortable in making contact with the possibility of accessing a pastoral space and identifying how they might use the space. We might tailor our pastoral supervision to the uniqueness of the person, and I am aware that some individuals reading this might question that idea, believing that we currently offer an individual and unique service to our supervisees. Yet, as the wife of the pastor, I may want to bring a situation that I was not directly involved in, but yet I am directly involved with, in that I am impacted by virtue of being married to the clergyperson. For example, I wrote earlier of the clergyperson who might have had a very difficult church council meeting which has left him/her experiencing a range of emotions and wondering about giving up. What I might take to supervision, as the clergy spouse, is how the experience of my husband has impacted me, or what it has been like for me to be the listener for my husband, or how I might feel about not being able to defend him. Our pastoral supervision practice may look similar, or very different, to our current practice, when supporting the clergy spouse. What is clear, is that we seek to work ethically and respectfully with this unique group, in a way that values all the nuances of the position of being a clergy spouse.

CONCLUSION

In this chapter, we have explored, to a small degree, the uniqueness of the clergy spouse in terms of being married to the clergyperson, and what that may mean regarding experiences and demands that are made on the couple's relationship and the ministerial relationship. The value and appropriateness of pastoral supervision has been explored, alongside factors to be considered within such relationships. I have invited you to consider your way of working as a pastoral supervisor, and to offer that parity, whether the clergy spouse is directly involved in their spouse's ministry or not, as each may be impacted by the clergyperson's vocation and may value the pastoral supervision space as a place to explore and have a voice. Finally, I would invite you to look at the ethical frameworks of the governing bodies to which you subscribe, to consider if the language that is used is inclusive, and to invite enquiries from individuals who are not directly employed in frontline church work, but who are nonetheless impacted as a spouse of a clergyperson. As the person closely aligned to the clergy person, the clergy spouse does not have anyone to speak to by way of support, and in some cases is not offered the same level of support that is offered to the clergyperson. I am hoping that this chapter will spark further conversation on a topic that is rarely discussed. As I close, I have received news of two recent and sudden deaths within two days that will impact on the pastoral community and their family. Both were related to clergy families, and it feels that the writing of this chapter is timely in terms of the value of pastoral supervision for clergy spouses.

BIBLIOGRAPHY

Baker, David C., and Jean P. Scott. "Predictors of well-being among pastors' wives: A comparison with non-clergy wives." *The Journal of Pastoral Care* 46, no. 1 (1992): 33–43. https://doi.org/10.1177/002234099204600107.

Drumm, Rene, Laurie Copper, Marge Seifert, Duane McBride, and David Sedlacek. "Love everybody, keep your mouth shut don't have an opinion. Role expectations among Seventh-day Adventist pastor spouses." *Social Work & Christianity* 44, no. 3 (2017): 94–114.

Finch, Janet. "Devising conventional performances: The case of clergymen's wives." *Sociological Review* 28, no. 4 (1980): 851–70.

Gardner, Deanne. "Responding to disaster in an Afro-Caribbean congregation," Pp. 134–45 in *Tragedies and Christian Congregations: The Practical Theology of Trauma,* eds. Megan Warner, Christopher Southgate, Carla A. Grosch-Miller, and Hilary Ison. London: Routledge, 2020.

———. "An Exploration of the Emotional Demands Made on Clergy Wives in The New Testament Church of God Tradition in the UK."Doctoral thesis, University of Chester, 2019.

Gubi, Peter Madsen. "Pastoral supervision for clergy and pastoral workers: A personal perspective." *Thresholds: Counselling with Spirit.* Summer (2016): 14–17.

Litchfield, Kate. *Tend My Flock: Sustaining Good Pastoral Care.* London: Canterbury Press, 2006.

McCann Lisa, and Laurie A. Pearlman. "Vicarious traumatization: A framework for understanding the psychological effects of working with victims." *Journal of Traumatic Stress* 3 (1990): 131–49. https://doi.org/10.1007/BF00975140.

Morris, Michael L., and Priscilla W. Blanton, "The influence of work-related stressors on clergy husbands and their wives." *Family Relations* 42, no. 2 (1994): 189–95. https://doi.org/10.2307/585322s.

Murphy-Geiss, Gail. "Clergy Spouses and Families in the United Methodist Church. Part 11: Local Church Expectations and What Clergy Spouses Most Want the UMC to Know." Chicago, Illinois: The Genera Commission of the Status and Role of Women, 2009.

Papanek, Hanna. "Men, Women and work: Reflections on the two-person career." *American Journal of Sociology* 78, no. 4 (1973): 852–72.

Pavalko, Eliza K., and Glen H. Elder Jr. "Women behind the men: Variations in wives' support of husbands' careers." *Gender & Society* 7, no. 4 (1993): 548–67. https://doi.org/10.1177/089124393007004005.

Smith, Magdalen. *Steel Angels: The Personal Qualities of a Priest.* London: SPCK Publishing, 2014.

NOTES

1. Magdalen Smith, *Steel Angels, The Personal Qualities of a Priest.* (London: SPCK Publishing, 2014).

2. Peter Madsen Gubi, "Pastoral supervision for clergy and pastoral workers: A personal perspective." *Thresholds: The Journal of BACP Spirituality Division* (Summer, 2016): 14–17.

3. Association for Pastoral Supervision and Education. www.pastoralsupervision.org.uk.

4. Deanne Gardner, "An Exploration of the Emotional Demands Made on Clergy Wives in The New Testament Church of God Tradition in the UK" (Doctoral thesis, University of Chester, 2019).

5. Gardner, "An Exploration of the Emotional Demands," 64–67.

6. Eliza K. Pavalko and Glen H. Elder Jr. "Women behind the men: Variations in wives' support of husbands' careers." *Gender & Society* 7, no. 4 (1993): 548–67.

7. Hanna Papanek, "Men, Women and work: Reflections on the two-person career," *American Journal of Sociology* 78, no. 4 (1973): 852–72.

8. Kate Litchfield, *Tend My Flock: Sustaining Good Pastoral Care.* (London: Canterbury Press, 2006).

9. Gail Murphy-Geiss, "Clergy Spouses and Families in the United Methodist Church. Part 11: Local Church Expectations and What Clergy Spouses Most Want the UMC to Know." (Chicago, IL: The Genera Commission of the Status and Role of Women, 2009).

10. Rene Drumm, Laurie Copper, Marge Seifert, Duane McBride, and David Sedlacek. "Love everybody, keep your mouth shut don't have an opinion. Role expectations among Seventh-day Adventist pastor spouses," *Social Work & Christianity* 44, no. 3 (2017): 94–114.

11. David C. Baker and Jean P. Scott, "Predictors of well-being among pastors' wives: A comparison with non-clergy wives," *The Journal of Pastoral Care* 46, no. 1 (1992): 33–43. https://doi.org/10.1177/002234099204600107.

12. Michael L. Morris and Priscilla W. Blanton, "The influence of work-related stressors on clergy husbands and their wives," *Family Relations* 43, no. 2 (1994): 189–95. https://doi.org/10.2307/585322.

13. Baker and Scott, "Predictors of well-being among pastors' wives," 33–43.

14. By 'integral ministerial position,' I mean a position taken by the spouse that is informed by the calling to serve alongside the clergyperson which integrates roles that are undertaken including offering support to the 'shepherd.'

15. Janet Finch, "Devising conventional performances: The case of clergymen's wives," *Sociological Review* 28, no. 4 (1980): 851–70.

16. Litchfield, *Tend my Flock*, 143.

17. Smith, *Steel Angels*, 7.

18. Deanne Gardner, "Responding to disaster in an Afro-Caribbean congregation," in *Tragedies and Christian Congregations: The Practical Theology of Trauma,* ed. Megan Warner, Christopher Southgate, Carla A. Grosch-Miller, and Hilary Ison. (London: Routledge, 2020), 134–45.

19. Lisa McCann and Laurie A. Pearlman, "Vicarious traumatization: A framework for understanding the psychological effects of working with victims," *Journal of Traumatic Stress* 3, no.1 (1990): 131–149.

20. Litchfield, *Tend My Flock*, 63.

Index

About the Contributors

Sally Bubbers, MSc, UKCP Reg., is a psychotherapeutic counsellor who is registered and accredited with UKCP. She is an active pastoral supervisor and a Trustee of the Association for Pastoral Supervision and Education, a Certified Internal Family Systems Therapist, and a Certified Sensorimotor Psychotherapist. She has worked as a counsellor within a medical practice and in a hospital occupational health department. She has been a workplace chaplain for the retail sector through Faith at Work in Worcestershire and has been the Bishop's Advisor for Pastoral Care for the Diocese of Lichfield. She has delivered trainings and workshops to therapists, clergy, and pastoral supervisors. She is now working in private practice. Sally has over twelve years' experience as a counsellor for clergy and their families and as a Church of England clergy wife, which led to her interest in pastoral supervision. She is a member of the Training, Research and Publication subgroup.

Dr Deanne Gardner, MA, DProf, UKCP Reg., is a Person-Centred psychotherapist and clinical supervisor. Her clinical work includes running a private practice where she offers counselling to individuals and couples and clinical supervision to groups and individuals. She has worked with a charitable organisation that provides counselling to adult survivors of childhood sexual abuse. As a clinical coordinator within the organisation, she offered clinical and pastoral support to volunteer counsellors. Her practice has recently developed to include providing a reflective practice space to headteachers and clergy. As a church minister's wife, she has an interest in pastoral support available for clergy spouses. Dr Gardner is a Trustee of the Association for Pastoral Supervision and Education and is a member of the Training, Research and Publication sub-group.

Revd Professor Peter Madsen Gubi, MA, MTh, PhD, ThD, DMin, FRSA, FHEA, is Professor of Counselling and Spiritual Accompaniment at the University of Chester, UK, and Honorary Professor of Practical Theology at Teofilo Kisanji University, Tanzania. He is a BACP Senior Accredited Psychotherapist, a BACP Senior Accredited Supervisor, and an APSE Senior Accredited Pastoral Supervisor in private practice, as well as being a Minister in the Moravian Church (British Province). Professor Gubi has researched and published extensively and is a strong advocate of pastoral supervision for all serving Clergy of any denomination and faith group. Professor Gubi is a Trustee of the Association for Pastoral Supervision and Education and is Chair of the Training, Research and Publication subgroup.

Rev Bill Mullally, MA, MProf, is a Methodist minister from Ireland and is currently serving as Director of Supervision at Wesley House, Cambridge, UK. He has been part of the team involved in the training, implementation and rollout of supervision within the Methodist Church in Britain. He has completed a Masters' Degree in Practical Theology with research into Ministerial Supervision. Bill is a Senior Accredited Supervisor with the Association for Pastoral Supervision and Education, has been a Trustee since 2018, and is a member of the Training, Research and Publication subgroup. He is committed to the ethos of reflective supervision and believes this should be an essential part of every professional person's practice.

Revd Dr Tuntufye Anangisye Mwenisongole, BD, MATS, MAPC, PGDE, DTh, is a Lecturer at Teofilo Kisanji University (TEKU), Tanzania. He specialized in practical theology and pastoral psychotherapy, and teaches various courses on practical theology such as pastoral care and counselling, pastoral theology, and Christian education. Among his most notable publications are his 2018 monograph, *Pastoral Counseling for Orphans and Vulnerable Children: A Narrative Approach*, and articles on addressing the AIDS crisis in East Africa. In addition to his work as a scholar and teacher, Dr. Mwenisongole is an ordained pastor in the Moravian Church in Tanzania, South-West Province, and has been active in preaching and church leadership. Dr Mwenisongole is a member of the Training, Research and Publication subgroup of the Association for Pastoral Supervision and Education.

Revd Dr Sally Nash, BA, PGCE (QTS), MA, DMinTh, PhD, SFHEA, has been involved with the support and supervision of people in ministry for over thirty-five years, and has twenty years' experience as a theological educator working with those training for lay and ordained ministry. She is a self-supporting Anglican priest, licensed to a parish in Birmingham, and is a freelance educator, researcher, mentor and Senior Research Fellow at St Padarn's Institute. Her PhD focused on shame and the church, which was completed as part of her ordination training. She continues to train, research, and write in this field.

Dr Michelle (Mish) Seabrook, DProf, MA, BA, MBACP Accred., has a special interest in the self-care of practitioners who work within the helping professions and supervision. She recently has completed her doctoral research into supervisee self-care in clinical supervision. She has worked in several roles within the helping professions for over twenty years and has been offering counselling and psychotherapy since 2008. She currently offers private practice and supervision consultancy across the helping professions. Dr Seabrook is the founder of 'Supervision Institute,' which is a hub for resources, support, workshops, and training on supervision, and is a member of the Training, Research and Publication subgroup of the Association for Pastoral Supervision and Education.